WIKI

GOVERNMENT

How Technology Can Make Government Better, Democracy Stronger, and Citizens More Powerful

Beth Simone Noveck

BROOKINGS INSTITUTION PRESS
Washington, D.C.

Library of Congress Cataloging-in-Publication data
Noveck, Beth Simone.
  Wiki government : how technology can make government better, democracy stronger, and citizens more powerful / Beth Simone Noveck.
    p. cm.
  Includes bibliographical references and index.
  Summary: "In explaining how to enhance political institutions with the power of networks, examines the Peer-to-Patent project. Discusses its design challenges faced in creating software to distill online collaboration into useful expertise. Explains how law, policy, and technology can be revamped to help government work in more open, participatory ways"—Provided by publisher.
  ISBN 978-0-8157-0275-7 (cloth : alk. paper)
  1. Political participation—Technological innovations—United States. 2. Wikis (Computer science)—Political aspects—United States. 3. Patent practice—Technological innovations—United States—Case studies. 4. United States—Politics and government—21st century. I. Title.
  JK1764.N68 2009
  320.9730285'675—dc22   2009000796

3 5 7 9 8 6 4 2

The paper used in this publication meets minimum requirements of the American National Standard for Information Sciences—Permanence of Paper for Printed Library Materials: ANSI Z39.48-1992.

Typeset in Sabon

Composition by Cynthia Stock
Silver Spring, Maryland

Printed by R. R. Donnelley
Harrisonburg, Virginia

For my digital mother,
DORIS BETTAUER NOVECK
and in memory of my analog father,
SIMON NOVECK
who brought the love of technology and the
faith in democracy together

CONTENTS

PREFACE

FOR SEVENTY-SEVEN DAYS, from election day to inauguration day, the Obama-Biden Transition Project convened in a nondescript office building in northwest Washington, D.C. Most of the transition work involved sending expert volunteers into federal agencies to research and write briefing binders for the incoming department heads. In addition, seven policy teams—a kind of protocabinet—"set the table" for the incoming president's first hundred days. In addition to Energy, Education, Health Care, Immigration, Foreign Policy, and Economy, there was a new kid on the policy block: Technology, Innovation, and Government Reform. We affectionately called ourselves the "TIGR" (think Winnie the Pooh) team.

President-elect Obama's mandate for government reform was to create unprecedented openness and innovation in government. Rethinking governance for the twenty-first century was not incidental to the president's agenda. In fact, Tech & Government was the original name of TIGR, and I was the group's original member. On his first day in office, President Obama issued a "Memorandum for the Heads of Executive Departments and Agencies" calling for the chief technology officer and the Office of Management and Budget to craft an Open Government Directive for greater *transparency, participation,* and *collaboration* in every agency.

The emergence of information-sharing technologies makes it possible, as a first step, to improve transparent publication of government data and faster commenting on that data. "Information maintained by the Federal Government is a national asset. My Administration will take appropriate action, consistent with law and policy," reads the memorandum, "to disclose information rapidly in forms that the public can readily find and use. Executive departments and agencies should harness new technologies to put information about their operations and decisions online and readily available to the public." Metaphorically speaking, the Internet can lead to the twenty-first-century version of C-SPAN, whereby government operations are more accessible via the Internet. Greater transparency also enables people to make use of information and hold government more accountable. For example, the District of Columbia requires every agency to make "feeds"—subscriptions to updates of government data—available from a central website. The District's chief information officer launched a contest to get citizens, nongovernmental organizations, and the private sector to develop new software applications using those data. The D.C. approach is not simply about transparency for its own sake but also about creating an ongoing collaboration between government and citizens for the betterment of public life. The federal government is launching recovery.gov to make economic indicators more transparent, and will eventually launch other data repositories. Still nascent, these data portals make it easier for communities to find—and to make valuable social use of—public information. The quantity and quality of posted data will grow. It is anyone's guess how people will make use of the information or the new ways they will take action.

The memorandum also calls for more participation: "Public engagement enhances the Government's effectiveness and improves the quality of its decisions. Knowledge is widely dispersed in society, and public officials benefit from having access to that dispersed knowledge. Executive departments and agencies should offer Americans increased opportunities to participate in policymaking and to provide their Government with the benefits of their collective expertise and information. Executive departments and agencies should also solicit public input on how we can increase and improve opportunities for public participation in Government." By soliciting expertise (in which *expertise* is defined broadly to include both scientific knowledge and popular experience) from self-selected peers working together in groups via the Internet, it is possible to augment the know-how of full-time professionals. The public can help with gathering data, evaluating information against performance benchmarks, recognizing patterns, making decisions, and measuring compliance.

But the vision of Open Government expressed in the memorandum goes beyond improving citizen participation to address the emerging opportunity for meaningful collaboration—as distinct from participation—across levels of government and between government and citizens. Collaboration catalyzes new problem-solving strategies, in which public and private sector organizations and individuals solve social problems collectively. As President Obama has said, "The challenges we face today—from saving our planet to ending poverty—are simply too big for government to solve alone. We need all hands on deck."

Knowing how to use technology to get all hands on deck and create more effective and efficient government institutions is the focus of this book. Collaboration is necessary not for its own sake but to generate creative solutions to challenges and to share the work of oversight and accountability. "Collaboration actively engages Americans in the work of their Government. Executive departments and agencies should use innovative tools, methods, and systems to cooperate among themselves, across all levels of Government, and with nonprofit organizations, businesses, and individuals in the private sector. Executive departments and agencies should solicit public feedback to assess and improve their level of collaboration and to identify new opportunities for cooperation," the president's memorandum notes. There are far too few opportunities to collaborate in governance. With new technology, government could articulate a problem and then work with the public to coordinate a solution among and across government institutions and with nonprofit organizations, businesses, and individuals. Instead of only promulgating a law or a regulation to mandate safety in school science labs, for example, it is now possible to organize a volunteer corps to survey the labs and distribute goggles. Instead of enacting sweeping policies on broadband deployment, technology might make it possible to map Internet penetration locally and devise more targeted technical and legal approaches. Instead of prescribing the solution, the government might offer a prize to elicit ten new solutions.

We have arrived at a moment in time when we can multiply the number and diversity of opportunities for engagement to respond to the complex problems that confront us today. Law, policy, and technology might be brought to bear to organize the work of many eager volunteers working across a distance to address common problems. While technology is necessary to undertake collaboration efficiently and at scale, creating better governance is not a question of technology. Rather, effective governance structures are needed to improve process effectiveness.

This is the core idea of *Wiki Government*; namely, that legitimate democracy and effective governance in the twenty-first century require collaboration. In an earlier technological age, this country organized power in representative structures with professional decisionmakers. Because of the high costs of coordination, the public participated in governance only once a year, at the polling booth, to choose its representatives. Citizens would remind those representatives of their obligations by means of indirect pressure from the press, lobbyists, and interest groups. Reformers also created innovations in deliberative democracy, wherein neighbors would convene face to face to talk about and influence the work of government officials. Deliberation has the added value of creating occasions for the public exchange of reasoned ideas that help to blow off social steam and resolve differences peacefully.

But in an era when information and communications technology makes it possible for many more people to work together, we can redesign our institutions and create more diverse mechanisms for solving problems. If we proliferate many more ways of working together, these collaborative practices can change the culture of governance. This change will also create a new kind of democratic legitimacy, deriving its egalitarianism through many small venues in which a large number of people engage.

In *Wiki Government,* I explain how to accomplish collaborative governance by telling the story of Peer-to-Patent, a participatory and collaborative method for those with the scientific expertise to make a difference in the patenting process. The Patent Office has examined patent applications in more or less the same way since Thomas Jefferson founded it over two hundred years ago. An official reviews the application, researches the relevant scientific literature, and then makes a determination about its patentability. As the number of applications has risen, reform strategies have focused on traditional approaches: hiring more examiners to do the work, changing the judicial standard for the review of patents once granted, or asking Congress to alter the scope of scientific subject matter eligible for a patent.

In 2005 it was radical to suggest that the Patent Office should change the way it makes decisions and suggest it use social networking technology to create teams of volunteer scientists and technologists to do the research and participate in decisionmaking. Since citizens traditionally participate either as individuals in one-off commenting processes or through donations to interest groups, the notion that we could construct new kinds of collaborative communities that tapped public expertise was exciting. It took only a million dollars (now it would be half as much) and two years to design, build, and launch a pilot program to integrate a volunteer network of self-selecting scientists and technologists into the formerly closed and secretive patent examination process.

In retrospect, Peer-to-Patent was incremental. But because it was the federal government's first social networking project, it generated attention as a model for what government might do next. Eric Schmidt, the chief executive officer of Google, publicly asked regarding Peer-to-Patent: "Why is that not true of every branch of government?" Now we are beginning to foresee that participation does not have to be only *in* government as it is already constructed but also *with* government in new, collaborative arrangements, some of which might involve government communicating priorities and people taking action in civil society in response.

The fact that the country is in the midst of an economic crisis and facing unprecedented job losses is more reason, not less, to invest effort in fixing the workings of government. Current institutions have failed to avert catastrophe. With the benefit of social and visual technologies, however, the architects of the new public institutions in the digital age can *design* better institutions. This requires developing and adapting tools to this end, but it also requires galvanizing the political will to change the institutional processes for making decisions and wielding power.

Cyberspace is dead. That is to say, it has receded into the background as a ubiquitous feature of modern life. There is increasingly little distinction between online and off. Social technologies make it possible to join groups online for shared work and play. As a result, there has been much public discussion and scholarship about the impact of the Internet on *me*, namely how individuals are responding to life online. Now we are beginning to tackle the question of how it affects us, namely how society organizes and manages itself through institutions. At this political juncture, the future of governance in the digital age is not simply a descriptive inquiry but also a normative opportunity to change those institutions.

Done right, it is possible now to achieve greater competence by making good information available for better governance, improve effectiveness by leveraging the available tools to engender new forms of collective action, and strengthen and deepen democracy by creating government by the people, of the people, and *with* the people.

ACKNOWLEDGMENTS

DIPLOMAS NOTWITHSTANDING, I received much of my education during and after university in the cafes of Vienna. There I learned about the joy of good coffee and better conversation. The Institute for Information Law and Policy at New York Law School, which boasts one of the finest assemblages of faculty versed in technology yet committed to the values of democracy, is a return to the fellowship of the *Kaffeehaus*.

Over coffees, dinners, and "conspiracies," my colleagues generated the intellectual heat and light that forged the theory of collaborative democracy and my understanding of the impact of technology on public sector institutions. No one knows more about technology law than James "Godfather of Cybersoul" Grimmelmann, who has applied his prodigious smarts to figuring out how to create greater public access to knowledge by communities via the Internet. Molly Beutz, an international lawyer by training, explores the relationship between web 2.0 technology and global human rights. Dan Hunter, when not chatting up the ladies under the guise of researching trademarks and knock-off handbags, has been writing some of the best and the first articles on technology and democracy and the relationship to virtual world technologies. One crucial year David Post passed through and kibitzed; if he could write about Jefferson and cyberspace, it was possible to write about patents and World of Warcraft in the same volume. Rudy Peritz, expert in intellectual property and antitrust, sparked the first conversations that led to the Peer-to-Patent project, while Richard Sherwin's contagious interest in the cultural influence of social and visual media pervades everything about this project. Dean Richard Matasar, who is friend, mentor, and "intellectual venture capitalist," has nurtured this vibrant and humane culture of inquiry. He not only had the foresight to bring us together but has also joined in the fun, sharing his wisdom and enthusiasm on all our projects, especially Peer-to-Patent. Naomi Allen, institute manager and "office Mom," keeps us together (as well as organized, on time, and informed about every theatrical and culinary development in town).

Thanks to Judy Johnson for lending David Johnson, the father of cyberlaw, to the New York Law School institute. A prodigious intellect, David is both classic Renaissance man and future-thinking netizen. His ability to produce new ideas is matched only by the enthusiasm he shows for learning. The importance of more collaborative, complex, and interesting forms of group interactions—and the role of the screen in helping to produce them—is something David talked about the first time we met. I am glad that it took me as long as it did to plumb the depths of his insights, as this afforded the opportunity for all the wonderful meals and conversations I have had the honor to share with him over the years.

A debt of gratitude must also go to the students at New York Law School and Stanford University who signed up for Law, Technology, and Democracy and patiently let me persuade them that the contemporary lawyer must be a problem solver who wields the tools of software code as well as legal code. I have learned an extraordinary amount from their insights.

Students at the law school set up and ran every aspect of the Peer-to-Patent project. From summarizing the applications for a lay audience to managing the relationship with the USPTO to bug-testing the website, Joseph Merante, Yeen Tham, Rahan Uddin, and Christopher Wong worked tirelessly at night, on holidays, while going to school, and while taking exams. Not only would there be no Peer-to-Patent, but there would be no book about it if Mark Webbink, former general counsel and senior vice president of Red Hat software, had not miraculously arrived to head up the Center for Patent Innovations and to run Peer-to-Patent— with aplomb. Suzanne Davidson has made all our grants possible. With Bridgette Johnson's help, good cheer, and fashion tips the public peer review project has thrived. Special thanks to the student research fellows at the institute who also applied themselves to the footnotes in this book with such good humor: Stephanie Figueroa, Marc Miller, Brian "Laborer" Pyne, Elizabeth Reilly, and Will Stock.

The United States Patent and Trademark Office professionals were willing to a take a risk and embark on this historic experiment. The Honorable Jay Lucas, then deputy commissioner for patent examination, was the first to say yes, with the support of Commissioner John Doll and Director Jon Dudas. With the help of his team, Jack Harvey has shepherded Peer-to-Patent from proposal to pilot to official project of the agency.

The New York Law School and the Patent Office are two-thirds of a triumvirate in this collaboration. I never cease to be amazed by the depth of knowledge and commitment demonstrated by our industry partners during the course of this project. In 2005, when Peer-to-Patent was but a mere idea in a blog posting, Dave Kappos and Manny Schecter of IBM shared the belief that it could become a reality. Numerous IBMers gave of their time to the project planning, including Marc Ehrlich, Susan Murray, and Marian Underweiser. Kaz Kazenske of Microsoft and Q. Todd Dickinson, then of General Electric, both former Patent Office leaders, lent their gravitas and know-how to the success of the project. Adam Avrunin at Red Hat, Curt Rose of HP, Steve Klocinski and Jim Saliba of CE, Scott Asmus and Pat Patnode of GE, and Matt Rainey at Intellectual Ventures rounded out the Steering Committee, contributing money and, perhaps more important in the case of such busy professionals, their time.

As I discuss in *Wiki Government,* it was the collaborative nature of the design and planning that enabled smart ideas to find the project. Colleagues at Harvard, Stanford, the University of Michigan, and Yale hosted workshops that convened the myriad experts in patent law, technology, social media, and design whose insights are reflected in the Peer-to-Patent project and, by extension, in this book. Thanks to Lauren Gelman, Colin Maclay, Eddan Katz, John Palfrey, and Paul Resnick for organizing and pushing this project forward. Michael Messinger and Steven Weiner were particularly helpful and engaged in lending expertise about patent examination, while Mark Lemley and Arti Rai provided insights on patent law, and Terry Winograd brought the design perspective to bear. Their names, and those of the other generous members of the project's advisory board, are captured on the project website.

Two special people must be singled out for their extraordinary contributions to the Peer-to-Patent project. It is their work more than anyone else's involved that is reflected in what lives now on the Internet. Pablo Aguero's artistry is visible on every page. He cured me of ever using the term *ASAP* in an e-mail by working tirelessly against impossible deadlines but with gorgeous results. Eric Hestenes is the lead architect of Peer-to-Patent. There are not enough thanks that I can express for all that he has done. Most of all, he took a flying leap of faith in committing himself to this venture. In the true spirit of a start-up, he served not only as chief technology officer but also as chief cook and bottle-washer and participated in every aspect of the planning, including teaching himself the minutiae of patent law and procedure and crisscrossing the country to make Peer-to-Patent a reality.

Without the unflagging generosity of the Omidyar Network and its general counsel, Will Fitzpatrick, none of this could have happened. Period. While the MacArthur Foundation gave financial support, the most valuable contribution has been the conversations with John Bracken, Valerie Chang, Julie Stasch, and Connie Yowell.

In the MacArthur orbit, I collided magically with John Seely Brown, chief of confusion and kid extraordinaire, who tilted my intellectual universe on its axis and propelled me into new directions of unexplored fun. Similarly, I have benefited over many years and many bowls of moose-tracks ice cream from transformational conversations with Jack Balkin and the Swedish Chef. My work on technology and democracy had its origins at Yale Law School under Jack's tutelage and Carroll Stevens's encouragement. Yale Law School is a second home, and Jack and Margret, Carroll and Libby, second family.

Over the course of this project, many people have helpfully argued, including Mike Ananny, Harvey Anderson, Blaise Aquera y Arcas, James Au, Richard Bartle, Brian Behlendorf, Ben Barber, Yochai Benkler, Donald Brenneis, Herbert Burkert, Susan Crawford, Jim Fishkin, Seeta Ganghadaran, Ted Glasser, Seth Harris, Todd Huffman, Mitch Kapor, Ethan Katsh, Jim Kolenberger, Daniel Kreiss, Jaron Lanier, Steve Midgley, Ellen and Richard Miller, Craig Newmark, Cory Ondrejka, Andy Oram, Thomas Plunkett, Andrew Rasiej, Howard Rheingold, Graham Richard, Colin Rule, Clay Shirky, Micah Sifry, Lee Smolin, Fred Turner, and Darrell West.

Others have helpfully gossiped: Andrew Berman, Marinn Carlson, Laurie Claus, Ken Norz, Said Hoderi, Larry Levine, Paul Marino (who also did the original Peer-to-Patent logo), Brian Murphy, Eileen Twiggs, Sophia "Chicken" Yaliraki. Thank you to the intellectually generous participants in Tim O'Reilly's Foo Camps and the State of Play Conferences on law and virtual worlds at New York Law School, who will see their stories leavening this narrative.

I owe a debt of gratitude to President Barack Obama, who championed open and collaborative government in word and deed and inspired the movement that proved that people can and will work together for change. President Obama's leadership more than any technological, cultural, or legal development stands to transform how government works in the twenty-first century. Thanks to Julius Genachowski I had the honor to participate in shaping the administration's innovation and government strategy. His choosing me to lead the transition's Technology, Innovation, and Government Reform (TIGR) group and to put the ideas in *Wiki Government* into practice on a national level reflects a sincere commitment to democratic ideals as a driver of innovation. Thank you to Blair Levin for assuming that leadership so that I could finish this book. The members of the TIGR innovation in government team—Emily Bokar, Mark Chandler, Dan Chenok, Aneesh Chopra, John Leibowitz, Bruce McConnell, Tom Freedman, Tom Kalil, Vivek Kundra, Andrew McLaughlin, Kartik Raghavan, Alec Ross, Dan Siroker, Sonal Shah, Larry Strickling, and Irving Wladawsky-Berger—could have written this book. With many of them now in public service, America can be hopeful about the future.

This project only became a book thanks to the careful and loving ministrations of my extraordinary editor, Mary Kwak, and copyeditor Diane Hammond at the Brookings Institution. Clay Risen's insistent questions kept me on the grammatical straight and narrow. Thank you to my agent, Andree Abecassis, who believed in the author as much as in the ideas and endured countless disquisitions on copyright licensing.

Over the last year no hours were spent more pleasurably than in trading drafts with David Booth: his gorgeous novel for my book manuscript. Nabokov claims that the writer should have the precision of the poet and the imagination of the scientist. David has that special talent for visualizing and hearing through language that comes from having both a love and a reverence for words. His attention has made this a better book.

My family never grumbled when I stayed in to write the book instead of spending time with them. I owe my nephews many an outing. My mother, who introduced a ticker-tape machine into our house when I was four, bought the first-generation IBM PC, and is still the only senior citizen I know with an iPod, a BlackBerry, and a Roku box, is my role model and inspiration.

The most important thanks of all goes to the Peer-to-Patent community, the volunteers who give of their time and expertise for the betterment of government and the benefit of all.

Montaigne wrote that once an author has "mortgaged his work to the world, it seems to me that he has no further right to it." Thanks to the contributions of those who made this book possible, I am not sure I ever did. Everything good in here is thanks to their love and support.

PART ONE

Collaborative Democracy and the Changing Nature of Expertise

CHAPTER ONE

PEER-TO-PATENT: A MODEST PROPOSAL

You must do the things you think you cannot do.

—ELEANOR ROOSEVELT

PATENT LAW IS THE students' least favorite part of the semester-long class, Introduction to Intellectual Property, that I teach at New York Law School. In this survey course they learn about trademarking brands and copyrighting songs. But they also suffer through five jargon-filled weeks on how inventors apply to the United States Patent and Trademark Office (USPTO) to secure a twenty-year grant of monopoly rights. Despite the fact that patents signal innovation to the financial markets and investors and drive economic growth in certain industries, many dread this segment of the course.[1] Patent applications are written in a special language; patentese is a member of the legalese language family that only the high priesthood of patent professionals understands. Even applications for the most mundane inventions are written in dense jargon. The patent application for the sealed crustless sandwich (aka the peanut butter and jelly sandwich patent), which sought to give Smuckers a monopoly on a process to crimp crusts, reads as follows:

> Claim: 1. A sealed crustless sandwich, comprising: a first bread layer having a first perimeter surface coplanar to a contact surface; at least one filling of an edible food juxtaposed to said contact surface; a second bread layer juxtaposed to said at least one filling opposite of said

first bread layer, wherein said second bread layer includes a second perimeter surface similar to said first perimeter surface; a crimped edge directly between said first perimeter surface and said second perimeter surface for sealing said at least one filling between said first bread layer and said second bread layer; wherein a crust portion of said first bread layer and said second bread layer has been removed.[2]

To help my students understand how patents further Congress's constitutional mandate to "promote the progress of science and useful arts," I start by teaching the process by which the government decides whether to grant a patent.[3] While this process has its special rules, the decision to award or withhold a patent is not unlike a thousand other decisions made by government every day, decisions that depend upon access to adequate information and sound science. Just as an official of the U.S. Environmental Protection Agency (EPA) must consult epidemiological studies to determine acceptable levels of asbestos or mercury in air and water, the patent examiner must obtain the relevant technological antecedents—known as prior art—to judge if an invention is enough of an advance over what preceded it to warrant a patent. The patent examiner effectively decides who will control the next BlackBerry or the next life-saving cancer drug.

The Patent Office employs 5,500 patent examiners.[4] While the examiner might have an undergraduate degree in computer science, she does not necessarily know much about cutting-edge, object-oriented programming languages. She's not up on the latest advances coming out of Asia. She may not have seen anything like the patent application for bioinformatic modeling of the human genome or the application for a patent on poetry-writing software![5] She has not necessarily been to law school (you don't need a law degree to take the patent bar exam).[6] She does not necessarily have a Ph.D. in science, and there is little opportunity on the job for continuing education. As an expert in patent examination, she is not and is not expected to be a master of all areas of innovation.

To make things worse, the inventor is not legally required to give her any help—say, by providing background research.[7] Indeed, the inventor has an incentive not to supply the Patent Office with prior art, since the examiner might use it to determine that the invention lacks sufficient novelty and thus to reject the application.[8] Sometimes inventors deluge an examiner with background research, hoping the overworked official will be daunted by the task of sorting the wheat from the chaff. It is no wonder that even Thomas Jefferson, the first patent examiner, in 1791 sought outside help, consulting with University of Pennsylvania chemistry professor Joseph Hutchinson before issuing a patent on an alchemical process for rendering seawater potable.[9]

Today the modern patent examiner works alone (or at most with a supervisor). Her primary resource is USPTO databases (known as East and West) of old and foreign patents, patent applications, and the prior art citations they reference.[10] On average, she has just fifteen to twenty hours to research the patent application and write up her findings.[11] Worse yet, her supervisor (with Congress in the background) is breathing down her neck to move on to the next application in the backlog of a million pending applications.[12] Applicants wait upward of three years (and in certain fields closer to five years) to receive their first notice from the Patent Office, and that's usually just the beginning of a series of communications that will be exchanged before the patent is finally granted or rejected.

Even with more time, patent offices around the world still would not have access to the information they need. To know if a particular inventor is the progenitor of a chemical compound or software program, the examiner has to scour the literature. Government patent offices naturally have access to the historical corpus of patents, and they have access to excellent and up-to-date journals, but the information needed is not always found in traditional government or academic sources. Inventors in cutting-edge fields may discuss their work on the web rather than in print. John Doll, the U.S. commissioner of patents, complains of the dispersed databases and inconsistent search protocols that impede examiners' efforts to decide whether an invention is new, useful, and nonobvious—in a word, patentable.[13] The result is an inefficient, inaccurate process: of the 2 million patents in force in the United States, many would not survive closer scrutiny.[14]

All this got me to thinking. What if the patent examiner worked with the broader community? What if the public augmented the official's research with its own know-how? What if the scientific and technical expertise of the graduate student, industry researcher, university professor, and hobbyist could be linked to the legal expertise of the patent examiner to produce a better decision? What if, instead of traditional peer review, a process of open review were instituted, wherein participants self-select on the basis of their expertise and enthusiasm? What if, instead of a social network like Facebook, a scientific and technical expert network were built? I nicknamed this "peer-to-patent." The online tools available today could be employed to connect the government institution and the increasingly networked public to collaborate on an ongoing basis.

Such a process is already happening outside of government. Some business and nonprofit organizations recognize that processes that were once the purview of an individual might usefully be opened up to participation from a larger group. Cancer patients, for example, provide medical information to each other via the Association of Online Cancer Resources website and its 159 associated electronic mailing lists. The website Patients Like Me allows patients to share information about their symptoms and the progress of their diseases. Patients Like Me also has data-sharing partnerships with doctors, pharmaceutical and medical device companies, research organizations, and nonprofits to encourage patients to supply information to those who are working to develop cures.

Other examples abound. Amazon's web-based Mechanical Turk project outsources the work of answering simple questions, such as tagging people and places in pictures, measuring the size of molecules in a microscopic image, identifying land mines from photographs, and creating links to or from a Google map. YouTube depends on amateurs to post video content. Volunteers populate the Internet Movie Database (IMDb), which offers information about close to one million movie titles and more than two million entertainment professionals.[15] Almost 30,000 Korean-speaking citizen-journalists report on stories for OhMyNews.com, where "every citizen is a reporter."[16] Korean speakers also answer each other's search queries via the Naver search engine, which far outpaces the popularity of such algorithmic search engines as Google and Yahoo![17] The Mozilla Corporation, maker of the Firefox browser, enlists the help of several thousand of its 180 million users to work on marketing campaigns, respond to queries on Mozilla message boards, write or edit documentation for developers, and even create the software code for the browser.[18]

More than 9,000 companies participate in technology giant SAP's global partner networks, and 1.2 million individuals participate in its online discussion communities, which are designed to generate innovation for the firm while making individuals more successful at their jobs.

Inspired by these examples, once the spring 2005 term ended, I wrote up a posting for my blog entitled "Peer-to-Patent: A Modest Proposal."[19] I proposed that the Patent Office transform its closed, centralized process and construct an architecture for open participation that unleashes the "cognitive surplus" of the scientific and technical community. I called on the Patent Office to solicit information from the public to assist in patent examination and, eventually, to enlist the help of smaller, collaborating groups of dedicated volunteers to help decide whether a particular patent should be granted. Through this sort of online collaboration, the agency could augment its intelligence and improve the quality of issued patents. "This modest proposal harnesses social reputation and collaborative filtering technology to create a peer review system of scientific experts ruling on innovation," I wrote. "The idea of blue ribbon panels or advisory committees is not new. But the suggestion to use social reputation software—think Friendster, LinkedIn, eBay reputation points—to make such panels big enough, diverse enough, and democratic enough to replace the patent examiner is."

Just as I posted my thought experiment the phone rang. Daniel Terdiman, a reporter for *Wired News,* was trolling for stories. "Heard anything interesting?" he asked. I reeled off three or four initiatives of various colleagues. "That's all well and good, but what are *you* up to?" Daniel probed, hoping I might have something to report. "Catching up on my blog and making improbable proposals to revolutionize the Patent Office, improve government decisionmaking, and rethink the nature of democracy," I modestly replied.

On July 14, 2005, *Wired News* ran an article titled, "Web Could Unclog Patent Backlog."[20] As a reporter who wrote about videogames, not government, Daniel was uninhibited about calling the patent commissioner for a quote. Commissioner John Doll responded: "It's an interesting idea, and an interesting perspective." Peer review, he added, "is something that could be done right now, and I'm a little surprised that somebody hasn't started a blog" for that purpose.

THE MODEST PROPOSAL TAKES OFF

The day the article appeared, Manny Schecter, the associate general counsel and managing attorney for intellectual property at IBM, sent me an e-mail: "I saw the story on Peer-to-Patent. We should talk." Manny

Schecter, Marian Underweiser, and Marc Ehrlich are known as the 3Ms of the intellectual property law department at IBM. Responsible for the company's 42,000 patents (28,000 in the United States alone), these three senior attorneys and their staff ensure that IBM continues its unbroken fifteen-year streak as the holder of the largest patent portfolio in the world. The firm now receives between 3,000 and 4,000 U.S. patents each year. In addition to strengthening the competitive position of IBM's products, these patents generate $1 billion annually in licensing fees from other businesses wishing to incorporate IBM's scientific inventions into their products and services. The size of IBM's patent portfolio signals to the market that the firm is an innovator, which may be responsible for its rising share price and increased shareholder value.[21]

As the USPTO's biggest client, IBM is one of the companies with the most to gain from an efficient patent system. It also stands to lose if the patenting process breaks down. With the pace of patent examination out of sync with the pace of innovation, firms like IBM are forced to wait ever longer for patents. And these innovations, on which their licensing strategies depend, may even turn out to be invalid. In addition, critics charge that the granting of undeserved patents, in combination with growing uncertainty over patent quality, has led to an increase in costly litigation. Patents provide a license to sue others for damages for using a patented invention. Companies with deep pockets, such as IBM, are more likely to be sued for patent infringement than smaller firms. Software patents, which represent the bulk of IBM's portfolio, are more than twice as likely as other patents to be litigated.[22] The cost of defending such a suit, even for the victorious, makes the game not always worth the candle, especially when the alternative is to pay the plaintiff a five- or six-figure fee.

The 3Ms, therefore, had been contemplating ideas for patent reform that were similar to Peer-to-Patent. The company had been experimenting internally with technology for distributed collaboration for a long time, and senior executives credit IBM's rescue from the brink (it is one of the 16 percent of large companies tracked from 1962 to 1998 to have survived) to the digitally aided development of a culture of collaboration.[23]

IBM's lawyers were intrigued by the simplicity and promise of the Peer-to-Patent proposal, particularly since it could be implemented, at least as a pilot, without legislative or Supreme Court action. By spring 2006 they were ready to help the idea become reality. The 3Ms at IBM offered a research grant to New York Law School to allow me to (iron-ically) take a break from teaching Introduction to Intellectual Property and to flesh out the blog posting into a design for a practical prototype. Little did I know that by yielding to the temptation of a semester off to write a research paper I would end up launching an experiment to improve the flow of information to the Patent Office and running the government's first open social networking project.

In short order, corporate patent counsel at the major technology firms began to hear about Peer-to-Patent, and Microsoft joined the project with a commitment to submit patents for public review and to contribute much-needed additional sponsorship. After all, it would smack of regulatory capture and delegitimize the work if the largest customer of the Patent Office were to be the sole supporter, designer, and funder of a plan to reform it. Then came Hewlett-Packard, followed by Red Hat, General Electric, CA (Computer Associates), and finally Intellectual Ventures, the invention company founded by former Microsoft chief technology officer Nathan Myhrvold. These companies not only offered to submit their patent applications through this process but also contributed money to the development of the legal and technical infrastructure. In addition, New York Law School received support from the MacArthur Foundation and the Omidyar Network, the organization that channels the philanthropic activities of eBay founder Pierre Omidyar.

Dozens of lawyers, technologists, and designers gave their time and expertise to refining the design of the project. The result was a series of workshops at Harvard, Yale, Stanford, the University of Michigan, and New York Law School during 2006–07. The planning of Peer-to-Patent created educational opportunities for New York Law School students, who practiced law reform and acquired professional skills by running the project at every stage. They produced educational videos about patent law and prior art (think Schoolhouse Rock for the patent system). They wrote the directions for each page of the website, explaining to new users how to find and upload prior art in connection with a patent application or how to comment on prior art submitted by others. Students also drafted privacy and copyright policies, terms of use, and solicitations to inventors to invite them to submit their applications. Above all, they learned how to work as a team, using technical, legal, and communication tools to implement a solution to a complex problem in the real world.

FIGURE 1-1. PEER-TO-PATENT HOME PAGE AT WWW.PEERTOPATENT.ORG

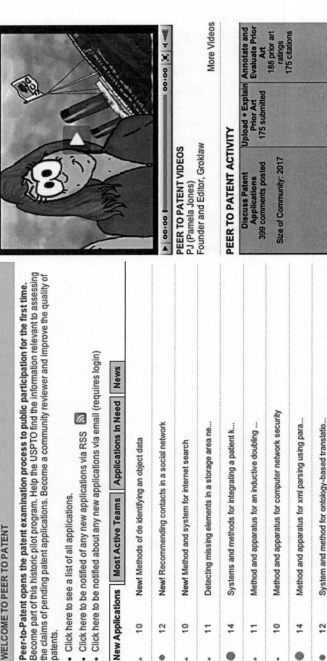

Most important, despite the first-of-its-kind nature of the plan, the USPTO was on board by the end of 2006. Sold first on the idea of channeling more information to overworked patent examiners from the website and second by a promise we made to forward only the ten most relevant public submissions, the Patent Office agreed to conduct this pilot in "open" patent examination. New York Law School hired Eric Hestenes, former vice president of technology for a large financial services firm, to lead a team of programmers in developing the million-dollar software platform that would help create teams of self-selecting scientific and technical experts to contribute information to the Patent Office online. (Not only have the cost of these tools come down, but options are available that would obviate designing from scratch. Strategies like cloud computing and shared services could enable many collaboration pilots to run off the same infrastructure.) A steering committee of corporate patent law experts and an advisory board comprising academics, journalists, and independent patent experts spent the next six months devising policies and designing the processes that would be enabled by the Peer-to-Patent website.

The USPTO then convened a team of eight executives to manage the project for the agency. Headed by the deputy commissioner for patent examination, Jay Lucas (later succeeded by John Love), and run by Jack Harvey, the director responsible for computer technology patents, the group collaborated with us on drafting the legal consent requirements. We agreed the pilot would include a maximum of 250 applications (enough to generate useful data without overwhelming the agency) relating to software and computer hardware (so-called Technology Center 2100 inventions), with a maximum of 15 applications from any one firm.[24] The USPTO chose and trained the examiners who would take part in the pilot, crafted the workflow processes for managing the receipt of public information and the distribution of feedback to the public, and circulated surveys to participating officials.

By 2007 press reports began to mount in anticipation of Peer-to-Patent's rollout. *Fortune* profiled the project in August 2006, and the *Washington Post* devoted a front-page story to Peer-to-Patent in the spring.[25] Finally, on June 15, 2007—twenty-three months after my initial blog post—New York Law School, in cooperation with the USPTO, launched the Peer-to-Patent website.[26] (A screenshot of the home page is shown in figure 1-1 and can be found at www.peertopatent.org.) The first five patent applications in the pilot came from HP, IBM, Intel, and Red Hat. The applications involved a wide range of computer technology relating to wind farming, virtual collaboration, and social networking. As an incentive to participate in this peer review process, the USPTO offered to examine Peer-to-Patent applications first, allowing companies to jump the million-application queue.

IMPLICATIONS FOR THE FUTURE: FROM WIKIPEDIA TO WIKILAW

In brief, here's how the collaboration works. As part of the process by which the patent examiner determines whether a patent application meets the legal standards set forth by the Patent Act, the Peer-to-Patent website solicits the public to submit information—namely prior art—relevant to evaluating a pending application. Because participating in this process requires enthusiasm and expertise, those who respond to the Peer-to-Patent invitation are self-selecting volunteers. Anyone can join but only an expert would. Participation requires working on an application in collaborative teams. Several team members might research the application, uploading relevant publications and suggestions for further research for use by the patent examiner. Others might comment on the relevance of submitted pieces of prior art. Following online discussion, each team vets the submissions made by its members. The group votes on which ten submissions are most relevant. Those are then forwarded to the Patent Office.

In the pilot's first year, inventors submitted eighty-four applications through Peer-to-Patent, and over 2,000 volunteers signed up to offer their expertise through the website. The numbers were small but the results demonstrated that the public is indeed in possession of information not readily accessible to the patent examiner and that, despite the complexity of the patent examination process, the public will take the time to contribute to it. At the end of the pilot's first year, 89 percent of participating patent examiners reported that the materials they had received from the public had been useful; 92 percent indicated they would welcome the opportunity to examine another application with public participation; and 73 percent wanted the Peer-to-Patent program implemented as regular office practice.[27] (This last number is quite high considering that examiners had no way of knowing if institutionalized public participation would eventually put them out of a job!)

In June 2008 the USPTO extended the pilot for a second year and expanded the subject matter of Peer-to-Patent from computer software to include so-called business methods, or patent applications pertaining broadly to methods and processes for doing business (such as the one-click shopping cart). Support for this experiment in collaborative governance also came from outside the Peer-to-Patent community. Among many media mentions, the head of the Ewing Marion Kauffman Foundation, Carl Shramm, and its vice president for research and policy, Bob Litan, also wrote in *The American* that, "assuming this experiment proves to be as promising as it sounds, the next president should urge the PTO to adopt and Congress to accept this new way of assessing patents much more broadly."[28] Jonathan Schwartz, CEO of Sun Microsystems, named Peer-to-Patent one of the "leading institutions promoting . . . patent reform."[29] In his campaign's technology platform, President Barack Obama called for incorporating Peer-to-Patent into USPTO's regular procedure.[30] The U.S. Chamber of Commerce endorsed the adoption of Peer-to-Patent.[31] In addition, Peer-to-Patent was nominated for the Prix Ars Electronica cyber arts prize for digital communities and the Silicon Valley Tech Museum Award for technology benefiting humanity.

To build on this incipient success, New York Law School established the Center for Patent Innovations to promote and facilitate public participation in the patenting process around the world. The patent offices of the United Kingdom and Japan were the first to follow the USPTO's example, adapting Peer-to-Patent for their own national patent systems and launching similar websites in 2008 and 2009. The patent offices of Australia, Canada, and Europe are exploring online public participation for their own examination processes. The Trilateral Cooperation (the European Patent Office, the Japan Patent Office, and the USPTO) has begun to discuss a multioffice pilot to network the global scientific community to the national patent offices. Pending versions of patent reform legislation left over from the 2007–08 legislative calendar all include provisions to allow for third-party commentary on applications. These bills would also expand the regulatory authority of the USPTO to enable the agency unambiguously to adopt innovations like Peer-to-Patent.

But the implications of Peer-to-Patent reach far beyond the field of intellectual property. Far from being unique to the patent system, the lessons we learned about soliciting far-flung, self-identifying expertise to improve government decisionmaking can be applied to a broad range of environmental, educational, and other policy domains. The technology and social processes that drive Peer-to-Patent can be used to solicit participation in governance on the basis of professional expertise, or local context and experience, or willingness to do research and hard work. For example, the web could be used to structure participation by local communities in EPA decisionmaking about clean air and water. Technology could connect experts in every level of government to one another to solve problems more effectively and more efficiently. An online network of independent university experts—an online brain trust—could be created to advise. Citizen juries could be appointed to oversee the work of every cabinet official or agency head and generate greater accountability. Local groups could even be empowered to spend agency money, report back on how they addressed specific problems, and thereby become eligible for more funding. So much innovation is still possible.

Public conversation about the power of networks is already proliferating. Books such as the *Starfish and the Spider, Here Comes Everyone, Crowdsourcing,* and *Momentum* describe ordinary people coming together into caucuses mediated by technology to promote change. But while the new literature includes inspirational stories about the power of social networking tools, there is still a need for deep and serious thinking about how to apply what is learned about technology to the betterment of public policymaking—or how, in other words, to enhance political institutions with the power of networks.

Connecting the power of the many to the work of the few in government has little precedent, making it difficult to visualize its potential. As the NYU media scholar and critic Jay Rosen comments, "Crowdsourcing will not create any genuinely new things unless people know what is being asked of them."[32] Users of Wikipedia know what to do because they understand what it means to write an entry for an encyclopedia. People share a common image of that collective goal. But despite the growing popularity of online collaboration, experience is fairly limited when it comes to participating in government decisionmaking.

There are new networking tools available to go from Wikipedia to "Wikilaw." The first government authority to start a blog was the Transportation Safety Authority, and that wasn't until 2008![33] While Silicon Valley and Route 128 develop increasingly powerful tools to connect people, policymakers downplay the role of technology in governance. They have not come to grips with the disruption created by this new way of working. This should not come as a surprise. Few institutions readily invite their own obsolescence. The *Encyclopaedia Britannica* did not create Wikipedia. The *New York Times* did not create Craigslist classifieds. Record companies did not create the MySpace social networking and music-sharing site. Existing institutions lack clear incentives to change their own business plans. More important, they lack a blueprint for doing so. Were it only a matter of more technology and a faster Internet, collaborative governance would have come to government long ago.

THE CORE IDEA

In a speech at the New America Foundation, Google CEO Eric Schmidt said about Peer-to-Patent:

> At the Patent and Trademark Office, which is as overloaded as it has ever been, they're running a very significant experiment where they publish the patent applications early for public comment. And guess what? All the players who cared deeply about this bizarre and nerdy patent really go after it because there's no way where their patent examiners can fundamentally get all the insight that the wisdom of crowds can do. Why is that not true of every branch of government? It makes perfect sense, use all those people who care so passionately, and who have a lot of free time, to help you.[34]

The presidential campaign generated unprecedented public engagement. The American public turned out in record numbers to vote and also to participate in getting out the vote. Thousands of experts joined policy committees to advise the Obama campaign via closed listservs, and tens of thousands of "ordinary" people participated in online policy discussions via the open transition website (change.gov). President Obama championed volunteerism with the launch of a national service initiative in honor of Martin Luther King's birthday. The campaign drew—or just drew attention to—a groundswell of enthusiasm for involvement, giving rise to the question, What next?

The Peace Corps and Americorps already offer opportunities for full-time engagement. Now VolunteerMatch and other web-based services help to hook up and reduce the coordination costs for the vast majority who prefer to do part-time community service. While the Internet may have increased participation in mass campaigns and enabled individual participation in civic life, both are divorced from the work of governing.

There is too little diversity of participation in the work of managing society, both participation in traditional government practices and innovative technological strategies that might connect government to the public to solve problems in new ways. While people can take full-time jobs in government, there is no equivalent of VolunteerMatch to connect a network of doctors to the Department of Health and Human Services or to allow a team of scientists to assist with evaluating climate change data for the EPA or the economist and the physicist to collaborate on modeling economic forecasts for Treasury. More to the point, government is not articulating priorities that enable the venture capitalist and the entrepreneur to build new businesses. There are too few projects where government articulates a problem and then the public coordinates the solution, such as NetDay did in the 1990s, when volunteers collaborated to connect local California schools to the Internet, in response to and with the encouragement of the federal and state governments.[35] While there are myriad public-private partnerships, these singular events do not address the opportunity for sustained collaboration and institutional redesign.

After Election Day, those who participated in the 2008 political campaign had the opportunity to engage in government directly. Traditional public participation practices, like peer review or federal advisory committees, select participants by means of complex vetting processes. But only a handful can ever serve. Yet outside of government people are coming together every day coordinated by Internet technology to strive toward common outcomes. Schmidt was therefore right to ask why there are not more opportunities for people to participate in governance.

It is overdue to rethink the legitimacy of attenuated participation in a small number of representative institutions. Instead, democratic theory and the design of governing institutions must be rethought for the age of networks. The opportunity now is to move toward collaborative democracy (of which Peer-to-Patent is an exemplar), in which institutions afford the public the opportunity to select themselves to participate actively in diverse ways.

Collaborative democracy is a new approach for using technology to improve outcomes by soliciting *expertise* (in which expertise is defined broadly to include both scientific knowledge and popular experience) from self-selected peers working together in groups in open networks. By lending their expertise and enthusiasm, volunteer experts can augment the know-how of full-time professionals and coordinate their own strategies. By taking advantage of technology's cost savings, hierarchies can be transformed into collaborative knowledge ecosystems and radically change the culture of government from one of centralized expertise to one in which the public and private sector—organizations and individuals—solve social problems collectively.

The private sector has been quicker than government to recognize that making better decisions requires looking beyond institutionalized centers of expertise. Don Tapscott and Anthony Williams have chronicled this phenomenon in the private sector in *Wikinomics*.[36] In this IBM 2006 global study that asked chief executive officers where they looked for fresh ideas, they cited clients, business partners, and employees far more than their research and development labs.[37] IBM conducts digital brainstorming sessions known as *World Jams,* which allow IBM employees across the globe to make and refine proposals collaboratively for the improvement of the company. Far from being gimmicky online happenings, World Jams are taken so seriously by the blue chip company that the CEO of IBM established a $100 million fund to implement the ten best resulting ideas.[38]

A handful of employees in an institution—any institution—cannot possess as much information as the many dispersed individuals who make up a field. This is why Eli Lilly set up Innocentive Inc. to farm out problems from life sciences companies to a network of 160,000 "solvers." One company recently paid a $1 million bounty for the solution to a complex chemistry problem. The solver was not even a scientist but a lawyer with a knack for chemistry. He answered the intractable question in fewer than four hours! In technology, this insight has been popularized as Joy's law: "No matter who you are, most of the smartest people work for someone else."[39] This quip, attributed to Bill Joy, cofounder of Sun Microsystems, pinpoints the core problem faced by all organizations in an exploding information ecosystem, including government: most knowledge lies outside the boundaries of the institution.

Collaboration is distinct from the concept of crowdsourcing. Jeff Howe, an editor at *Wired* magazine, coined the term *crowdsourcing* to describe the burgeoning phenomenon of "taking a job traditionally performed by a designated agent (usually an employee) and outsourcing it to an undefined, generally large group of people in the form of an open call."[40] (He does use Peer-to-Patent as his one public sector example.)[41] But whereas crowdsourcing generally refers to aggregating the responses of individuals across a network, collaborative democracy aspires to the kind of intentional peer production and shared group effort of Wikipedia, in which volunteers sign up to write encyclopedia entries as a group. While crowdsourcing activities like prediction markets aggregate individual preferences, collaboration implies more robust and diverse coordinating structures that enable people to divvy up tasks and roles. Collaboration does not so much imply throwing people at a problem as coordinating the right people in different roles. Role differentiation not only helps to structure work done across a distance, it also conveys the sense of working as a team. Unlike peer production, which includes purely civic, bottom-up activities, collaborative democracy emphasizes shared work by a government institution and a network of participants. Collaborative participation is the "smoke-filled aquarium"—to borrow an overheard coinage—that combines open-source volunteer participation with government's central coordination, issue framing, and bully pulpit.

In *Wiki Government*, the case for a collaborative vision of democratic theory is bolstered by three arguments woven through the book: collaboration as a distinct form of democratic participation, visual deliberation, and egalitarian self-selection.

First, collaboration is a crucial but not well understood claim of democratic practice. There is a belief that the public does not possess as much expertise as people in government. Furthermore, the technology has not previously existed to make collaboration possible on a large scale. These spurious assumptions have produced an anemic conception of participatory democracy. Participation has generally referred to once-a-year voting or to community deliberation, in which neighbors engage in civil dialogue and public opinion formation on a small scale. New social and visual technologies (sometimes referred to as web 2.0) are demonstrating that people are knowledgeable about everything from cancer to software and that, when given the opportunity to come together on a network and in groups, they can be effective at solving problems (not only deliberating about them). We must therefore distinguish between deliberation and collaboration as forms of participatory practice (which we'll do more of in chapter 2). *Wiki Government* explores many examples of ordinary people joining together to do extraordinary things coordinated via the Internet. Peer-to-Patent is a paradigmatic case of database programmers and wind-farming experts working with patent examining professionals to make a better decision.

Second, the medium matters. To enable collaboration at scale requires designing the practices to make participation manageable and useful and then enabling those practices by means of technology. While the forms of participation will differ when information gathering or priority setting or data analysis is required, the technology should always be designed to reflect the work of the group back to itself so that people know which role they can assume and which tasks to accomplish. This second insight is what I term *visual deliberation*. In traditional deliberative exercises, strict procedures for who can talk govern the public conversation. But collaboration depends, instead, on having tools that convey the structure and rules of any given collaborative practice. This kind of social mirroring can be communicated through software. Peer-to-Patent uses visualizations to communicate the work flow by which information goes from the government institution to the public and back again. The website helps to convey what it means to review a patent application. It exploits rating and reputation techniques that help each group work together as a group, even across a distance. Hence, designing new democratic institutions also depends on designing the appropriate collaborative practices and embedding that design in software.

Third, collaboration is a form of democratic participation that is egalitarian—but egalitarian in a different way than the traditional understanding of the term. Typically, mass participation like voting is thought of as being quite democratic because everyone can participate in the same way. By contrast, Peer-to-Patent is not mass participation. It demands highly technical expertise. Successful participation depends upon the participant's interest in and knowledge of patents. If Peer-to-Patent were the only example of collaborative participation, it would not be egalitarian. But Peer-to-Patent multiplied by a thousand would be more institutionally diverse and complex. If the patent expert and the doctor and the teacher each has a vehicle for engagement, contexts would be created in which they each uniquely possess expertise and derive meaning.

In other words, people do not have to participate in the same exercise. One person may want to work on Peer-to-Patent, another may want to get involved in health care debates. One person may want to work on energy policy; another may want to organize a corps of energy "scouts" to go door-to-door and help neighbors evaluate their energy usage. The ability to self-select to participate in the arena of one's choosing is what makes collaborative democracy egalitarian. A person may be an expert on wetlands because she possesses professional credentialing. Another person may be an expert on wetlands because she lives near one. Perhaps it is a level of know-how or the enthusiasm to commit more time that generates status in other domains. For every project, there is a different kind of expertise, which could be sought. Experts will flock to those opportunities that exploit their intelligence. In this choice lies the equality of opportunity.

What does collaborative democracy look like in practice? In the old way of working, the bureaucrat might decide to repair a bridge in response to an opinion poll or vote that randomly obtains feedback. Or the bureaucrat might publish a fully developed plan to repair the bridge, ostensibly soliciting comment in response to a notice of proposed regulation, attracting participation by formal interest groups and lobbyists but not ordinary citizens, who can never hope to match the power and influence of corporate interests. Community groups might use the web to lobby for bridge repair but with no greater opportunity to get involved in detailed decisions. The government or a nongovernmental organization (NGO) might organize a face-to-face deliberative discussion about the bridge and hope to use the event to trigger a newspaper article that will influence the decision. A similar online discussion may or may not attract attention.

Under a collaborative strategy, the bureaucrat establishes the process, then frames and asks the questions that will get targeted information from bridge users (the truck driver, the commuter), from an engineer, and from the informed enthusiast. The public can contribute evidence and data to help inform specific decisions, analyze data once gathered, and share in the work of editing, drafting, and implementing policies. Alternatively, if officials articulate the priority of bridge safety, they might spur private sector businesses, nonprofits, and individuals to develop their own strategies, such as organizing a volunteer corps of bridge safety inspectors who log their work on a shared website. Citizens are no longer talking about the process: they are the process.

The future of public institutions demands that we create a collaborative ecosystem with numerous opportunities for those with expertise about a problem) to engage. There is a Plum Book, which lists government jobs, and there is a Prune Book, which lists the toughest management positions. The pluot is supposed to be the sweetest variety of plum (or plum plus apricot). Yet there is no Pluot Book cataloging opportunities for part-time participation in government! When participatory democracy is defined to include diverse strategies for collaboration, when these thousands of opportunities to self-select come to light, a Pluot Book may well be needed.

OVERVIEW OF THE BOOK

This book offers a rethinking of the meaning of participatory democracy in the digital age. At the same time, it is a how-to guide for bringing about collaborative democracy and the practices of collaborative governance using the tools of law, policy, and technology. Practical experience with the Peer-to-Patent program enhances understanding of the core problem: a failure to grasp the changing nature of expertise in the digital age and the resulting misconception of both effective institutional practices and legitimate democratic theory.

Chapter 2 argues that the "single point of failure" in government can be transformed through new mechanisms for obtaining expertise. Decisionmaking is currently organized around the notion that the government official knows best. In reality, agencies make decisions every day without access to the best information or the time to make sense of the information they have. Citizen participation traditionally focuses on deliberation but, in the Internet age, it will not be as successful as collaboration in remedying the information deficit. The broader mandate is to use technology to upend the outdated theory of institutional expertise and replace it with collaborative practices for gathering and evaluating information and transforming raw data into useful knowledge.

Chapters 3 and 4 tell the story of the Peer-to-Patent pilot. Chapter 3 illustrates the single-point-of-failure problem by showcasing the crisis of patent quality—the problem to which Peer-to-Patent was designed to respond. Whether or not one knows or cares about patents—though there is plenty of reason to do both—the information deficit faced by the Patent Office is paradigmatic of the practices of centralized decisionmaking in government. The aim in chapter 3 is therefore to provide a detailed account of how the Patent Office gets—or fails to get—the information it needs to make important decisions and to detail the consequences of this failure.

Chapter 4 begins to explain how to move toward a collaborative solution to the governance challenge described in chapter 3. It describes the development of the Peer-to-Patent website—what it is, how it worked, and why it worked—to illustrate the process through which innovative participatory practices can be designed and adopted. The story of Peer-to-Patent begins with an in-depth exploration of the innovative role of technology design in making citizen participation practices manageable. Instead of designing for deliberation—pure talk—I argue for what I term *visual deliberation,* namely, ways of using the computer screen to mirror the work of participating groups back to themselves so that they can organize and function as networked publics. Creative uses of the interface through which people interact with the computer and therefore with each other also make information manageable and intelligible and reduce the problem of information overload. From talking about the design of the collaborative project, the chapter concludes with a discussion of the collaborative design process that led to the creation of the project.

Perhaps the most important chapters of the book are those in part 3, "Thinking in Wiki." These chapters generalize from the Peer-to-Patent project to online participation in other arenas of governance.

Chapter 5 focuses on the role of information in collaboration, arguing for a government information policy that enables the collection and distribution of information in ways that engender participation. Data can become more useful as a result of group participation. Groups not only can help to visualize information in graphic formats that make it more intelligible but these graphical formats can also focus the work on solving problems. As a baseline condition, information must be transparent—accessible, searchable, and usable—to lend itself to collaboration.

Chapter 6 examines the history of citizen collaboration and its future. This chapter situates Peer-to-Patent against the backdrop of transparency and participation legislation and regulation. The aim is to uncover why—despite past attempts to introduce innovative and participatory practices into administration, including those that exploit Internet technology—agencies have not always had access to enough information nor have citizens enjoyed meaningful participation in government decisionmaking.

Chapter 7 asks what will produce such innovations in government. Peer-to-Patent was brokered by an outside organization that pushed for this citizen participation effort, building on the momentum of web 2.0 technologies. But to transform the culture of government and create lasting change, there has to be evangelism from within as well as without. This should be the job of the senior leadership, such as the new role of U.S. chief technology officer created by President Obama. Senior government management should use the bully pulpit to exhort public institutions to put collaborative democracy into effect. The CTO can be the champion of participatory innovations to connect institutions to public expertise. I offer examples of such innovations, including the policy wiki and the citizen jury, which might produce more open, and ultimately more legitimate, ways for government to work.

Finally, chapter 8 offers lessons for designing better practices to engage the public in government. These lessons apply both to information-gathering projects like Peer-to-Patent and to policy wikis, citizen juries, online brainstorming, and other innovations in participation. Collectively, these lessons form the basis of a new design science of government. Designing for democracy requires law, technology, and policy to create more effective institutions. Such a design approach has the potential to enhance the legitimacy of government; it also empowers participants. Ordinary citizens have more to offer than voting or talking. They can contribute their expertise and, in so doing, realize the opportunity to be powerful.

This book speaks to three audiences: those interested in the story of Peer-to-Patent as a lesson in patent reform; those aficionados of web 2.0 interested in a specific case study of how to apply collaboration in the government arena; and government reformers interested in improving decisionmaking. The chapters of the book unwind the argument about collaborative democracy and the role of social and visual technology in enabling collaboration. Patent experts may want to skim the patent problem in chapter 3 and focus, instead, on the specifics of Peer-to-Patent in chapter 4 and subsequent chapters that describe the lessons learned. Web 2.0 enthusiasts who already "get" collaboration but do not know the government context can skim the book's justification, articulated in chapter 2, and dig right into the story of Peer-to-Patent (chapters 3 and 4) and the challenge of collaboration in government (chapters 5 through 8). Government reformers with no particular patent bent will want to read the opening chapters 1 and 2 carefully to understand the distinction between deliberation and collaboration and then focus on the lessons of Peer-to-Patent in chapters 5 to 8.

Peer-to-Patent is an experiment. But that's the point: the best strategy is to try something: to see what works to bring about a more engaged citizenry. Peer-to-Patent demonstrates a way to solicit help from those with know-how, passion, and enthusiasm.

CHAPTER TWO

THE SINGLE POINT OF FAILURE

The world is full of amateurs: gifted amateurs, devoted amateurs. You can pick almost any group that has any kind of intrinsic interest in it, from dragonflies to pill bugs to orb-weaving spiders. Anybody can pick up information in interesting places, find new species or rediscover what was thought to be a vanished species, or some new biological fact about a species already known.

E. O. WILSON

THE PATENT SYSTEM IS just one example of how government institutions create single points of failure by concentrating decisionmaking power in the hands of the few, whether legislators in Congress, cabinet officials in the executive branch, or bureaucrats in agencies. Administrative practices are constructed around the belief that government professionals know best how to translate broad legislative mandates into specific regulatory decisions in the public interest. Governance, the theory goes, is best entrusted to a bureaucracy operating at one remove from the pressure of electoral politics and the biased influence of the public at large.

THE CLOSED MODEL OF DECISIONMAKING

The rationale for this closed model of decisionmaking, as explained by such theorists as Max Weber and Walter Lippmann, is rooted in the assumptions of an earlier age. Although citizens may express personal opinions, they are thought to lack the ability to make informed decisions on complex policy matters. Moreover, democratic pessimists warn, government officials must be protected from the factionalized public that Madison so feared in *Federalist 10*. To ward off this danger, centralized power is concentrated in the apolitical professional or, in Weber's words, "the personally detached and strictly objective expert."[1] Only government professionals possess the impartiality, expertise, resources, discipline, and time to make public decisions. Or so it is assumed. The assumption is not unjustified insofar as the technology has not been available before to organize participation easily. Participation in a representative democracy is largely confined to voting in elections, joining interest groups, and getting involved in local civic or political affairs.

Thus the patent examiner, like her counterparts throughout government, must act as an expert in fields far outside her ken. The process of determining which inventor deserves a patent demands that she analyze and synthesize scientific and technical information about cutting-edge areas of innovation over which she has no real mastery. In any given subject area there are scientists, engineers, and lawyers with greater expertise, as well as laypersons with valuable insights, but the patent examiner has no access to them. In this she is not alone. In a survey of environmental lawyers, for example, only 8 percent of respondents thought that the EPA has sufficient time to search the relevant science before making a decision about environmental policy, and only 6 percent believed that agencies employ adequate analysis in their decisionmaking.[2] The bureaucrat in Washington often lacks access to the right information or to the expertise necessary to make sense of a welter of available information. This can pose a challenge to good decisionmaking and to creativity in problem solving.

The single point of failure results not just from a lack of time or resources or technology. It goes much deeper than that. Simply put, professionals do not have a monopoly on information or expertise, as the social psychologist Philip Tetlock observes. In his award-winning book *On Political Judgment* Tetlock analyzes the predictions of professional political pundits against modest performance benchmarks. He finds "few signs that expertise translates into greater ability to make either 'well-calibrated' or 'discriminating' forecasts."[3] While smart people can explain, they often cannot predict and therefore make decisions based on spectacularly bad guesses.

Pacifists do not abandon Mahatma Gandhi's worldview just because of the sublime naïveté of his remark in 1940 that he did not consider Adolf Hitler to be as bad as "frequently depicted" and that "he seems to be gaining his victories without much bloodshed"; many environmentalists defend Paul Ehrlich despite his notoriously bad track record in the 1970s and the 1980s (he predicted massive food shortages just as new technologies were producing substantial surpluses); Republicans do not change their views about the economic competence of Democratic administrations just because Martin Feldstein predicted that the legacy of the Clinton 1993 budget would be stagnation for the rest of the decade; social democrats do not overhaul their outlook just because Lester Thurow predicted that the 1990s would witness the ascendancy of the more compassionate capitalism of Europe and Japan over the "devil take the hindmost" American model.[4]

It turns out that professional status has much less bearing on the quality of information than might be assumed and that professionals—whether in politics or other domains—are notoriously unsuccessful at making accurate predictions. Or as Scott Page, the University of Michigan author of *The Difference,* pithily puts it: "Diversity trumps ability"—this is a mathematical truth, not a feel-good mantra.[5]

Moreover, government or government-endorsed professionals are not more impervious to political influence than the impassioned public that bureaucrats are supposed to keep at arm's length. Often the scientists and outside experts who are asked to give impartial advice to government are lobbyists passing by another name. The National Coal Council, made up almost exclusively of coal industry representatives, sits on the Department of Energy's federal advisory committee on coal policy: the department has adopted 80 percent of the Coal Council's recommendations.[6] White House officials regularly replace experts on agency advisory panels with ideologues and political allies (or eliminate advisory councils altogether). An Environmental Working Group study finds that the seven EPA panels that evaluated proposed safe daily exposure levels to commercial chemicals in 2007 included seventeen members who were employed by, or who received research funding from, companies with a financial stake in the outcome.[7]

In a published statement titled *Restoring Scientific Integrity in Policy Making,* over 60 preeminent scientists, including Nobel laureates and National Medal of Science recipients, lambasted George W. Bush's administration for having "manipulated the process through which science enters into its decisions."[8] In 2008, 889 of nearly 1,600 EPA staff scientists reported that they had experienced political interference in their work over the last five years.[9] But if the Bush administration is among the more egregious violators of the presumed wall between politics and institutionalized expertise, its actions only go to show how easy it is for any executive to abuse his power while claiming the mantle of expertise.

Taking a historical view, the journalist Chris Mooney, in his book *The Republican War on Science,* persuasively explains that the marriage of big business to the religious right in the Reagan era has resulted in a systematic abuse of science in regulatory decisionmaking.[10] What began during World War II as an intimate relationship between science and politics—the flames of whose passion were fueled by the competitive jealousy of the cold war and the attentions of an intellectually inclined Kennedy administration—has now waned. The rise of conservatism spurred a movement to create alternative sources for scientific information. Hiding behind the skirt of science, antievolution and antiabortion politics create pressure to misrepresent science to serve political ends. At the same time, the fear by big business that scientific research might impel expensive environmental and consumer regulation further contributes to a distortion of the use of science in policymaking. Mooney readily acknowledges that the Left as well as the Right makes decisions on the basis of political value judgments rather than facts. But whereas Democrats, he contends, sometimes conduct politics in spite of science, choosing to ignore the data in pursuit of a normative end, Republicans dress up politics as science and attempt to name such positions "creation science" behind a veneer of scientific legitimacy.

The problem of relying solely on professionals is compounded by the practice of confidential decisionmaking. While federal government agencies are required by law to conduct meetings in the open (and many state governments have similar sunshine laws), this spirit is violated by regular backroom dealings with lobbyists.[11] Under the Bush administration, the attorney general changed the presumption of disclosure under Freedom of Information Act requests away from the prevailing standard to make it more difficult for agencies to release information and allow agencies to defend decisions to withhold records "unless they lack a sound legal basis."[12] President Obama changed it back. It is not surprising that the American people perceive government to be taking place behind closed doors (three-quarters of American adults surveyed in 2008 view the federal government as secretive, an increase from 62 percent in 2006).[13] Massive financial bailout measures taken late in 2008 met with concerns that these troubled asset relief programs lacked transparency or monitoring. There have been myriad instances of information being deliberately hidden.

The Bush administration threatened to shut down the award-winning economic indicators website, which combines data like GDP, net imports and exports, and retail sales to make it convenient for viewers to assess the state of the economy.[14] The administration also announced it would no longer produce the Census Bureau's Survey of Income and Program Participation, which identifies which programs best assist low-income families, and stop publishing its report on international terrorism, making it more difficult for citizens to find important and useful news.[15] The Bush administration has taken down reports about mass layoffs and, by executive order, limited the publication of presidential records.[16] Until 1999 the USPTO did not publish patent applications until they were granted.[17] Even today, the office is circumspect about Internet research to avoid compromising the privacy and confidentiality of the decisionmaking process.[18] The less those outside the government know about its activities, self-evidently, the greater the need to rely on internal experts. When the public cannot see how decisions are arrived at, it cannot identify problems and criticize mistakes. Accountability declines and so does government effectiveness.

New Technologies and Civic Life

Technology enables collective action in civil society and helps some people to route around the logjam created by the single point of failure. Countless civic groups already use new communication and information-sharing tools to promote political action, operate an opposition movement, or mobilize community activism. Collaborative governance needs to be distinguished from this kind of civic action that is independent of government—change.org instead of change.gov.

The Carrotmob project in San Francisco uses the "carrot" of consumer buying power to encourage small businesses to help the environment.[19] Web-based tools are used to organize a consumer "flashmob," which channels business to stores that commit to environmental improvements. Carrotmob organizer Brent Schulkin asked local businesses how much they would be willing to invest in environmental improvements if the group he convened were to organize a buying spree directed toward that business. The result for the winning bodega in San Francisco's Mission District: more than triple the sales of an average Saturday, lots of free advertising, oodles of community goodwill, and a scheme to pay for improvements that, in turn, will save the business money over the long run.

Similarly, Obama Works, a corps of self-organizing citizen volunteers with no connection to Barack Obama's presidential campaign, used Internet technologies to organize neighborhood cleanups not only on a local scale but also on a national scale.[20] Tech for Obama similarly galvanized support for the campaign within the techie community.[21] Supporters, independent of the campaign, even went so far as to create "campaign offices" to recruit volunteers and organize voters. The largest one, in Silicon Valley, California, started on December 15, 2007.[22] Its Neighborhood Teams project geocoded the records of 1.5 million voters and used them to help over 40,000 neighbors find each other and volunteer in support of Obama. They produced and sent daily e-mail newsletters to 5,000 people. Its thirty-five-person technology team built its own tools to overcome inefficiencies in the organizing process. For its part, the official Obama campaign organized a summer program for Obama fellows (students and recent graduates who were recruited online) to come together and spend six weeks learning basic organizing skills from grassroots leaders. Senator Obama also spoke out publicly about creating a grassroots civic structure that could survive the campaign and continue to work on community issues after the election. In addition to meeting face to face, these volunteers used the Internet to form groups, organize, and bring about social change.

Both Carrotmob and the activities swirling about the Obama campaign are vivid examples of the use of new media technologies to convene and organize groups of people who, working together, can be more effective than any individual acting alone. Other examples include powerful online netroots organizations and blogs, ranging from MoveOn.org on the left to Red State at the other end of the political spectrum.

Civic groups are also taking advantage of new technologies to shine the light of greater transparency on government from afar. These third-party brokers of transparency are helping to do what government is not doing enough of for itself. The Cato Institute's Jim Harper launched the WashingtonWatch program to track bills in Congress and estimate their cost or savings, if implemented into law.[23] The Center for Responsive

Politics started OpenSecrets; and the New York Gallery Eyebeam launched Fundrace (now part of the Huffington Post blog) to make the Federal Election Commission's databases easier to understand and search.[24] PublicMarkup.org used collaborative editing software, known as a wiki, to mark up the Transparency in Government Act of 2008 and the various economic stabilization and bailout proposals floated during the economic crisis in the fall of that year.[25] MapLight.org shines the light of transparency on money politics by illuminating who contributed to which politician and how he or she subsequently voted.[26]

But while online communities to date may have enabled people to click together instead of bowling alone, they are not yet producing changes in the way government institutions obtain and use information. These purely civic programs are disconnected from the practices and priorities of government. They may circle around political themes and issues but are not tied into institutional processes. They are, therefore, limited in what they can accomplish. A few pioneering programs, such as Connecticut's CityScan program, suggest forms that such change might take were we to redesign rather than try to route around the workings of government.[27] Launched in the mid-1990s by the Connecticut Policy and Economic Council, CityScan helped city governments in Bridgeport and other municipalities collaborate with local communities to rescue derelict land-use sites. The organization secured a promise from each city to assist with the cleanup of a given number of parcels. Senior citizens and young people used first-generation digital cameras and handheld devices to photograph and track the progress of the work in their own communities. They mapped conditions on a website. The community groups communicated local information about land use that the government would not otherwise have had. They worked alongside the government while holding it accountable.

The government, in turn, worked with the CityScan teams, taking action based on their input and thereby giving relevance and impetus to these volunteer efforts. Technology helped both sides to organize the collaboration and to visualize its success. But the crux of CityScan was not the tools. The practices that CityScan evolved for robust collaboration between groups of citizens and local government are what differentiated this work from that of most civic action.

Collaboration and collective action, of course, are not new. Since the early nineteenth century members of the august Athenaeum Club on Pall

Mall in London have penned questions in a shared book, which was left in the club's leather-chaired drawing room for other members—including Dickens and Thackeray—to answer.[28] The book is still there.

As Stephen Kosslyn, chair of the Harvard Department of Psychology, explains, working together allows people to utilize many different tools. He says that, because we "simply do not have enough genes to program the brain fully in advance," we must extend our own intelligence with what he terms *social prosthetic systems*.[29] At the most basic level, we need to pool our diverse knowledge and skills. Even institutions need prosthetic extensions to make themselves smarter and more effective. Virtually all activities of public life, including activism and organizing, depend on the work of teams. Until recently, however, most teams have relied heavily on physical proximity.

In the pre-Internet era, when working at a distance was not possible to the same extent (I had to be near you to join you), participation would have demanded a far greater time commitment to a cause. In the decade leading up to the American Revolution, the colonies organized Committees of Correspondence to communicate their practices of self-governance and fortify their opposition to the British.[30] Through the exchange of ideas about successful ways of working, they coordinated decentralized efforts at resistance across a distance. But they were committed to this all-important cause. Anything less and one would still have had to attend meetings to accomplish shared goals or alternatively pay dues to an organization to work on one's behalf. The ability now to use new technology to organize shared work makes it possible to work in groups across distance and institutional boundaries. Technology can reinforce the sense of working as a group by recreating some of the conditions of face-to-face work environments that build trust and belonging. The ability to organize collective activity puts more power in the hands of individuals by making it possible for people to self-organize and form teams around a boundless variety of goals, interests, and skill sets. And technology can support the formation of larger and more complex teams than previously imaginable.

Not surprisingly, the software community has been in the forefront of efforts to tap these benefits. Harvey Anderson, general counsel of the Mozilla Foundation, which makes the Firefox browser, says of the Mozilla community of volunteer programmers: "Many is better than one." He echoes a common refrain among those who work on open-source governance: "Whenever we confront a problem, we have to ask ourselves: How do I parse and distribute the problem? How might we build feedback loops that incorporate more people?"[31]

The volunteer efforts extend the capacity of the full-time staff at Mozilla. By asking a community to help fix bugs in the software and rewrite the code, the organization begins to rely more and more on its community of volunteers, most of whom are not full time and most of whom may not even be known to the central project leadership. Instead, by articulating a set of common goals the Mozilla Foundation helps disparate groups of people organize themselves and perform practical, concrete tasks toward a shared end.[32] What begins as a process of information gathering builds steam and ends up creating a culture of engagement. Whereas the Mozilla organization makes the final decision about which software version to release, and when, the centralized organization cannot make these decisions without the help of the community of volunteers upon whom it relies to do the work. As the community comes to be more involved, actual decisionmaking becomes a more amorphous concept, and control becomes dispersed. Everyone in the network has an influence.

Similarly, when a policy problem is divided into smaller parts, so that it can be distributed and worked on by collaborative teams, the drive toward openness and innovation begins. This openness may help government do its job better by bringing better information to the institution. But it can also introduce the institutional priorities to more people so that competition for solutions can emerge. Impelled by government mandate, the private sector and civil society might suggest their own solutions, evolving more robust public-private approaches, which may produce greater legitimacy than government currently enjoys. It may also help to solve complex economic and social problems faster and more efficiently.

New networking technologies, such as those embodied in Peer-to-Patent, provide an opportunity to rethink the closed practices by which agencies gather information and make decisions. In 2007 the U.S. Congress mandated, and the president signed, a complete changeover by 2014 from incandescent bulbs to new, energy-efficient but mercury-containing lightbulbs. Congress instructed the EPA to implement the law into regulations. The agency, however, did not yet have a plan for disposing of the 300 million new mercury-containing bulbs sold in the United States in 2007—a number that will only increase as the mandate approaches.[33] The EPA could have solved this problem at little additional cost by setting up a simple online platform to involve a network of concerned citizens and organizations in identifying both the challenges raised by the new law and possible solutions—a lightbulb clearinghouse. Private sector companies might have stepped up to offer mercury reclamation programs sooner; foundations might have funded prizes to social entrepreneurs who devised effective solutions; interest groups might have run competitions among their members for effective recycling practices; scientists could have pointed out that they were working on the creation of a "nanoselenium" cloth to clean up mercury spills.[34] Creating new channels of communication would not only inform and improve information gathering, but it could also lead to improved decisionmaking and greater citizen involvement.

Policymakers have been slow to seize these opportunities. Innovation is not emanating from Washington; instead, the practices of government are increasingly disconnected from technological innovation and the opportunity to realize greater citizen participation—and therefore more expert information—in government. At the very least, this means that government institutions are not working as well as they might, producing declining rates of trust in government. (In 2008 the approval rating of both Congress and the president declined below 30 percent and, in some polls, even below 10 percent.)[35] At the very worst, there is a crisis of legitimacy. Clearly, relying on a small number of institutional players to make important decisions is not the only or the best way to confront complex social problems.

One explanation for this government failure lies in the unfamiliarity with technology displayed by many policymakers, including those responsible for its regulation. In the debate over net neutrality, then Senator Ted Stevens of Alaska, vice chair of the Senate Subcommittee on Science and Innovation, infamously referred to the Internet as "a series of tubes."[36] While tubes could arguably be a reasonable metaphor, history has not been kind to Senator Stevens, whose literal remark has now become iconic (it has its own Wikipedia entry) of Washington's ignorance of technology. But lack of technical knowledge is not the only cause of the government's slowness to capitalize on the promise of networked, online groups. An even more fundamental explanation lies in the outdated theory of participatory democracy that drives the design of government institutions.

PARTICIPATORY DEMOCRATIC THEORY
IN THE AGE OF NETWORKS

After the advent of the World Wide Web, many anticipated that the Internet would revolutionize government, enabling an increase in political participation: an e-democracy as well as an e-commerce revolution. Pundits heralded a new Periclean Golden Age and celebrated the civic opportunities of the new communications and information technologies.[37] The deliberative ideal of people with diverse backgrounds and differing viewpoints debating and even voting on public issues was about to become a reality. It did not happen.[38]

THE FAILURE OF DIRECT DEMOCRACY

Proponents of direct democracy (sometimes called pure democracy) hoped that the Internet would promote participation unmediated by representative politics by allowing citizens to express themselves through voting (referenda, initiatives, recalls) more often on a wider range of issues.[39] Direct democrats argue for the use of technology to bolster such forms of direct participation as the initiative and referendum as a way to speed up the pace of governance.

During his presidential bid Ross Perot celebrated the direct democratic ideal and advocated that the president communicate directly with the American public via new media and encouraging the public to vote regularly and directly from home on issues.[40] Auburn University houses a center dedicated to teledemocracy—large-scale, Internet-enabled, direct democracy.[41] Aficionados of proxy voting like the idea of using the web to allocate one's votes to a trusted interest group of one's choosing to render direct democratic voting better informed and more practical to administer.[42] A now-defunct Swedish company pioneered online proxy voting in the political arena, a practice in common use in the corporate sector.[43]

But security and reliability problems have plagued the rollout of both electronic, kiosk-based, voting and Internet-based vote-from-home technologies in the United States. Annual political elections are hard enough to run without introducing yet more possibilities for voter fraud and abuse. Instead, new services, such as Smartvote.ch from Switzerland, use the Internet to inform voting at the polling booth. Smartvote allows the user to plug in opinions in response to questions. The software then tabulates which candidate or proposal is closest to the user's own views. Countless informational websites have sprung up around the electoral process, whether it is the *Washington Post*'s subscription service to inform the reader every time her elected official casts a vote or one of myriad webcasts of online legislative coverage designed to inform and render the political process more accountable by virtue of its being transparent.[44]

But the notion of widespread, push-button democracy in whatever form does little to address how to institutionalize complex decisions in particular cases. It is no wonder that the vision of participation by direct democratic voting has not taken off.

THE TIMIDITY OF DELIBERATIVE DEMOCRACY

Deliberative democracy has been the dominant view of participation in contemporary political theory. At its center is the Habermasian notion that the reasoned exchange of discourse by diverse individuals representative of the public at large produces a more robust political culture and a healthier democracy.[45] It has almost become a commonplace that people of diverse viewpoints should talk to one another town-hall style in public (this despite the fact that some recent empirical research even suggests that talking to people of differing viewpoints correlates to *reduced* participation in community life).[46] It is a normative, democratic ideal unto itself and a means to the end of enhancing legitimacy in governance.

With the reduction in the cost of communications since the Internet, the hope had been that new information technologies would result in more widespread deliberation. Early e-democracy thinkers were optimistic that new technology could promote open discourse, equal participation, reasoned discussion, and the inclusion of diverse viewpoints. By allowing diverse participants to come together regardless of the boundaries of geography and time, the Internet could help overcome the hurdle of groupthink—a state in which like-minded people fail to consider alternatives adequately and fall prey to their own ideology.[47] Like direct democrats, advocates of deliberative democracy have also been disappointed. While social-scientific experiments in deliberation proliferate, deliberative theory founders on the practical reality of present-day political decisionmaking. In practice, such conversations have been difficult to achieve, especially on a large scale.[48]

The weakness of the deliberative approach is not that it reaches too far (as direct democracy may) but that it does not reach far enough. By making talk the centerpiece of its normative aspirations, deliberative democracy's proponents assume that people are generally powerless and incapable of doing more than talking with neighbors to develop opinions or criticizing government to keep it honest. In theory, convening people of diverse viewpoints can have a beneficial impact on policy—assuming that the political system is structured to translate those viewpoints into meaningful participation in decisionmaking.[49] But in practice, civic talk is largely disconnected from power. It does not take account of the fact that in a web 2.0 world ordinary people can collaborate with one another to do extraordinary things.

The anthropology of deliberative participation leads to practices designed to present the finished work of institutional professionals, spark public opinion in response, and keep peace among neighbors engaged in civic discourse. The goal is not to improve decisionmaking, for "there is no one best outcome; instead, there is a respectful communicative process."[50] The desire for civilized discussion and dispute resolution lead to a requirement of demographically balanced representation in the conversation. This may ensure inclusion of all affected interests but does not, as Alexander Meiklejohn said, necessarily result in an airing of all ideas worth hearing.[51] Deliberative democracy relegates the role of citizens to discussion only indirectly related to decisionmaking and action. The reality of deliberation is that it is toothless. Perhaps it is, as Shaw once said: The single biggest problem in communication is the illusion that it has taken place.

In 2002, for example, the Civic Alliance to Rebuild Downtown New York (with the help of AmericaSpeaks, a civic group that organizes public deliberation, and the sponsorship of the Lower Manhattan Development Corporation) convened Listening to the City, a demographically representative deliberation exercise that brought 4,500 New Yorkers together in person and 800 online to talk about the first set of designs for the World Trade Center site.[52] After hearing a presentation of the proposed plans, the group was highly critical. The high-profile, public nature of the event attracted a front-page story in the *New York Times*. It led directly to officials scuttling the plans and initiating a second round of designs.

The people power, as the populist historian Howard Zinn might say, of a large number of people massing in physical space created political pressure.[53] But people were neither expected nor invited to offer advice and expertise to inform the new plans. In this carefully orchestrated deliberation, they did not have an opportunity to get involved in the cleanup nor to identify problems or solutions to the mounting environmental and economic development challenges in the area. The problem was not presented in ways that could have led to private sector assistance either in the government's effort or as an adjunct to it. Nothing about the weekend changed or improved the way government works. Arguably, the Lower Manhattan Development Corporation used the Listening to the City exercise to appear responsive to citizens' concerns while obscuring the real power politics at play, ultimately depriving New Yorkers of the chance to participate rather than simply react.[54]

The political sociologist Michael Schudson writes about the "monitorial citizen," who is too busy to play an active role in government.[55] While it is important and useful that government is responsive to the watchful citizen, this passive vision does not recognize the full potential of ordinary people to share expert information and effort with government. Among members of the public are scientists, engineers, doctors, lawyers, students, teachers, and nonprofessionals with a wide range of experience and enthusiasm who can contribute to an understanding of energy independence by submitting data. Others can analyze information given to them about endangered species or participate in the drafting of policies about transportation. There are expert conferences daily, where instead of presenting disconnected academic papers great minds might also be enlisted to solve pressing social problems. These potential resources for public decisionmaking are largely going to waste.

DISTINGUISHING DELIBERATIVE AND COLLABORATIVE DEMOCRACY

There is a difference within participatory democracy between the two related but distinct notions of deliberation and collaboration. Deliberation focuses on citizens discussing their views and opinions about what the state should and should not do. The ability for people to talk across a distance facilitates the public exchange of reasoned talk. But deliberative polls, neighborhood assemblies, consensus councils, citizen panels, and other conversation-centered experiments, whether online or off, have not translated into improvements in decisionmaking practices. The underlying Internet and telecommunications infrastructure is essential to conversing across a distance, but the Internet by itself is not the "killer app." If it were, the history of citizen participation in government institutions, which I describe in chapter 6, would already look very different.

While both deliberation and collaboration may be group-based, deliberative democracy suffers from a lack of imagination in that it fails to acknowledge the importance of connecting diverse skills, as well as diverse viewpoints, to public policy. Whereas diverse viewpoints might make for a more lively conversation, diverse skills are essential to collaboration.

Deliberation measures the quality of democracy on the basis of the procedural uniformity and equality of inputs. Collaboration shifts the focus to the effectiveness of decisionmaking and outputs.

Deliberation requires an agenda for orderly discussion. Collaboration requires breaking down a problem into component parts that can be parceled out and assigned to members of the public and officials.

Deliberation either debates problems on an abstract level before the implementation of the solution or discusses the solution after it has already been decided upon. Collaboration occurs throughout the decisionmaking process. It creates a multiplicity of opportunities and outlets for engagement to strengthen a culture of participation and the quality of decisionmaking in government itself.

Deliberation is focused on opinion formation and the general will (or sometimes on achieving consensus). Consensus is desirable as an end unto itself.[56] Collaboration is a means to an end. Hence the emphasis is not on participation for its own sake but on inviting experts, loosely defined as those with expertise about a problem, to engage in information gathering, information evaluation and measurement, and the development of specific solutions for implementation.

Deliberation focuses on self-expression. Collaboration focuses on participation. To conflate deliberative democracy with participatory democracy is to circumscribe participation by boundaries that technology has already razed. In fact, the distinctions between deliberation and collaboration become even more pronounced in the online environment, whose characteristics are increasingly making collaboration easier.[57] New technologies make it possible to join ever more groups and teams. Such familiar websites as Wikipedia, Facebook, and even videogames like World of Warcraft inculcate the practices of shared group work, be it writing encyclopedia entries or slaying monsters, at a distance.

New technology is also making it possible to divvy up tasks among a group. "Digg-style" tools for submitting and rating the quality of others' submissions have become commonplace ways to sort large quantities of information. Finally, the digital environment offers new ways to engage in the public exchange of reason. With new tools, people can "speak" through shared maps and diagrams rather than meetings. Competing proposals, using computer-driven algorithms and prediction markets, can evolve. Policy simulations using graphic technology can be created. Social networking tools enable collaborative making, doing, crafting, and creating. Yet most of the work at the intersection of technology and democracy has focused on how to create demographically representative conversations.[58] The focus is on deliberation, not collaboration; on talk instead of action; on information, not decisionmaking.

CHALLENGES FOR COLLABORATIVE DEMOCRACY

Critics might suggest that there already exists an architecture of participation, involving a wide array of actors in policymaking processes. Corporations participate through lobbyists and notice-and-comment rulemaking. Nongovernmental organizations, too, funnel information to government through think tanks, white papers, and publications. Interest groups lobby and enlist their members to respond—usually through postcards and e-mail—in rulemaking and legislative policymaking. Scientists and others participate in deliberative, small-group, federal advisory committees that give advice to officials. And more public deliberation exercises, when they take place, help to generate opinion formation.

What is lacking, though, are effective ways for government to be responsive to the public, as opposed to corporate interests, large stakeholders, and interest groups. These citizen participation strategies suffer from the problem of "capture"—excessive political influence. Nominees are often subjected to ideological litmus tests. Lobbyists use their ability to participate to stall rather than inform the regulatory process. The use of notice-and-comment periods (in response to agency-proposed rule-making), which solicit individual participation, is typically late in the process, when policies are all but finalized. And people are too busy anyway to do the work of professionals in government.

What will prevent new, networked publics from becoming as entrenched as the lobbying culture that has produced the failures of current politics is that collaborative democracy seeks to proliferate many smaller opportunities for openness. The EPA doesn't need 100,000 people to work on the issue of asbestos or mercury. While some issues attract a huge number of people, obscure (yet important) decisions are made every day in government that could be made better if technology were used to open participation and oversight to a few dozen experts and enthusiasts: those that blogger Andy Oram calls the microelite: the 5 or 10 or 100 people who understand a discrete question and who are passionate about getting involved in a particular way.[59] Collaborative democracy is about making it easier for such people to find the areas where they want to work and contribute.

Some will counter that more active involvement in government by self-selecting private citizens would only increase the risk of corruption. Their fear is that opening up channels of participation would create a whole new class of online lobbyists and campaigns that participate to serve their own financial interests. Perhaps. But if the practices of twenty-first-century government were designed to split up tasks into many small fact-gathering and decisionmaking exercises, technology would diversify against that risk. It is harder to corrupt a system with many parts. This approach would also make it easier for busy people to participate. And if government decisions were designed to be made in groups, group members would keep each other honest and blow the whistle if corruption occurs.

The primary challenge when engaging in deliberation is to avoid capture and corruption by those who speak with the most influence. In a collaborative governance environment the greatest challenge is one of design: organizing the work most effectively to tap outside expertise. The bureaucrats who design the collaborative processes might be tempted to set them up in such a way as to promote participation by particular vested interests over others. But open processes that enable people to evaluate one another's participation help to preclude the risks. At the very least, technology makes it possible to organize decisionmaking in ways that might overcome abuses familiar from the offline world. If governance is thought of as a granular and focused set of practices, ways can be designed to delegate greater power to citizens to gather facts, spend money, and participate in making decisions.

Giving ordinary people—as distinct from corporations and interest groups—the right and ability to participate enables them to form new groups better suited to address new problems. Alone, there is not much any one person can do to bring about change or to participate meaningfully and usefully in a policymaking process. But working together a group can take meaningful action. Online groups can also change their collective goals in response to pressing problems more quickly than traditional organizations that lock in their own institutional and individual priorities.

Government need not—it must not—fear new technology and the opportunity it creates to invite participation from those with the experience in the field. Reinventing democracy as collaborative democracy will create work for government. Having a blog requires someone to respond to comments. Posting a wiki demands following the changes as they evolve. Creating a web form to invite input from the public necessitates honing in on the right questions and listening to the resulting answers. Participation will require staffing and technology to manage. But a collaborative culture does not place the burden on government or the public alone to address complex social problems. Instead, by organizing collaboration, government keeps itself at the center of decisionmaking as the neutral arbiter in the public interest and also benefits from the contributions of those outside of government. Joseph Nye explains the collaborative imperative for governments:

> The very nature of leadership has changed in today's interdependent, globalized world. In information-based societies, networks are replacing hierarchies, and knowledge workers are less deferential. Business is changing in the direction of "shared leadership" and "distributed leadership," with leaders in the center of a circle rather than atop a hierarchy. . . . Modern leaders need an ability to use networks, to collaborate, and to encourage participation. They need to be able to make decisions within rapidly changing contexts. They need to attract followers into new identities—both individual and social—and provide meaning in a disruptive world of globalization. In short, they need to

use the soft power of attraction as well as the hard power of force and threat, both at home and in foreign policy.[60]

In other words, collaboration offers a huge potential payoff in the form of more effective government. Effective government, in turn, translates into better decisionmaking and more active problem solving, which could spur growth in society and the economy.

Let's say that the Environmental Protection Agency wants to pass a regulation protecting a certain endangered species. As currently designed, public input comes too late for anyone but a lobbyist to effectively have a say. But the Internet makes it possible to design methods for soliciting better expertise sooner from private citizens. Or imagine that the United States Postal Service wants to cut its energy bills by 30 percent over the next three years. An online best-practices website would enable the USPS to generate many solutions from crowds of people. Those crowds could include self-selected experts across federal, state, and local government as well as motivated members of the public. Imagine that a series of economic events triggers a crisis of confidence in the economy. Technology could make it possible to track economic data in a more transparent, collaborative, verifiable way.

Innovation in the practices of governance will require investment. But if government can design effective mechanisms—law, policy, and technology—to build the bridge between institutions and networks, it can enhance its legitimacy and value. Look what happened to the entertainment industry. Fearing a loss of ad revenue from consumers' home taping, the movie studios and television broadcasters initially feared the new tools. They (unsuccessfully) sued the makers of the Betamax personal video recorders (the precursor of the DVD and the VCR) in an effort to put the consumer electronics companies out of the Betamax business altogether.[61] People wanted to watch movies at home and would not be stopped. Eventually, the home video rental market, far from threatening the incumbents, flourished and vastly increased their markets.

Similarly, in response to the advent of digital technologies that reduce the cost of making and distributing nearly perfect copies of music, the record labels proposed legislation to criminalize new forms of copyright infringement. They began suing twelve-year-olds and grandmothers for illegally sharing music files via peer-to-peer networks and filed suit to put the makers of these new digital technologies out of business.[62] But the law is out of step with society's music consumption practices: while traditional business models wane, iTunes, eMusic and other alternatives innovate and embrace the power of new technology. Instead of cheating or routing around the music laws, these new entrants are helping to reengineer and reshape the industry. If institutions don't work with the networks, networks will work around them, rendering government practices increasingly disconnected, ineffectual, and brittle.

PART TWO

Peer-to-Patent and the Patent Challenge

CHAPTER THREE

PATENTS AND THE INFORMATION DEFICIT

I know well the difficulty of drawing a line between the things which are worth to the public the embarrassment of an exclusive monopoly and the things that are not.

—THOMAS JEFFERSON

JACK HARVEY HAS RISEN through the USPTO ranks to become the director of Technology Center (TC) 2100, one of eight clusters of officials deciding who gets a patent.[1] Born and raised in New York, Harvey loaded tractor-trailers by night to put himself through college (in pursuit of a degree in electrical engineering) before parlaying his technical expertise into a position as an examiner with the USPTO in Alexandria, Virginia. He has worked on applications relating to computer networking innovations, database storage solutions, novel computer programs, and devices like memory sticks and hard drives.

Now, twenty years later, as head of the USPTO center with jurisdiction over computer hardware and software, Harvey is responsible for deciding whether Google—or perhaps a small inventor working out of her garage who might create the next Google—will monopolize the latest high-technology invention. Not surprisingly in the Internet age, software is one of the fastest growing areas of patent activity, and accordingly Harvey directs one of the largest examination groups in the Patent Office, with almost 1,000 (of almost 5,500) examiners reviewing close to 70,000 new patent applications annually (and close to 90,000 awaiting action).[2]

Under U.S. patent law, an inventor files an application with the USPTO describing the invention for which he seeks twenty years of monopoly rights.[3] For an invention to merit a patent, the examiner must determine that the application is "novel" insofar as the applicant must be the first inventor. The law also requires that the invention be "non-obvious"—or a sufficient enough advance over what came before to deserve the extraordinary rights of a patent. Even though the patent gives the inventor the exclusive right to exploit the patented invention, the inventor must also disclose the invention with enough specificity to enable a subsequent innovator to recreate it. Contrary to the popular misconception that patents must be kept secret, under current law the application has to be published by the USPTO (with some exceptions) after eighteen months.[4] A confidential trade secret and a patent are therefore mutually exclusive forms of intellectual property protection.

In deciding which inventions deserve this monopoly, Jack Harvey compares the novelty and nonobviousness of the invention to those of earlier innovations by sifting through the literature—earlier patents and patent applications, scientific journal articles, and product descriptions known as prior art. His job is not to determine the invention's commercial viability or social utility but to decide whether the patent application clearly and specifically describes a functioning original invention that advances the state of the art. In granting the patent, he is not giving the applicant the ultimate right to make the invention but the right to prevent all others from doing so. In other words, he decides whether businesses or researchers who want to use the applicant's patented invention—even if their goal is to cure cancer or invent the next iPod—must first request and most likely pay for a license from the patented inventor, assuming, that is, they can obtain permission at all. Failure to do so may result in a lawsuit and a demand for monetary damages or in an order to desist from activity related to that patent, even if that activity is noncommercial scientific research.[5]

Despite having traded his stevedore's cap for a Brooks Brothers suit, Harvey is still very much the straightforward New Yorker. In fact it may be the direct demeanor learned as a dockworker and Teamster, rather than the technical skills acquired as a patent examiner and engineer, that comes in most handy in his job. Examiners have reason to be unhappy. They have the increasingly difficult job of making legally enforceable decisions in the public interest without the benefit of enough time or adequate informational resources. With the exponential growth in the number and complexity of applications facing the patent examining corps, the challenges of finding and evaluating relevant information have only increased.

This chapter digs deeper into the information deficit plaguing the Patent Office, paying particular attention to the information the Patent Office uses in examining a patent application and the particular relationship it creates to expertise.[6] By understanding the shortage of time and lack of access to adequate information to make the best possible decision in the public interest, it becomes clear how difficult it is—even with the best intentions—to possess the necessary expertise. The patent case is paradigmatic of decisionmaking under constrained resources. To envision how an open network like Peer-to-Patent might be useful to Jack Harvey and his team (and how such a system might apply in other contexts), one must first know something about the internal practices of the Patent Office: How does it give out patents? What information goes into making the decision? What procedures do examiners follow? And what are the shortcomings that risk producing "low-quality" patents?

Most books and articles about the patent system focus on what makes a good or bad patent, whether the software industry needs patents less or more than the pharmaceutical industry, or what kinds of damage awards are appropriate in patent infringement cases. In contrast, here the focus is on the inner workings of the institution. A brief tour of the historical rationale behind patents provides the necessary context for this discussion about patent practice.

THE WHY OF PATENTS

Patents are intended to advance technological and scientific knowledge by stimulating investment in new products, methods, and concepts. By creating barriers to competitive entry, patents increase the prospective return on investment in innovation. As Abraham Lincoln said, "The patent system add[s] the fuel of interest to the fire of genius."[7] This is considered particularly important for capital-intensive industries, in which research and development costs are high, and for individual inventors, who rely on patents to get the financial boost they need to progress from invention to product to company. In addition, some firms commoditize their patents by licensing the right to use the invention to end users and other businesses. According to the Association of University Technology Managers, university licensing revenue skyrocketed from $186 million in 1991 to roughly $1.4 billion in 2006, and the annual number of licenses granted nearly tripled.[8]

Support for patents is not universal. Patent abolitionists argue that the patent system should be dismantled altogether. These critics lambaste all legally backed monopolies that put control over broad areas of science and technology in the hands of a single entity. The Columbia law professor Eben Moglen explains the abolitionist perspective with a powerful metaphor: "If you could feed everyone by baking one loaf of bread and pressing a button, what would be the moral case for permitting the price of bread to be higher than the poorest hungry person could pay?"[9] From the abolitionist perspective, the patent monopoly takes the bread of information, science, and knowledge out of a hungry society's mouth. By creating incentives for higher prices and lower output, patent monopolies may limit access to life-saving products and cures.

Moreover, as the Nobel Prize–winning economist Joseph Stiglitz argues, patents often do little to stimulate innovation.[10] In many fields, broad patent protection may even lock up innovation and slow technological development. Inventions do not occur in isolation; usually multiple firms are working on the same idea at the same time, and when one gets a patent, it might then be able to stop or slow its competitors.[11] Edison's invention of incandescent lighting was clearly innovative, but Edison received a broad patent in 1880 and subsequently litigated competitors out of the market.[12] The more successful Edison was at securing injunctions or infringement awards, the slower the pace of innovation. The same is true of the Wright brothers and their sweeping patent on aircraft design. These three men are rightly considered inventive pioneers, but their reliance on the patent system likely retarded further development in their fields.[13]

Other analysts see value in patents only in the small number of industries with enormous start-up costs, such as pharmaceuticals and biotechnology.[14] Those who financed Biogen's development and clinical testing of alpha and beta interferon and a vaccine for hepatitis B depended on the promise that a patent would protect their investment from competition. And it worked: although Biogen never manufactured the drugs, it was able, through the protection of the patent, to license its discoveries to manufacturing companies. More broadly, however, the empirical relationship between patenting and innovation is weak. In a handful of industries enormous start-up costs justify barriers to competitive entry. In others, the case is far less clear. As James Bessen and Michael Meurer conclude, "The evidence certainly is consistent with the notion that patents encourage American pharmaceutical R&D. But otherwise, it is hard to find evidence suggesting patents are a major factor spurring R&D investment, that patents contribute to economic growth, or even that the patent system is a source of great wealth to important inventors and innovators (outside of a few industries like pharmaceuticals)."[15]

The confusion over the value of patents is further compounded by uncertainty regarding the actual grant rate of patents. The percentage of patent applications that become patents is unknown.[16] Some claim that 97 percent of applications become patents.[17] Others estimate 75 percent but with divergences among industries (more pharmaceutical applications are likely to be accepted than high technology applications) that may, at least in part, be the result of pressure on the USPTO to curb the grant rate because of dissatisfaction over low-quality patents.

This chapter does not pick a side in the debate over patent abolition, or even in the narrower debate over what should be patentable. Instead it focuses on the lack of efficacy in the administration of the patent system.[18]

CHALLENGES OF PATENT EXAMINATION

The Court of Claims described the difficulty of trying to capture the essence of scientific innovation in the limited confines of words and text:

> An invention exists most importantly as a tangible structure or a series of drawings. A verbal portrayal is usually an afterthought written to satisfy the requirements of patent law. This conversion of machine to words allows for unintended idea gaps, which cannot be satisfactorily filled. Often the invention is novel and words do not exist to describe it. The dictionary does not always keep abreast of the inventor. It cannot. Things are not made for the sake of words, but words for things.[19]

The crucial job of converting words back into machines, for the purpose of determining whether those machines are sufficiently innovative to be patentable, falls to patent examiners.

Thomas Jefferson instituted the patent examination system in the United States in 1791.[20] Within two years, the pressure of running the

Patent Office while at the same time warring with Hamilton over how to put down the Whiskey Rebellion and whether or not to have a national bank, in addition to trying to pick sides in the French Revolution, prompted Jefferson to shift to a registration system.[21] But the Patent Office reverted to an examination system and instituted prior art searching in 1836 in order to improve the quality of patents. It has remained in place ever since.

Today, after checking the patent application for completeness, the USPTO assigns it, based on subject matter (manufacturing, computer technology, pharmaceuticals, and so on), to an examiner in one of the "art units," such as Jack Harvey's TC 2100. The examiner's responsibility is to determine whether a patent should be granted (because it is novel and nonobvious) and, if so, to ensure that the boundaries of the resulting monopoly are circumscribed and clearly articulated. As a first step, the examiner must read and understand the recondite incunabula of the patent application so that she can determine the relevant antecedent inventions. She must research the precursors—the prior art—to be able to compare the application's "claims" to what came before and to determine if (from the viewpoint of the person with specialization in that field of science and technology) the invention is truly new, nonobvious, and clearly drafted.

Claims are the dense, paragraph-long, nuggets that describe the "metes and bounds" of the invention and define the scope of the resulting patent. Although the patent application also contains a narrative explaining and touting the invention, a description of how the invention might be implemented in practice, as well as illustrative drawings, the claims matter the most. And these claims rarely reveal all their secrets at first sight. For example, the 2004 patent for the "Lawsuit board game" describes the invention as "an educational, legal-based game and method for players [that] has a board with spaces on which the players land. The spaces instruct players to bring a simulated lawsuit or to act as a result of a simulated circumstance associated with the legal profession."[22]

But the examiner must parse the claims of the patent application, the first of which reads, in part:

A method of playing an educational and legal profession-based board game for a plurality of players, comprising the steps of: providing a game board containing a series of spaces on which each player can land, the spaces including a first plurality of spaces instructing a player to bring a simulated lawsuit and a second plurality of spaces instructing a player to act in accordance with a simulated circumstance associated with the legal profession, the second plurality of spaces including at least one space associated with simulated circumstances involving at least one of simulated legal education, simulated legal training, and simulated legal licensing of the player; providing a fund of play money; providing a set of lawsuit cards, each having thereon a lawsuit scenario including a fact pattern and a positive or negative monetary result; randomly determining a number of spaces on the game board to be moved by each player in turn, for each player to land on a space on the board; a player landing on one of the first plurality of spaces taking a lawsuit card and having an option of complying with the monetary result by either paying into the fund of play money, a negative result of the taken lawsuit card, or drawing from the fund of play money, a positive monetary result of the taken lawsuit card.

Working from such dense verbiage (and that's only the first half of the first claim), the examiner must identify and compare relevant precedents, including earlier invented board games as well as games specifically pertaining to law, such as the "Professional malpractice board game apparatus," patented in 1978, to decide if this application deserves a patent.[23]

Or take another example. For $49.95 one can buy the Big Daddy Driver golf club and weed whacker all in one. (Even Oprah recommended it.) But as readily intelligible as the product might be to the average consumer, the examiner's obligation is to analyze sixteen specially drafted patent claims that begin:

A weed-cutting golf club comprising: a shaft terminating in a club head, the club head defining a compartment having a downwardly directed opening; a power source carried by one of the club head and the shaft; a motor carried within the compartment and coupled to the power source; a drive shaft extending in a downward direction from the motor through the opening and terminating in a hub; and cutting members extending from the hub.[24]

The examiner may have had to research the 27,677 golf utility patents issued since 1976 (and earlier, if relevant), comparing the claims against the most analogous ones, before issuing the patent—all in a matter of hours.

As the Supreme Court said in 1892, "The specification and claims of a patent . . . constitute one of the most difficult legal instruments to draw with accuracy."[25] The difference between one word and another in the drafting of a patent claim can mean the difference between a valuable and a voidable patent. *In Senmed Inc.* v. *Richard-Allan Medical Industries,* the judgment of infringement of a surgical skin stapler—and potentially millions of dollars in damages—turned on the meaning of the word *on* in the claim relating to the place where the staple is actually formed; *on* being held to require physical contact rather than close adjacency to the stapler's anvil surface.[26]

Faced with claims that often defy comprehension, the examiner's job, in a sense, is to prove the unprovable—that never in recorded history has there been another inventor with the same invention. As old and obvious as an idea might seem, finding or even knowing where to look for the prior art to invalidate it is often quite difficult. Consider the litigation over the BlackBerry, one of the most important and widely used technologies today. The patent-holding company, NTP, alleged that Research in Motion (RIM), the manufacturer of the BlackBerry, had infringed on NTP's patents on transmission of electronic mail over a radio frequency. RIM forced the Patent Office to reexamine those patents by turning up a crucial piece of prior art. That prior art was a planning memorandum for a mobile data network taken from a technical manual of the Norwegian phone company and found only in a Norwegian library. The manual was dated 1986. The plaintiff's invention was dated 1991. It was hardly surprising that the patent examiner failed to uncover this piece of prior art in the first place; litigation ensued.[27]

RIM had a strong incentive to comb the world for prior art. Patent applicants, in contrast, do not always help examiners in their search. For example, Microsoft's application for "Off-line economies for digital media," one of the first applications made available for public review in the Peer-to-Patent pilot, contains twenty-two short claims but not a single reference or citation.[28] This is hardly unique to Microsoft. In a random sample of applications conducted by the USPTO in 2005, of the approximately 12,000 applications checked 3,500 cited no references whatsoever, while another 2,000 cited three or fewer. The USPTO chief counsel, James Toupin, estimates that more than 50 percent of new patent applicants either cite no prior art references or cite so many (more than twenty) as to be too many to read.[29]

Here's why this happens. The initial burden of showing that a claimed invention is obvious, and thus not patentable, is statutorily placed upon the examiner. To balance that burden, the *United States Code of Federal Regulations* places on applicants "a duty of candor and good faith in dealing with the Office, which includes a duty to disclose to the [PTO] all information known to that individual to be material to patentability."[30] However, this does not necessarily impose a duty upon applicants to uncover prior art actively. In fact, many lawyers counsel their clients to avoid researching the background to their inventions so as to remain ignorant of any information they would then be required to submit, potentially against their own interests in obtaining a broad patent. In the best interests of their clients, attorneys are also disinclined to search lest they be required to disclose information that could be used to attack competitors in future lawsuits. But even acting in good faith, a patent applicant may not know of inventions in the field.

In 1999 Congress amended the Patent Act to provide that after eighteen months most applications will be published and, once published, the public may submit written evidence of prior art without annotations, commentary, or explanation.[31] The public must pay a $180 fee to submit such art.[32] But competitors, who are the only entities likely to know about the publication of the patent and willing to pay the cost, could be subject to treble damages if they are later found to have willfully infringed the resulting patent.[33] The third-party submission will become evidence that they already knew about the patent when it was filed. So it is not a surprise that in 2007 the Patent Office received only 112 such third-party submissions, containing 600 items of prior art.[34] There is no record yet if any of these were used. Examiners are required to read these submissions but are not allocated any time to do so.

Patent examiners are thus essentially on their own. Under current law they are expected to be scientifically adept enough to discover the prior art. They cannot pose a question on a blog or listserv nor call a professor of computer science or business administration to discuss an application and the meaning of its claims.[35] That's because Congress directed in the Patent Act that the USPTO structure its procedures to prevent "protest or . . . pre-issuance opposition."[36] Virtually all the examiner has to go by are the databases available at the USPTO for navigating the past, issued, published, and pending patent literature; these databases are known as East, West, and Plus. East (examiner's automated search tool), a Windows-based client, and West (web examiner's search tool), a browser-based interface, are mechanisms for searching expired and current patents, published patent applications, and the literature cited in those patent documents. West is essentially a web-based version of East. Plus is a query-by-example search system for U.S. patents since 1971. It is intended to produce a list of the most closely related patents to the application being searched.[37] When these databases came into being in the early 1990s, the National Intellectual Property Researchers Association filed two lawsuits to stop the destruction of paper backups, suspecting that the integrity of patent files had been compromised and that the databases were not comprehensive.[38]

The USPTO makes use of other nonpatent databases, but as was once said about the Oxford don, the USPTO "know[s] everything, and nothing about everything else."[39] In other words, the office has excellent patent-related resources, but its other databases are not comprehensive sources of knowledge about the scientific state of the art. John Doll, the patent commissioner, asserts that "we have everything we need; we have state-of-the-art search systems."[40] Yet significant shortcomings are evident. Even Doll acknowledges that even though the office spends $60 million each year on database access, the examiners must deal with databases with different protocols for organizing information and different search techniques and without the necessary date stamps to determine whether a source predates the patent application.[41] It is extremely difficult for an examiner working under time pressure to search each one appropriately.

Broader searches of the scientific literature are not happening. In a recent study of the references submitted by the inventor or dug up by the examiner in the course of the examination of 502,687 utility patents, 41 percent of the citations to previous U.S. patents came from examiners, but examiners accounted for only 10 percent of references to nonpatent prior art in the issued patent. The study concludes that this gap is due to inferior search capabilities for prior art other than U.S. patents.[42]

"Complaints have mounted as the computer spits out more and more references to journals not available at the PTO," writes the *Patent Office Professional Association Newsletter*.[43] "The average return time on interlibrary loans is four days, with about three in fifteen hundred taking over sixty days." A study done in 1989 indicated that over 1,000 journals were ordered via interlibrary loan, with 275 ordered at least five times.

The USPTO agreed to purchase microfiche copies of these 275 journals and to take paper copies "if private industry will donate them." As late as the late 1990s, the examiners' union was still negotiating for travel time to account for the work of going to get files from the library. Management granted two minutes per round trip to examiners whose primary search files were on another floor, up to a maximum of thirteen hours a year.

Patent examiners are painfully aware of the shortcomings of their own capacity to do adequate research.[44] While 89 percent of examiners surveyed in 2006 and 91 percent in 2002 expressed confidence in the importance of their work, only about 40 percent were satisfied with the training they receive in information retrieval and research methodologies.[45] Although computerization and electronic filing alleviates some of the practical problems associated with fetching and finding files, the need for information in a short amount of time is still a challenge. And the examiners' union newsletter rarely has an issue without an article complaining of the shortcomings of automation at the USPTO. Complaints range from worry about the health effects of radiation exposure from too much computer usage to concern over the inadequacy of computer resources for searching information. According to the *Patent Office Professional Association Newsletter*, "What we have here is a failure to communicate: a monumental system for patent examination is being put into place by automation specialists who seem to spurn information from those for whom the system is allegedly being designed . . . render[ing] the chances for writing software that meets our needs a near impossibility."[46]

Unlike a movie in which the heroine could be saved simply by not venturing down the dark, eerie staircase and instead turning on the lights, there is no simple solution to the problem of lack of information, for instance by subscribing to more journals. Many kinds of information are not to be easily found even with the best search tools. Physicists no longer publish in journals when they can publish in Arxiv, the online repository with 500,000 physics preprints.[47] But some fields do not publish in readily searchable sources online or off. For example, computer science does not have a culture of universal academic publishing. Industry and academic programmers publish their computer code repositories on the web, generally unindexed, unclassified, and undocumented, making that code accessible to other programmers familiar with the subject matter but making it harder for examiners to find and cite.[48]

In many disciplines, journals take years to publish scientific findings. Meanwhile, inventions pertaining to cutting-edge research are more likely to be discussed around the water cooler at Microsoft or Genentech or at a university graduate student party than in an academic journal. Many inventions that might be directly relevant to a determination of novelty and nonobviousness may not be documented at all. While some software coders are compulsive about annotating their code, just as many simply want to see if it works and are not interested in archiving to create a knowledge base of patent information. The rise of open-source software licensed for reuse and redistribution has made software prior art even more widely available to the public but also difficult for the USPTO to locate. As Christopher Wong, the project manager of Peer-to-Patent, writes, "The examiner is unlikely to know about the open or closed source code, products or processes, websites, or prior publications that ordinary people in the community know about from their personal experience."[49]

Does the Internet come to the rescue? The world's library is now at people's fingertips. Google delivers it. And yet examiners, including those in Jack Harvey's group, are not at present permitted to search Google and the Internet. The Patent Office worries that the privacy and security of inventors may be compromised by open Internet searching.[50] The examiner's searches, if traced, might reveal too much about the inventions, which are not made public until eighteen months into the examination process. While anonymous searching technologies could be deployed (and the USPTO is currently investigating such solutions), they would not solve the problem of the haphazard, poorly organized, and difficult-to-find nature of scientific information. This might explain why examiners, perhaps surreptitiously, are the largest users of the Wayback Machine, an Internet archive and nonprofit search engine that allows a search of the historical Internet.[51] Though an excellent resource, the Wayback Machine is still incomplete and erratic.

Previously, the USPTO had considered outsourcing the research function to private firms and paying others to look up information for it.[52] But as examiners will readily assert, this is not a process that can be either automated or done by someone without knowledge of the interpretation of the claims. It is not a matter of simply searching for a keyword in related scientific publications but of knowing what is relevant.

PATENT EXAMINATION TODAY

In recent years, a number of trends have compounded the difficulty of the patent examiner's task. The expansion of the subject matter and lengthening of the term as well as the strengthening of patent law in favor of the patent holder have spurred unprecedented growth in patenting activity. This in turn creates an administrative challenge for the Patent Office, which has to examine all these new and varied patent applications.

NUMBER OF APPLICATIONS

The number of applications doubled during the Reagan years and again in the last ten years from 1997 to 2007.[53] Patent activity worldwide rises by 4.7 percent a year.[54] The USPTO now receives upwards of 420,000 applications each year.[55] The backlog has reached Borgesian proportions, and it feeds on itself: The patent examiner has less time to review more applications. Reviews become less rigorous. The easier the application process becomes, the more inventors apply. The backlog is currently 1 million applications, and of that stack, 120,000 are "on Jack's desk." The Japan Patent Office (JPO) works under similar (if not greater) pressure than the PTO, receiving more than 400,000 patent applications annually while maintaining a backlog of about 750,000. The JPO employs only 1,358 patent examiners, roughly a third the number at the PTO.[56] Compounding the challenge, the USPTO cannot retain its skilled workforce with the lure of a government paycheck. The number of examiners per 1,000 patent applications is down by 20 percent.

Perhaps people are more inventive now than before, or perhaps they are under greater pressure from their investors to seek a patent to bar competitors from entering the marketplace. Or perhaps they think it is getting easier to obtain a patent. Regardless of the reason, the volume of patenting activity depresses the time examiners have to search and evaluate.

SCOPE OF PATENTS

The increase in quantity is, in part, caused by the expansion in the scope of subject matter that the USPTO and courts now consider to be patentable. The USPTO is examining applications in over four hundred

classes and thousands of subclasses of inventions from A-frame structures and abacuses to zithers, zootechny, and Zwieback (toast patents?).[57]
Among the more popular classes of inventions are those related to silicon chips and golf equipment.[58] Having to master research in so many
different types of science and technology creates an added challenge for
the examiner workforce.

The Constitution leaves it to Congress and the courts to determine
what can be patented. In addition to traditional "utility patents"—such
as technological, manufacturing, and biochemical inventions—Congress
also enacted protection for plants and industrial designs.[59] Because of the
perceived competitive and scientific value of patents, they expanded the
scope of what was patentable and the duration of the patent monopoly
beginning in the 1980s. In 1982, the Supreme Court pronounced in
Chakrabarty, "everything under the sun is patentable," including a bacterium. This expansion in the scope of patentable subject matter paved
the way for the growth of the biotechnology industries.[60] But once the
Supreme Court opened the Pandora's box of patentable subject matter,
lower courts opened the way for patenting computer software, business
and financial methods, and genetic technologies.[61] The expansion, in
turn, opened the floodgates of patent prosecution activity.

Fortunately, in the same year as the *Chakrabarty* ruling, Congress created the Court of Appeals for the Federal Circuit (CAFC)—a specialty
patent appeals court—to iron out discrepancies among rulings by different regional appeals courts.[62] The Eighth Circuit Court of Appeals, head-
quartered in St. Louis and St. Paul, for example, had not held a patent
valid in ten years, whereas the Fifth Circuit, based in New Orleans, had
ruled in favor of patent holders more than 80 percent of the time.[63] The
CAFC created more uniformity and therefore more certainty in the
process and increased the likelihood that a patent would be upheld if
challenged.[64] The widening of patentable subject matter has been controversial, with reformers arguing that it has become an exercise in reduc-
tio ad absurdum to distinguish between an idea (like a mathematical formula), which is not patentable, and a practical invention, the use of that
formula to power a computer program that produces a result.[65]

The Supreme Court's decision to read the subject matter of patentability broadly to include both computer software and business methods has
contributed to the growing breadth of cases. This has a negative impact
on the USPTO's preparedness to examine applications. Software did not

begin to be patentable until the early 1980s. As a result, there is no well-developed database of prior literature. And while mechanical inventions can be illustrated with pictures, business methods (such as a software program to allocate financial risk or investment or to hedge nonqualified deferred compensation, or infamously the "one-click shopping cart" process for transacting on the Internet) often elude easy description. Information in these fields is also evolving rapidly, preventing the Patent Office from keeping up.

LENGTH OF TERM

In addition to the expansion of subject matter, Congress also extended the term of patents to favor patent holders. In the 1984 Hatch-Waxman Act, Congress extended the patent term of new drugs (to account for delays in obtaining FDA approval).[66] A little more than a decade later, Congress changed the duration of patent protection from seventeen years from the date of invention to twenty years from the date of filing to conform to the World Trade Organization's Agreement on Trade Related Aspects of Intellectual Property Rights (TRIPS).[67] The lengthening of the term has met with criticism from those who argue that twenty years is unnecessarily long in a world in which technologies change so rapidly, especially the high-technology industry. In addition to keeping prices for consumers artificially high, a longer term may suppress the incentives for follow-on innovation by competitors.[68]

COMPLEXITY OF PATENTS

Patent applications are growing in complexity as well as in number and length.[69] John Doll, the commissioner of the USPTO, complains of broad and ambiguous claims. Drafted by lawyers, the claims are often, he says, unintelligible to the inventors themselves let alone to the examiners.[70] This is not necessarily malicious. Lawyers are simply doing the best job they can to obtain the strongest and broadest possible patent for their clients.

Over the last thirty years, the number of words in a patent application—specifically in the written description—has almost doubled, as has the number of claims.[71] While overall patent applications generally contain around two dozen claims, the number varies dramatically. One application contained only a single claim for "Element 95."[72] There have been applications, particularly involving complex biotechnology inventions such as pharmaceuticals, submitted with hundreds or even thousands of claims. Shell Oil filed a patent application with 8,958 claims.[73] Inventor Ronald Katz has earned a Wikipedia entry for his infamous applications that usually include hundreds of pages of claims, designed to overwhelm and outwit the examiner.[74] The proliferation of claims and the ever-expanding length of applications, without a concomitant increase in time for the examiners, prompted the USPTO in late 2007 to require applicants retroactively to limit their initial filings to 25 claims.[75] An inventor wishing to file a longer application was to have been required to do some of the heavy lifting by paying a hefty premium and submitting his own record of research and analysis of the earlier literature. But a federal court in Virginia enjoined implementation of the rules for exceeding the regulatory authority of the USPTO.[76]

EXAMINERS' WORKLOAD

Jack Harvey's examiners are working with closed databases of a limited subset of scientific information, with twenty hours to do the job of reviewing an application that may be poorly drafted, with a hundred broad and vague claims, about a subject they may not know, and about which the inventor has provided no additional background information. If that were not pressure enough, examiners are given a financial incentive (in the form of productivity bonuses) to grant patents as quickly as possible.

In response to a recent survey, only 11 percent of examiners agreed with the statement, "The current production system allows the examiners time to produce quality products."[77] The chief complaint is that they have no more than twenty hours to do the job.[78] That means reading and digesting the meaning of the application's claims, researching the relevant literature, and applying the legal standards of novelty and nonobviousness to the scientific facts. The examiner also has to write up the decision. The workload, by putting stress on the USPTO, is revealing the fault lines in the structures that have been established to make decisions about patentability. The patent examiners bear the brunt of this strain. As the head of the examiners' labor union complained, "Ancient proverb: fewer people will do less work. PTO management corollary: unless you beat the people harder."[79]

Outside the USPTO, these complaints are matched by the industry outcry that the office is granting too many patents of low quality. The

Board of Patent Appeals and Interferences, the administrative appeals body at the Patent Office, complains that cases they receive from examiners "often contain administrative errors, inadequate support for the examiner's final rejection, and other unanswered questions or omitted information about the patent's claim that should have been addressed."[80]

Though the USPTO generates a revenue surplus from patent filing fees, the money is not used to hire more examiners. Congress siphons the surplus into the general budget, despite the fact that "there is no substitute for having adequate numbers of trained personnel with sufficient time to exercise their considered judgment," as the National Academy of Sciences has noted.[81] Moreover, "even if the Patent Office could magically expand its ranks," writes John Squires, chief counsel on intellectual property at Goldman Sachs, "it still faces the formidable challenge to train, manage, and even find desks for its increased examination corps."[82] Giving current examiners more time is also not a practical solution. Inventors are already waiting simply to start the application process with the USPTO. The average time until a final action by the Patent Office is now thirty-one months (up from twenty-four in 2001, though the Patent Office is working to reduce the number).[83] While adding more examiners to alleviate the pressure could be helpful, it is not practical in tight economic times and also is not a substitute for improved search technologies, more efficient workplace practices, and turning to those who know the relevant information firsthand.

Pendency in Jack Harvey's art unit averages about thirty-one months to first office action, with an average pendency of about forty-three months to final determination. If you're unlucky enough to be filing an application relating to interactive video distribution, your wait is fifty months. Delays in finance, banking, and accounting are up to fifty-two months.[84] Applicants relate stories about waiting seven years to hear from the Patent Office, during which time the technology has long since been surpassed and the business opportunity missed. Considering the usual life cycle for any new technology, three years vastly exceeds the economic viability of products in certain fast-paced industries. The Patent Office's effort to speed up the process by creating an expedited examination known as "petitions to make special" has not solved the problem. Pendency continues to increase, and the Patent Office cautions that if reforms are not implemented these pendency rates will double.

CONSEQUENCES: THE CRAB IS TRAVELING BACKWARD

The constitutional patent scheme enshrined in Article I was one of the only constitutional clauses incorporated without debate.[85] The delegates to the Constitutional Convention may have felt, as Mark Twain later expressed it, that "a country without a patent office and good patent laws was just a crab and couldn't travel any way but sideways or backwards."[86] After all, a similar scheme had existed in Venice, Italy, since the fifteenth century and in England since the early eighteenth.[87] The practical reality was that a private property right in inventions (as distinct from the alternatives of a subsidy or prize) was an inexpensive way for the new federal government saddled with revolutionary war debt to promote innovation. Today, however, there is a growing chorus of complaints that the crab is traveling backward. One federal circuit judge has melodramatically described the crisis of patent quality as being "akin to rearranging the deck chairs on the Titanic—the orchestra is playing as if nothing is amiss, but the ship is still heading for Davy Jones's locker."[88]

Critics across the political spectrum complain of a crisis of quality in the patent system. The secretary of commerce estimates that the USPTO is spending "more than 55 percent of its examination resources to examine applications that do not warrant a patent."[89] This might be fine if examiners regularly rejected those nonmeritorious applications. But rushing to get through the backlog, officials all but rubber-stamp the applications that come across their desks. There are many examples of patents that are anything but nonobvious. The "Method of swinging on a swing," awarded to a five-year-old boy is paradigmatic.[90] The boy (and his attorney father) claimed a method for swinging "in which a user positioned on a standard swing suspended by two chains from a substantially horizontal tree branch induces side-to-side motion by pulling alternately on one chain and then the other." Following great public ridicule, the commissioner of patents ordered a reexamination and canceled the patent, but by then many hours had been wasted.

The grant of a patent allows the inventor to sue for infringement anyone who "without authority makes, uses, offers to sell, or sells any patented invention" without any obligation to produce the invention. Regardless of quality, patents enjoy a presumption of validity, making them hard to challenge in court and giving some patent holders an incentive to litigate. Adam Jaffe and Josh Lerner summarize the problem in

Innovation and Its Discontents: "The patent office has been granting patents on old ideas because it has inadequate examination resources, and also because it is not very good at finding information about the relevant existing technologies, particularly in new, fast-moving technological fields. And when patents are granted on ideas that are not new, other firms have no practical recourse other than the risky and expensive prospect of challenging the patent in federal court."[91]

The doubling of patent prosecution resulted in a concomitant doubling in patent litigation in the 1990s. Apple, for example, has witnessed an increase in the number of patent infringement lawsuits filed against it—from seven in 2006 to twenty-one in 2008.[92] Microsoft reportedly defends an average of thirty-five to forty patent infringement lawsuits a year, at a cost of $100 million.[93] In addition, aggressive patent holders are able to disrupt markets by merely suggesting the infringement of their patents and extorting license fees as a payment to avoid expensive litigation. Companies pay inestimable millions of dollars in license fees to undeserving patent holders who threaten litigation.

The law on patent damages only encourages the avid plaintiff. A plaintiff windshield-wiper manufacturer can recover damages for the value of the car; the claimant for an infringed hinge is allowed to sue for the value of the laptop or the piano to which the hinge is attached. As a result, awards are often way out of proportion to damages. The Administrative Office of the U.S. Courts calculates that the median award in a federal patent trial is $1,694,000, the third-highest-grossing type of suit, surpassed only by antitrust and asbestos litigation.[94] Pricewaterhouse-Coopers estimates average damages in 2003 at $29 million and the median award at $3 million.[95] Individual cases are even more shocking. In 2006 Rambus Technologies was awarded $307 million in a suit over dynamic random access memory (the award was subsequently reduced to a mere $133 million).[96] TiVo won $74 million against EchoStar for infringing TiVo's technology that allows viewers to record one television program while watching another.[97]

Further, because patent law permits (with limitations) injunctive relief, a litigant can stop a defendant from using the invention altogether. Such strike suits effectively hijack a competitor's business. The request for enormous compensatory damages or an injunction may be meritorious, but the amounts involved also create an attractive nuisance to those wishing to profit from litigation alone. The potential size of damage awards and the presumption of validity, coupled with favorable jurisdictions (such as the Eastern District of Texas, which rules in favor of patent plaintiffs 78 percent of the time, compared with the national average of 59 percent), encourages those who use patents to profit from litigation.[98]

These litigious parties are known colloquially as patent trolls, firms that seek patents not to engage in productive economic activity but solely for the purpose of initiating infringement actions or extorting licensing fees from competitors. Trolls and their attorneys strenuously justify the legality of what they do, painting themselves as patent enforcers. Some go further, to assert that they are helping to realize economies of scale by acting as middlemen to pool patents and thereby lower the costs of licensing them. Of course, aggressive and litigious trolling is not in itself an indication that the holder is the owner of substandard patents. Nevertheless, the incentives to sue combined with low-quality patents contribute to the litigation explosion and cannot easily be disentangled. And in any case the litigation boom, regardless of the cause, imposes staggering costs incommensurate with any increase in patent activity. For a case with more than $25 million at stake, the American Intellectual Property Law Association estimates the cost at $3 million per side just through discovery and $5 million to verdict.[99] That's $10 million for one trial! Even in a small matter where less than a $1 million is at risk, the cost is estimated to be $350,000 through discovery and $600,000 to the end game.[100] And that's on average.

While the data vary, they point to the same trend: patent litigation is expensive. Paying royalties for a license from the patent holder is often the path of lesser and cheaper resistance and is preferable to a defensive lawsuit. At the same time, the cost creates a hurdle to companies or universities wanting to challenge the validity of nonmeritorious patents in their industries. For those who want to sue others to recover damages for infringed patents (and who have no other costs, since they are not running productive businesses), it is simply a cost of doing business.

Ultimately, increased litigation diverts money from research and development to unproductive lawsuits. The Phoenix Center for Advanced Legal and Economic Policy Studies, a Washington-based, free-market-oriented think tank, estimates that the grant of substandard patents diverts $21 billion annually, or 7 percent of annual R&D spending in the United States, from legitimate research activities. When litigation is factored in, that number rises to $25.5 billion.[101] As IBM assistant general counsel Manny Schecter has written, "Less than 4 percent of the approximately 3,000 patent lawsuits filed each year reach trial. In addition, the 4 percent figure overlooks the far greater number of settlements reached prior to the filing of suit. Thus the innovation tax caused by invalid patents is literally billions of dollars per year."[102] The economists Bessen and Meurer have pointed out that the more R&D a firm performs, the more likely it is to be sued, effectively imposing a tax on scientific research.[103] Especially in information-based industries and those without high investment costs, low-quality patents may produce unmeritorious monopolies and create the risk of unjustified holdups. How can it be that Test.com invented online test taking? But lacking time and intellectual resources, the Patent Office still has a hard time finding the information to prove a lack of novelty. Test.com has already approached various universities, including Regis University and the University of Tulsa, demanding license fees.

Some innovators now choose to forgo patent protection altogether; eBay, for example, built its multi-billion-dollar auction business without a single patent. (It got its first patent only after the company went public.)[104] If the trend continues, the patent examination process will have decoupled the patent process from marketplace innovation to the point of commercial irrelevance (and eventually political illegitimacy). If it is true that patents promote innovation in certain sectors, then the longer that inventors need to wait to secure this protection, the more detrimental the impact on the economy will be.

WHAT'S AT STAKE?

The patent system leaves no one indifferent. This is an era of both technological innovation and economic dislocation. The future of the patent system is emblematic of both. It signals exploding levels of inventiveness and ingenuity, contributing to the largest increase in scientific know-how in the span of human history. Rhetoric against reform of the system frequently invokes such American icons as Jefferson, Franklin, Edison, and the Wright brothers (though the share of U.S. patents issued to non-U.S. companies is increasing). The argument is that reform will only increase the cost of getting a patent and thereby disadvantage small entities needing a patent to attract investment. A full-page advertisement in opposition to patent reform, published in the *New York Times* by the

Professional Inventors Alliance, is captioned, "If this Congress is allowed to destroy the U.S. Patent, this Congress will destroy America."[105]

At the same time, the United States is precariously balanced on the edge of economic decline. Shifting geopolitics, economic downturn, and environmental uncertainties contribute to a real and perceived deterioration in America's fortunes. The country wonders how long it can remain dominant in a world that rejects its tarnished politics and laughs at its currency (but wants its shiny new technology). The U.S. Patent Office once was the standard-bearer for quality examination. But now the institution that should reflect the nation's scientific and technical success is increasingly mired in dysfunction. Like an emperor without clothes, it decreases legitimacy when it issues patents of low and no quality. While the legal principles may be strong, there is a consensus that the institution of the Patent Office no longer commands the respect it once enjoyed.

No single bad patent—even the patent application for "Method and instrument for proposing marriage to an individual" (dating not necessary, says the application)—has crippled an industry or stopped scientific research.[106] But if the Patent Office keeps producing too many patents that do not meet the test of novelty or nonobviousness, it raises doubt about whether the country is innovating anywhere but in the courtroom. Reformers invoke the rhetoric of patent "failure," "crisis," and the immorality of a system that is out of touch with the ways in which innovation is practiced today. The system ought to work better to fulfill the constitutional mandate to "promote the progress of science and useful arts."

If poor examination results in low-quality output (a patent that is not sufficiently novel or is too broad and imprecise to apprise the public of the actual boundaries of the invention), the resulting patent then increases uncertainty and costs. With low-quality patents a competitor has a hard time knowing if it is infringing the patent once granted. After all, according to one analyst, running an online e-commerce business today arguably implicates 4,319 different possible patents.[107] It's a minefield out there. There are those who argue that only the quality of economically important patents—namely, those patents that trigger litigation or upon which viable businesses are built—matter. But there are societal costs associated with the issuance of all low-quality patents. The patent owner risks litigation; the rest of the world risks the patent being used unfairly to lock up innovation. Investors have to expend resources to vet patents, raising the cost of capital to fledgling enterprises. Given the risks of litigation and licensing fees, not to mention the uncertainty created in a marketplace that does not know how to assess the worth of its patents, it is an economic and moral imperative that the patent examiner does the job right the first time.

CHAPTER FOUR

DESIGNING FOR COLLABORATIVE DEMOCRACY

Americans of all ages, all stations in life, and all types of disposition are forever forming associations. There are . . . a thousand different types— religious, moral, serious, futile, very general and very limited, immensely large and very minute.

ALEXIS DE TOCQUEVILLE

PEER-TO-PATENT GROUNDS THE idea of collaborative democracy in a concrete strategy to remedy the problem of information deficit in the Patent Office. The challenges facing patent examiners described in the previous chapter cannot be fixed through legislative or judicial reform alone. Legislative proposals that would change the standards of patentability require extraordinary political capital. Judicial reform to raise the standards of review and ensure that low-quality patents are harder to enforce is slow and piecemeal and comes too late in the patent process to make a difference for the majority of patents that are never litigated and yet are used to extract licensing fees. Balancing the needs of large and small inventors, patent holders and licensees, legitimate plaintiffs and wrongly accused defendants across different industries further complicates the ability to arrive at a consensus on how to ensure that the USPTO remains the agency of citizen innovation, not citizen litigation.

While negotiating these traditional legal approaches is also necessary (were the patent system only so easy to fix with a single law, court case, or software program), collaboration enabled by software can help to introduce greater expertise in a manageable fashion before decisionmaking, improving both the quality of the participation and the resulting decision. After explaining how Peer-to-Patent works, this chapter asks why it works, examining the design of the technologies that were used to communicate to the group of volunteers how to do their work. I explore two key insights. First, designing granular and group-based rather than individual participation ensures a manageable and useful process in which decentralized volunteers have a clear understanding of what is expected of them. Second, designing a reputation-backed system provides feedback to participants, conveying a sense of belonging to a group and fostering collaboration. This use of the available technology, in particular the graphic screen to mirror and reflect the work of the group back to itself, is what I term *visual deliberation,* as distinct from deliberation in which the tools are used for talking and typing. Visual deliberation may produce what John Seely Brown terms "screen learning," which helps to teach effective collaboration across a distance.[1] The chapter concludes by exploring the collaboration that was at the heart of organizing Peer-to-Patent itself and assessing how well it has worked so far.

VISUAL DELIBERATION

Visual deliberation can communicate the group's "physics"—the organizational and governance rules that structure how participants interact as a group.[2] Is an online team legally incorporated or simply a loose agglomeration? Does the group have an explicit policy about who can join and what membership requires? Who makes the decisions and by what means? Physics may be embedded in legal rules, but the concept encapsulates more than just governance. Physics includes all the forces that dictate the workings of the group, including informal norms and even social practices encoded in software and made intelligible through on-screen visualizations.

Physics can be hard to achieve in the online environment. Without the familiar structures and rules for coordinating behavior we know from face-to-face interactions, it becomes increasingly difficult to manage interpersonal relations at a distance. While network connectivity has made it possible to start a conversation about poker or poodles, web technology has not made it easy to transform that conversation into a group or to structure the group to take action and accomplish a goal.

Not enough websites clearly articulate the way the group is supposed to function or offer opportunity for groups to set and change those rules.

In addition to physics, the technology design can also reflect and strengthen the group's culture—its values, identity, and purpose—to help forge a sense of trust among participants. There is much similarity between the physics of conveying clear rules and the culture that conveys a shared sense of mission. If physics describes how the group forms, culture explains how a group sustains itself over time. Culture, like physics, has been hard to create in cyberspace. Working at a distance in the absence of face-to-face clues and cues often impedes that sense of belonging to a common group—there are no virtual pheromones. Without a shared sense of community, a spammer can substantially diminish the value of an online e-mail list that might otherwise create a valuable contribution. A sock puppeteer (one who creates a false online identity) can adulterate a wiki, causing constructive participants to spend their time removing offensive or irrelevant material. But the right design of today's screen can strengthen the group's sense of itself.

As we shall see with Peer-to-Patent, the highly granular process communicated via visualizations helps to ensure successful governance (physics) of the open, all-volunteer, wiki-style community. At the same time, the Digg-style rating and reputation tools and other feedback mechanisms bind group members closer to one another (culture). Designing the screen to communicate the rules and forge a sense of trust—visual deliberation—could allow institutions to work better with distributed networks of experts.

To be clear, by *visual* I am not referring to video or to three-dimensional modeling or to any one kind of technology. In fact, my favorite metaphor to describe the notion of visual deliberation is a pile of rocks. Despite the absence of immediate gain or self-interest, hikers in the American West stop and take the time to contribute to the cairn, a mound of stones marking the path for the next hiker.[3] While sometimes a solo hiker places a marker, I imagine and have seen beautiful cairns, more artwork than signpost, that are the result of one person after another lovingly placing a new stone on the pile. Hikers use the technology of the rock pile to solve the problem of finding the path, and they do this by means of mass collaboration, namely the building of a cairn. The cairn is a visual totem that reflects back to each hiker the presence of a shared community.

HOW PEER-TO-PATENT WORKS

Steve Pearson is a senior software engineer at IBM in Portland, Oregon, who designs databases for a living. He holds a patent for a way to improve the protection of information stored in databases.[4] Informed by his employer about the opportunity to become a Peer-to-Patent volunteer and review competitors' patent applications relating to database technology, Pearson went to the Peer-to-Patent website at www.peertotpatent. org the week it was launched in June 2007.

There he found a list of published patent applications submitted by participating companies and deemed eligible for the pilot by the USPTO. At the behest of the Patent Office, the New York Law School posts each of these applications online for a three- to four-month period of public consultation.[5] After registering on the website by providing his name and e-mail address, Pearson filled out an optional public profile with information about his employment history, education, and expertise. Though the information is not authenticated (a participant need not provide a credit card to corroborate his identity and may use a pseudonym to preserve anonymity), a first name and last name rather than only a "handle" are required in an effort to elevate the level of discourse. Only 130 of over 2,300 users in the first year indicated (by checking a box) that they were using a pseudonym. Of the actively participating users (1,627 of 2,300), most have gone to the trouble of adding more information in their personal profiles, also suggesting that they are also using their real names.[6]

Pearson quickly found a patent application that interested him: Hewlett-Packard's application for a "User-selectable, management-alert format." According to HP, this invention relates to "electronic computing, and more particularly to a computing system that implements user selectable management alert format. . . . This application describes a system for improving efficiency of remote access by displaying to the user a list of formats available (as determined from the devices attached to the computer system being remotely accessed) and allowing the user to select a single format for all of the devices to use."[7]

Something made it even easier for Pearson to identify this as an application about which he had some knowledge. Users had labeled—or tagged, as it is known in web parlance—the application with common technological terms: bios (a basic input/output system) and boot (loading an operating system). Tagging is a way to assign a short (one- or two-word) label to an item of content. Web users are accustomed to captioning their photos in online albums with such short tags as "puppy," "Mom's birthday" and "my vacation." The USPTO assigns an arcane classification to every patent application. But the government schema does not correspond to the ways in which technical and scientific experts most affected by the patent system classify information. This imposes a linguistic barrier, preventing those with the most knowledge from contributing to the process. Hence Peer-to-Patent encourages participants to add their own designations (and most do). This kind of supplementary community self-tagging, called a *folksonomy*, lets the users associate a patent with a technology or concept familiar to them.[8]

It is not possible to participate in Peer-to-Patent solo. Rather, Pearson joined the application's team of reviewers. From a graphic visualization on the website, Pearson could see that twenty-nine people had already volunteered to review this HP application collectively. The group included four engineers, thirteen technologists, five lawyers, two students, two academics, a "laborer" (who was actually my New York Law School research assistant, keeping an eye on the process), and two others. An activity map (based loosely on a tree map, a free information visualization tool from the University of Maryland) showed Pearson how many discussion postings, prior art submissions, and annotations had been submitted both for the HP application and for the site as a whole (figures 4-1 and 4-2). Tree maps use colors, intensity of color, and size of quadrants to indicate hierarchies.[9] For Peer-to-Patent, changing size and color in the diagram reflects the changing size of the team and the level of its activities. Yet another graphic on the website explained how Peer-to-Patent works and the various roles Pearson could fill as a member of the team, such as uploading prior art, or making suggestions to the patent examiner for further research, or rating other people's submissions of prior art or research.

After reading HP's application, Steve Pearson entered his team's discussion space, where members deliberated about the application's focus and quality, decided what research needed to be done, discussed where prior art might be found, and divvied up the work of finding it. Each new posting appeared in Pearson's e-mail in-box automatically so that he would not have to continuously check the site for updates.

Discuss Patents Applications
30 comments posted

Size of Community: 30

Upload + Explain Prior Art
9 submitted

Annotate and Evaluate Prior Art
22 prior art ratings

9 citations

Research Prior Art
6 research notes

FIGURE 4-2. PEER-TO-PATENT PROCESS MAP

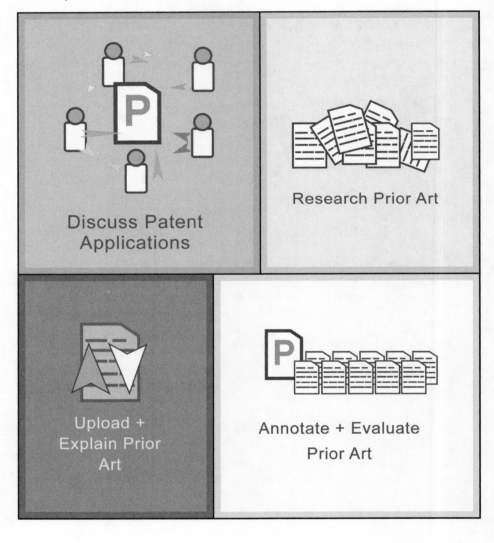

Discuss Patent
Applications

Research Prior Art

Upload +
Explain Prior
Art

Annotate + Evaluate
Prior Art

Discussion of the HP application was very lively, generating thirty comments and a highly responsive back-and-forth.[10] Because Pearson clearly demonstrated active interest in helping out, the New York Law School students administering the website invited him to act as the team's facilitator, which meant that his discussion postings appeared in a special color and he was tasked with helping to keep the discussion on track. In addition to talking about the application, the team submitted nine pieces of prior art over a two-month period, including old patents, a computer program, and a computer manual from the Intel corporation (Pearson's contribution). The Peer-to-Patent software helped ensure that these items were relevant to the application by requiring the submitter to provide the publication date of each piece of prior art.

Pearson's Intel manual predated the HP invention by two years, making it eligible for consideration by the examiner as a source to disprove the invention's novelty and nonobviousness. In response to directed questions in a web-based form, Pearson also identified the specific claims that the prior art addressed, inserted a hyperlink to the document, and uploaded a copy. (To preserve the intellectual property rights of the prior art's author, this copy was not published on the website, nor was it available for downstream duplication. Instead, New York Law School forwarded the single copy to the USPTO.) There exists a tension between protecting the rights of the prior art author and facilitating discussion among peer reviewers, who might benefit from being able to read the original document. But this work-around makes the process possible (and suggests that intellectual property laws, procurement policies, and other stumbling blocks that might impede participation are surmountable with the right design of social practices).

To ensure that the public participation aids the examiner in decision-making, the website asks participants to cite prior art with exactitude by indicating the pages, paragraphs, and phrases relevant to the claims of the patent application. In addition, it requires anyone submitting prior art to explain its relevance, for the benefit of both the community and the patent examiner. Precisely that which was forbidden by law under the paper-based system—namely, commenting on submissions of prior art by third parties—is essential to extracting information most useful to the USPTO.[11] The Peer-to-Patent website makes possible what was not only impractical before but also illegal.

Once a piece of prior art is submitted via the Peer-to-Patent website, the group collectively decides which submissions are most useful. Members of the HP group were invited both to annotate each other's submissions and to vote on their relevance. For example, two participants gave Pearson's manual a thumbs-up, expressing their agreement that the Intel manual might be useful for the examiner.

At the conclusion of the public review process in September 2007, the team of New York Law School students maintaining the website prepared an information disclosure statement, or IDS, consisting of the prior art, the suggested research, the annotations on the submissions, and the thumbs-up ratings from the online review community; the team then forwarded this IDS to the USPTO. Just in case the link to the website with the Intel manual went down, the students printed the relevant portions of the manual and forwarded the hard copy, as the USPTO also requires. Had there been more than ten prior art references, the software would have tabulated the ones with the most thumbs-up votes, and the students would have forwarded only those. Promising the agency to share only the top ten submissions was crucial to ensuring that the participating reviewers would not overload the USPTO, creating inefficiencies for the agency.

Upon subsequent examination of the patent application in the normal course, the patent examiner conducted her own search for prior art, using the USPTO's standard databases. In addition, she reviewed the results of Peer-to-Patent's "human database," including Pearson's research. In deciding to reject HP's application in February 2008, the patent examiner cited the Intel manual that Steve Pearson had uncovered. HP filed an amended application two weeks later. Nonetheless, the examiner issued a final rejection in May 2008, disposing of the HP application outright as unpatentable in light of Intel's "Active Management Technology: Quick Reference Guide"—a piece of prior art the examiner never would have identified on her own.[12] Because the examiner used Pearson's prior art, the Peer-to-Patent team posted his name on the website under an icon of a patent application wearing a beret and holding a palette (figure 4-3). The Prior Artist title recognizes contributors who post prior art or research used by the USPTO in evaluating a patent application.

Peer-to-Patent is a simple process that rewards all sides. The patent examiner gains access to new information. The inventor benefits from

FIGURE 4-3. PEER-TO-PATENT PRIOR ARTIST AWARD

PATENT APPLICATION ARTIST AWARDS

 These contributors submitted prior art or annotations used by the USPTO in making the determination of patentability

Name	Type	Patent Application
Alexandre Eichenberger	Prior Art	Method and apparatus for an inductive doubling...
Gabriel Gomez	Prior Art	Image inversion
Sharat Mendu	Prior Art	Computer compliance system and method
Charles Peck	Prior Art	System and method for implementing a multi...
Jeff Morrill	Prior Art	Method of obtaining data samples from a data...
Christian Seifert	Prior Art	Honey monkey network exploration
Steven Pearson	Prior Art	Method and apparatus for selectively executing diff...
Susan Murray	Prior Art	Methods of enhancing media content narrative
Kathy Wang	Prior Art	Honey monkey network exploration
Mark Nowotarski	Prior Art	Tuning core voltages of processors
Walter Dietrich	Prior Art	System and method for retaining information in a...
Abhay Porwal	Prior Art	Smart drag-and-drop
Rob Cameron	Prior Art	Cipher method and system for verifying a decrypti...

the likely increase in the quality of the resulting patent and does not pursue a patent that will later prove to be unenforceable, risking costly litigation and unsuccessful enforcement. The public benefits from avoiding low-quality patents that potentially stifle future innovation. As programmers are wont to say: many eyes make all bugs shallow.[13] Having more people look at the patent application helps to identify weaknesses in this early phase, before a business strategy is built around a low-quality patent, which would then be prone to expensive legal challenges in court. While HP had its application rejected in this case, another dozen applications that went through public review arguably came out stronger and more litigation-proof as a result of having been scrutinized by many eyes. A Peer-to-Patent participant like Steve Pearson gets a unique opportunity to "bust" a nonmeritorious patent application in his domain of expertise before the USPTO approves it—as well as the chance to work with and gain the recognition of a community of his peers.

REFLECTING THE WORK OF THE GROUP BACK TO ITSELF

Jeremy Bailenson is a social psychologist at the Stanford Department of Communication who studies affective computing, or technology that influences emotional phenomena. He conducts experiments in which the human subjects look at an avatar, a digital image, of themselves on the computer screen.[14] (Derived from the Sanskrit *avatra,* meaning "descent," *avatar* connotes an incarnation or human appearance of a deity, particularly Vishnu. Chip Morningstar and Randall Farmer are credited with coining the use of the term in connection with an online character in the Habitat video game in 1986.) *Avatar* has since become common parlance for one's online persona and the common tool for social science research.[15] Bailenson manipulates his subjects' avatars. When he makes them unattractive, participants' sense of self-confidence and assertiveness in real life declines. Changing the computer screen undermines and changes human behavior.

When Bailenson shows the avatar engaged in exercise, the person is more likely to exercise in real life. (This phenomenon accounts, perhaps, for the success of the Nintendo WiiFit exercise game.) Bailenson has also demonstrated that people are more likely to vote for the political candidate who resembles them. This may explain, according to Bailenson, why in the 2004 election the Bush campaign darkened the president's image for advertisements in Hispanic and black neighbor-hoods.[16] But what happens when I can perceive the communities and groups of which I am a part via the screen? What happens when, instead of merely seeing my own avatar, I can see reflected back at me the mem-bership, rules, values, and goals of an online consulting group, a net-worked community of activists, or a Peer-to-Patent team? What if the computer reflects us instead of me?

Joan Morris DiMicco (formerly of the MIT Media Lab and now at IBM) is one of only a few people working on this question of the influ-ence of screens on group behavior.[17] She studies ways in which the com-puter screen can be used to reflect the behavior of a group back to itself and, in so doing, to make the group more than the sum of its individual parts by reinforcing its identity as a group. This is what she calls *social translucence,* or social mirroring: greater mutual awareness of actions that can result in more effective coordination as a group. She knows that such experiments will suffer from a Heisenbergian observer effect. By introducing visual reflections of social behavior into collaborative processes, she will change and influence those processes in uncertain ways. From such luminaries of the behavioral economics literature as Tversky and Kahneman, we know that small changes in the description of a decision can result in dramatic changes in the choices people make. It is precisely because the screen can have a persuasive effect that makes its impact potentially powerful.

DiMicco's research looks at how technology can be used in face-to-face settings to address the social factors that have a damaging influence on group decisionmaking, such as imbalanced participation and speak-ing habits. Her empirical tests with face-to-face groups have demon-strated that social visualization tools—things as simple as using voice recognition software to spot conversational topics and display them back to participants, or red and green lights to indicate who is talking more and less—can make communities more effective at sharing information and at participating in a collaborative process.

While DiMicco's research looks at how to correct deliberative group discussion processes, the results of her work have more general applica-bility. Visualizations make participants more aware of group imbalances and correct for them. "By altering its decisionmaking process," DiMicco comments, "a group can avoid the above communication flaws and over-reliance on others. For example, by allowing for minority viewpoints to be freely expressed, by continually scanning the available options, to find new alternatives that may work and by allowing for open dissent [from] the authority figure's opinion, the group . . . will more likely make the best possible hiring decision for the group."[18]

In one of her experiments, DiMicco used displays with light-emitting diodes (LEDs), which became redder if a person spoke more relative to others or greener if a participant spoke less, causing, in particular, those who were dominant to tone down their participation. Her testing deployed visualizations demonstrating the quantity and turn-taking of participants by means of automated diagrams and graphics. The visualizations had multiple, positive effects on interaction in groups. But as she admits, because she was only testing and playing with participation levels, these experiments did not produce better group processes to the full extent that might be possible had she experimented with a broader range of the group's decisionmaking processes.

GRANULARITY, GROUPS, AND REPUTATION

Peer-to-Patent is neither a blog nor a wiki. It is not a free-for-all. It is a structured process designed to elicit participation that is helpful to the USPTO by facilitating granularity, "groupness," and reputation (figure 4-4).

GRANULARITY

The New York affiliate of National Public Radio invited listeners to coproduce serious political programming via a wiki.[19] The project succeeded because the design of the wiki reflected the "physics" of participation back to participants via the screen; volunteers knew what was being asked of them. NPR did not simply request participation in general terms. The opportunities to volunteer were broken down into granular questions. The wiki outlined the desired content by discrete category: angles on the theme, possible guests to invite on the show, questions to ask, audio clips to use, links to research materials. People knew where to submit their answers and could participate in only one category or in all categories.

Typically, citizen participation, such as notice-and-comment rulemaking, invites people to respond in general to a draft rule. Each person has to submit his own complete comment. But for an open and collaborative process to work in a competitive and technical arena like the

FIGURE 4-4. HOW PEER-TO-PATENT WORKS

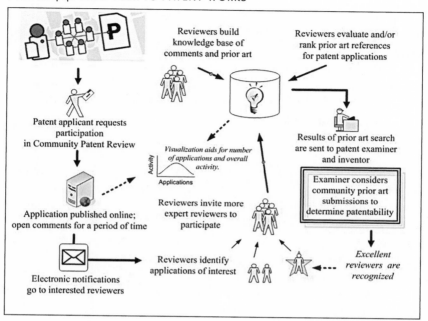

patent system, it was necessary to ask specific questions through the web-based form and thereby invite specific and useful responses. Also, asking nongovernment experts to participate demands identifying opportunities for part-time commitment, preferably of varying length, that require diverse forms of expertise. In Peer-to-Patent, participants can self-select to submit prior art or simply to comment on someone else's, to join the discussion, or to rate and rank a posting. Only 3 percent of Peer-to-Patent participants reported that they contributed daily; 42 percent went on the site only once or twice, 36 percent did so monthly, and 19 percent weekly. While on average a reviewer spent six hours working on an application, many participants may have simply reviewed the discussion and the group's work, posted one item of prior art, and never come back.[20]

Dividing the work into tasks enables members of the group to self-select different roles to take on and thereby to work together as a group most effectively. It is a truism in the world of open-source programming that asking people hard questions is the best way to engage them in a collaborative enterprise.[21] With patent review, it is particularly easy to "chunk" the work into manageable, discrete tasks that makes collaboration possible, because the questions are already well identified as a matter of law. Under the Patent Act, the examiner has to figure out if the invention is new compared to similar inventions in the same and related fields. This dictates asking the public for information relating to similar inventions. Patent examination lends itself particularly well to chunking, but all areas of policymaking could yield concrete, specific tasks that would benefit from collaborative attention.

Groupness

In the preweb world, visual cues as simple as a common uniform or a shared social space helped to create a sense of the groups to which we belong. The social rituals and visual totems that inculcate culture for a group in real space, however, have been absent in cyberspace in the past. Put another way, there are no sidewalks in cyberspace, and the decoupling of cyberspace from geography has impeded the purposive interaction that fosters belonging and friendship and allows groups to cohere.[22] But visual and social technologies are changing our ability to sustain virtual communities.

The wildly popular multiplayer video game World of Warcraft has 10 million subscribers. WoW, as it's called, is an adventure game that organizes people into "races," which in turn collaborate in "guilds." Races have specific attributes that translate into offensive, defensive, or more esoteric skills. Orcs are aggressive and warlike, with the power to stun, while dwarfs are frost resistant and good defensive players. Blood Elves are highly magical. The game assigns quests (slaying monsters, grabbing enchanted goblets, and other assignments à la *Lord of the Rings*) for the members of a guild to accomplish together. Joichi Ito, the globally successful entrepreneur and technologist (and custodian of a large WoW guild), attributes the success of WoW to the high level of structured role and task differentiation, which encourages collaboration.[23]

The diversity of social roles to be played in WoW guilds may be some of the game's appeal. The anthropology of WoW is so rich as to have merited a scientific conference sponsored by the National Science Foundation (that took place in the Earthen Ring in 2008).[24] No less august a publication than the *Harvard Business Review* published an article by John Seely Brown, the former chief scientist at Xerox Parc, about the complex social systems of today's "massively multiplayer" games:

Diversity is essential in the world of the online game. One person can't do it all; each player is by definition incomplete. The key to achievement is teamwork, and the strongest teams are a rich mix of diverse talents and abilities. The criterion for advancement is not "How good am I?"; it's "How much have I helped the group?" Entire categories of game characters (such as healers) have little or no advantage in individual play, but they are indispensable members of every team.[25]

The value of role differentiation to foster group collaboration holds true for real-world institutions as well. Stephen Kosslyn and Richard Hackman, who run the Group Brain project at Harvard, describe this phenomenon of people working together as a group, collectively responsible for their output, as a "brain-based approach."[26] The group is an emergent entity, akin to a brain, where in order to work together effectively people must be able to adopt roles in the team—distinct but interdependent brain systems. In other words, the successful group is a first-order social actor in which people can accomplish what they cannot do alone.[27] People are increasingly taking advantage of new technology to form such purposive groups to accomplish their goals. Group brain research (Kosslyn and Hackman have studied orchestras, groups of investment bankers, as well as teams of spies) empirically demonstrates that achieving successful outcomes depends on diversity of roles in the group, a conclusion echoed in the popular and scholarly book *The Difference*.[28]

In professional life, small, interdependent teams of lawyers work together to "do deals." (Yet law schools, infamous for the apocryphal custom of first-year students highlighting library books in black, rarely train young lawyers in the art of collaboration.)[29] Similarly, their counterpart analysts in investment banks work under time pressure on mergers and acquisitions. This is not dissimilar to the effective way that emergency room teams function: working as a group, under stressful conditions, with differentiated tasks and roles to achieve a clear outcome. "Evolution," Kosslyn observes, "has allowed our brains to be configured during development so that we are 'plug compatible' with other humans, so that others can help us extend ourselves."[30]

Bureaucracy, at least the way it is currently constituted, may operate under similar time pressure, but it is not set up for complementary, interdisciplinary, role-differentiated group work. Patent examiners sometimes get a "second set of eyes" to review an application, but generally they work alone. The public may participate in rulemaking processes by submitting comments to the agency, but communication is one to one: each individual submits a unique comment and has no means to comment on others. There is no dialogue or collaboration among members of the public. The burden falls to the official to wade through the discrete comments, making it very hard to organize on a large scale and losing the opportunity to benefit from the expertise of other members of a knowledgeable team. (Later we explore the shortcomings of existing group-based practices, such as negotiated rulemaking in which stakeholders work on hammering out consensus as a group.)

Getting people to think of themselves as a group—such as a distributed team of scientists working to aid the Patent Office or a guild in World of Warcraft—and to collaborate toward achieving a common purpose depends significantly on giving the group a nudge toward collaborative behavior that will make the collective more aware of itself, its goals, and the various roles members can play.[31] In much the same way as a wax seal provides the outward manifestation to strengthen the legal fiction of a corporation—which can sue, be sued, own assets, and make collective decisions—the computer screen may be able to provide that nudge to construct collaboration between networks and centralized decisionmakers. (Seeing human activity industriously eating away at the earth's biosphere in Al Gore's landmark film, *An Inconvenient Truth*, also helps us visualize a reality of global warming that we could hardly otherwise fathom.)

The ability to create a sense of groupness via the screen has been a key driver to the success of Peer-to-Patent. The design of the process offers a framework for volunteers to self-select unique roles as part of a collaborative effort. But the technology plays an important role in conveying that process to participants. The Peer-to-Patent website divides the work to be performed into clear and manageable tasks. People can choose how they want to participate. Some find prior art while others are good at annotating that art. Some discuss the patents while others fill in the bibliographic citations. The visualizations on the Peer-to-Patent website that show a picture of the membership and activity of the team also help to stimulate a sense of the group working together on an application.

While we might have subscribed more people faster had we not imposed the requirement to join a group, without a cohesive sense of community and a common sense of purpose, online communities frequently end up proving Godwin's Law. The adage, coined by online activist Mike Godwin in 1990, states that "as an online discussion grows longer, the probability of a comparison involving Nazis or Hitler approaches one."[32] Instead, collaboration in a team helps to overcome the distrust that stems from working anonymously at a distance.

Having groups makes it more practical to organize meaningful feedback. Teams in Peer-to-Patent range in size from one to forty-six, with an average of nine members per team. Across Peer-to-Patent participation has been diverse, with one-third of active participants reporting themselves to be technologists. Most significantly, only 9 percent of participants in the first year indicated that they were lawyers (those typically involved in the patent system). Participants help one another to understand the issues at stake in the course of discussing the application's twenty-one claims. Over the course of the first month, Pearson and his teammates talked about the exact nature of the technology at issue with reference to the patent's claims. (Typing the number of a claim between two brackets—[[claim 4]]—inserts a link to the content of that claim automatically, allowing people to cite specific provisions and bring the content directly into the conversation.)

The website's user-moderation features help facilitate productive discussion. Private-sector websites (from the book reviews on Amazon to the movie reviews on IMDb to the news postings on Slashdot, the technology news site) use what are known as collaborative filtering mechanisms to enable users to rate each other's postings and then filter what they wish to read. Peer-to-Patent allows participants to flag discussion postings as action items requiring attention, as unhelpful noise, or as spam by checking the appropriate box next to each posting.

The system tabulates the feedback so that Peer-to-Patent administrators can be alerted to inappropriate content and volunteer participants can sort the discussion by quality of submissions (for example, choosing to display the discussion without items marked by others as noise). As of this writing, there has been no reported instance of spam or abuse and no need to take down content from the website for violating the terms of service. Godwin's Law has yet to be proven. In fact, while the Patent Office is only obligated to review the prior art submissions, it also follows the discussions for insights into how to conduct its search. Slashdot, the popular technology news website, is the best known example of a publication that uses this kind of community moderation to make the flow of content more manageable. Selected from among active Slashdot readers, eligible community moderators rate posted articles on a scale of one to five, and then readers have the option of sorting and filtering what they read based on these ratings, perhaps eliminating information that falls below a certain threshold.[33]

RATING AND REPUTATION

In addition to flagging discussion postings, Peer-to-Patent makes public participation more useful and manageable by encouraging users to rate each other's submissions to the USPTO and, in turn, having the USPTO rate participants.

By evaluating prior art with a thumbs-up or thumbs-down (plus any written annotations), a volunteer expresses whether or not the public submission is relevant enough to the claims of the application to be forwarded to the agency. (In point of fact, we don't count the thumbs-down ratings, which we added for the same reason that elevators have a Close Door button.) These Digg-style ratings (as on the news site digg.com, where users can vote on the quality of postings; and Dell computer's IdeaStorm, where customers can evaluate ideas for new Dell products) provide a simple way to calculate the top-ten list and winnow submissions, if necessary.[34] Giving the community power to evaluate itself also reduces gaming by encouraging members to police each other. The USPTO can feel comfortable that an IBM employee like Steve Pearson is participating in examining the application of a competitor like Hewlett-Packard, because third parties have a way to signal if a public submission may be of low quality, irrelevant, or inappropriate.

Such community rating features will be especially useful when Peer-to-Patent (or projects like it) begins to handle a much larger volume of patent applications, teams, and prior art. In the early stages of the pilot, few applications attracted more than ten items of prior art; none had more than twenty. Generally, the public submits three to five items of prior art per application. Submissions may continue at that level, but if the volume rises, the ability to rate and filter will become essential.

Open, wiki-style, peer production enables many people to contribute information through the use of a common online environment for collaborative writing and editing. But Digg-style rating is what makes that volunteer participation manageable even on a large scale. Rating tools help to winnow a large quantity of information. The voting also creates opportunities for people to participate as evaluators of content even if they do not have their own know-how to share. For example, during the presidential campaign debates in 2008, the Presidential Debate Commission invited public submission of questions for the one town-hall-style debate. At least 25,000 questions were submitted online; it was up to NBC anchor Tom Brokaw to sift through them and pick six or seven.[35] Had the commission used the Peer-to-Patent and Digg technique to solicit public expertise as well as public questions, others could have done the job of culling the questions to a manageable number. By contrast, Netroots Nation, the progressive activism conference, enabled users to rate, up or down, questions to House Speaker Nancy Pelosi on askthespeaker.org, which she then answered at the annual convention.[36] Both presidential candidates in the 2008 race signed a statement endorsing this technique of bubbling up the questions from the public.[37] President Obama has committed to using this technique in his administration.

Successful companies and organizations have cultivated responsiveness from and to employees, suppliers, and customers, but government rarely has the opportunity to improve the quality of public consultation practices by giving or receiving feedback. Peer-to-Patent awards reputational honors—the Prior Artist award—to those who submit relevant material. The Prior Artist reputation scheme educates participants about what the agency deems to be useful performance. This feedback can help participants in future searches for prior art to know what is most useful. This reputation scheme encourages participation by enabling participants to receive professional recognition for their hard work. Professional patent searchers demonstrate research prowess, students attract prospective employers, technologists show mastery at their jobs.

By contrast, Ten Downing Street offers the e-petitions website, which invites people to submit petitions for the government's consideration but without meaningful direction or feedback.[38] These citizen-submitted petitions have thus far garnered 8.8 million signatures on 1,007 petitions. In one case, an individual started a petition against a proposed travel tax. Over 1.8 million people signed it.[39] Every petition with over 200 signatures, regardless of topic or merit, receives a pro forma response via e-mail. In the case of the travel tax petition, the prime minister himself drafted the message. But there are no reputational gains to be had as a participant. All petitions are the same and, as a matter of policy, none of them directly leads to action. (The travel tax is still in effect.) To do so would usurp Parliament's authority. The lack of reputational feedback based on outcomes is the reason that the project attracts so much frivolous participation. There are countless petitions to knight this one or that and no measures to teach desired participation practices.

Peer-to-Patent's reputational metrics might eventually be expanded to include volunteers directly rating each individual's broader participation. Such a reputational score could help team members and the examiner assign weight to submitted information. Similar dynamics may also extend outside the immediate Peer-to-Patent community. The lawyers who draft the applications under review may acquire a reputation for the precision or clarity of their language. At the very least, the ability to acquire a reputation in a professional community could create an impetus to increased participation.

The online auction site eBay allows members to award reputation points to trustworthy sellers (formerly, they allowed rating of both buyers and sellers).[40] This software-enabled reputation system translates into some sellers enjoying increased sales.[41] Similarly, automating the system of providing feedback in Peer-to-Patent about people and content may help to "bubble up" better information from self-selecting experts. But reputation in an online community can also emerge in more informal ways. As the project grows, community members may come to be known for the high—or low—quality of their reasoning or research. In this collaborative ecosystem of examiners and volunteers, the institutional decisionmakers may come to anticipate reading the submissions from certain participants. Because people are working together in teams, groups may earn their own reputations for successful participation—patent posses as distinct from individuals. A reputation scheme can help to evolve an open meritocracy of engagement, which may replace the exclusive access of patent professionals in the patent system (and lobbyists and other Washington insiders in other agency contexts).

Getting Everyone on Board

With hindsight, the benefits of soliciting outside expertise to inform decisionmaking now seem obvious. But when we started out, the idea that the web could improve the quality of patents was not self-evident, necessitating a process of cajoling and explaining in order to "sell" people on getting behind the project. Social networking technologies like Facebook and MySpace were not quite as familiar then. While what we were peddling was, in many respects, no more revolutionary than the twelfth-century innovation of the jury, we were asking a government agency to overhaul practices that had not been changed in generations. But to design it right and achieve the necessary consensus to implement this open strategy, we needed to work with the agency to ensure that what we would build would respond to its needs—its "pain" about information deficit and work overload.

After trying to make the case that the USPTO should open its own decisionmaking practices to public participation, New York Law School could not then run Peer-to-Patent as a closed-door cabal. The aim was not to create a Washington Beltway insiders' project, either. We needed to test the hypothesis that distributed, nongovernment, self-selected experts could assist the Patent Office by creating our own group. If we were to craft an effective solution, corporate lawyers had to sit down with Silicon Valley technologists and Washington policymakers, academics and corporate representatives, civic leaders and graphic designers. We needed a collaborative process to design a collaborative project!

As recounted in chapter 1, IBM was the first company to declare its interest in Peer-to-Patent.[42] The participation of IBM's lawyers transformed a solo blog post by a self-declared outsider to the patent world into the beginnings of a collaborative community. With IBM officially on board, Microsoft signed on almost immediately. This surprised many who have a knee-jerk animosity toward Microsoft's business practices, especially Microsoft's threat to bring patent infringement lawsuits against open-source software developers. But Edward "Kaz" Kazenske, the senior director of patent prosecution strategy and relations in Microsoft's Intellectual Property and Licensing Group, was personally committed to patent reform. As the former deputy commissioner of the USPTO for patent resources and planning, he had been responsible for budget and financial management, strategic operations, and business information technology at the Patent Office. He understood the need for better quality information resources to aid examiners and the opportunity that technology might provide. He dug up a 1966 report to President Johnson that he had been holding onto; one of the recommendations called for a confidential six-month window for public submission of prior art. This recommendation was never adopted.[43]

Kazenske's commitment to patent reform coincided with corporate self-interest. Perhaps Microsoft hoped that its participation would mitigate the open-source community's ire that had arisen after the company threatened to assert its patents against the Linux open-source software developers. By summer 2006, when Microsoft joined the Peer-to-Patent Steering Committee, a deal with Novell was in the offing that would allow Microsoft Windows to work with Novell's open-source, Linux-based servers.[44] Many in the open-source community greeted this arrangement with suspicion. Peer-to-Patent might have helped to dampen the backlash. Of course, Microsoft, like the other participating companies, also wanted to ensure that IBM, as the largest patent holder and licensor among them, would not monopolize the process or impose undue influence. And Microsoft desperately wants reform. With up to forty infringement suits against it pending at any given time, it is the high-technology company most sued for patent infringement.[45]

GE was the third company to join the project. The chief intellectual property counsel of General Electric at that time, Q. Todd Dickinson, was the former undersecretary of state for intellectual property and director of the USPTO (and therefore a colleague of Kazenske).[46] Dickinson had a personal commitment to creating greater transparency in the patent system. Popular during his tenure as head of the Patent Office, he instituted the 1.99 rule, allowing for limited third-party submissions without commentary. Dickinson and Kazenske, who had deep knowledge of the institution and its practices, added credibility to the project planning.

With IBM, Microsoft, and GE in the stable, Computer Associates (CA), Hewlett-Packard, Intellectual Ventures, and Red Hat agreed to support the project. These companies composed the Steering Committee, which met weekly by telephone for the better part of a year to lend expertise and direction. If New York Law School were to design a reliable process and a website to integrate successfully with the USPTO's own decisionmaking, it would need, however, to find additional financial support to build the software. At the same time, independent and disinterested voices from philanthropy and academia balanced out the interest, skills, and perspective of corporate insiders. The John D. and Catherine T. MacArthur Foundation and the Omidyar Network provided much-needed fiscal support but also the legitimacy of independent and trusted third parties.

The foundations participated in an Advisory Board along with renowned patent law and technology professors, heads of international patent offices, and representatives from the largest intellectual property law association—the AIPLA—and the National Academies of Science. The Advisory Board and the dozens of other academics and professionals who participated in the planning formed a counterweight to the corporate Steering Committee. The academics mediated any communication between the USPTO and the corporate participants to reduce risk of corruption and to ensure transparency. Together, a three-legged governance structure (the USPTO team, the corporate Steering Committee, and the Advisory Board) drove the project forward.

Finally, of course, the USPTO was the indispensable partner. Without its cooperation, Peer-to-Patent—and thus the first federal collaborative governance project—would never have become a reality. And there were many reasons for the agency not to cooperate. We were asking the USPTO to invite unknown outsiders to participate in the activities that made up its raison d'être—examining patent applications. Not without irony, we were trying to apply open-source principles in the monopolistic culture of the patent system. Traditional forms of public participation practices typically do not work well: the agency is either overwhelmed by too many or receives too few public comments. The New York Law School project asked the USPTO to break the mold of familiar forms of consultation—such as notice-and-comment rulemaking, advisory committees, and even traditional peer review—and embrace self-selected reviewers connected by the web. Moreover, we could provide no guarantee that those participating in the process would be experts in their fields or disinterested parties.

No agency had ever attempted to connect its institutional practices to an open, online, social network. While we were modeling our ideas on the jury and earlier forms of peer review, we would largely be improvising as we went along. That meant convincing the Patent Office to accept "rough consensus and running code"; that is, asking one of the most conservative, independent, process-oriented institutions to experiment with its core operations.[47]

But USPTO also had good reason to take part in Peer-to-Patent. The agency was under increasing pressure from industry and Congress as the backlog of patent applications mounted. Peer-to-Patent offered a partial solution to its problems—and other entities were offering to foot the bill.

But what ultimately convinced the USPTO to come on board was the fact that Peer-to-Patent would leave the final determination of patentability in the hands of its professional staff. The public would offer information that the examiners would be free to use or discard.

Peer-to-Patent did not seek to eliminate the agency or the examiner. It would not alter the substantive standards applied in reviewing inventions but, instead, augment the examination system with a self-selected corps of researchers, working through a structured interface to deliver information in a manageable quantity. We wanted to work within—to redesign, not route around—decisionmaking practices. With this assurance, Jay Lucas, the newly appointed deputy commissioner of patent examination—a life-long patent official who met his wife among the examiner corps and whose son also became an examiner—championed the Peer-to-Patent idea. Jack Harvey, who took over responsibility when Lucas assumed a judgeship in the Patent Office, approached the task of organizing the agency's role in Peer-to-Patent with creativity and enthusiasm, informed too by his experience as a rank-and-file examiner. Together, Lucas and Harvey convened a team of eight officials to shepherd the project.

So who was not at the table for this collaboration? Representatives of the biotechnology industry declined to participate. Pharmaceutical lawyers had no interest in a reform process that at the outset seemed doomed to fail (and, in any case, focused on the high-technology industry). The biotech industry is dependent on the status quo: strong patents to protect large, up-front investments in research and development. While it might seem counterintuitive that an industry so focused on patents would not want the best-quality ones, pharmaceuticals and biotechnology traditionally have shown little interest in reform that might curtail or limit patenting.[48] As an industry, biotech fights patent reform legislation. The biotech and pharmaceutical companies instead push to strengthen patent protection for their products by lobbying against legislative reform in the United States and for provisions guaranteeing exclusive marketing rights in the patent law of developing countries.[49] (With greater understanding now of what Peer-to-Patent is, pharma may participate in the future.)

Also absent was the Free Software Foundation (FSF), which is dedicated to promoting the development of free software and protecting users' rights to use and modify their software. Chaired by techno-evangelist Richard Stallmann and represented by Columbia law professor Eben

Moglen, the Software Freedom Law Center objects to patenting, especially in high technology. Patents lock up what should be free, notably software, which is a core form of expression in the digital age. From their perspective, patents allow companies to monopolize and control how others write code. An initial toe in the water with the FSF to test interest in the idea of Peer-to-Patent (we would ironically be applying collaborative open-source methods to the closed practices of the USPTO) confirmed that the abolitionists would not be complicit in software patenting in any form.[50] Other open-source groups like the Groklaw online community and the Linux Foundation, representing corporate users of the open-source operating system, have participated actively. Mark Webbink, executive director of Peer-to-Patent and the Center for Patent Innovations at New York Law School, was formerly the general counsel of Red Hat, the public open-source software company and an early supporter of Peer-to-Patent.

Nonetheless, by the time we were ready to think seriously about building Peer-to-Patent, we had a diverse and knowledgeable cast of characters who had joined forces.

THE DESIGN PROCESS

In 2006 our own group brain came together (in face-to-face workshops and online via listservs and e-mail correspondence) to teach and learn from one another—to have fun.[51] At the same table were the general counsel of Palm Inc. and the then twenty-nine-year-old founder of Slashdot. They brainstormed about whether Peer-to-Patent users should rate the public submissions on a one-to-ten scale, or with thumbs up and down, or with gold stars.

Stanford computer science professor Terry Winograd, one of the world's leading experts on human-computer interaction, had probably never before spent an afternoon with his Stanford colleague Mark Lemley, one of the country's foremost patent law academics. Winograd exhorted the group to pay attention to the needs of the potential audience; Lemley knows what those needs are. Graduate students in information science applied their knowledge of prediction markets to the problem of patent expertise. Visualization specialists, who normally develop tools to make usage patterns on the web or census data more intelligible via the computer screen, joined intellectual property litigators, who know something about how information needs to be presented to courts in complex intellectual property cases. Those who invented the eBay "power sellers" reputation system, where buyers award sellers stars for their timeliness and courtesy, contributed their understanding of how to design a rating system. They brainstormed with the programmers about how the same techniques might be applied successfully to patent information to create the top-ten list. Together, they devised a strategy for winnowing public participation into a manageable form. Even virtual world and video game designers shared their knowledge of how to make the Peer-to-Patent online community fun and keep people coming back.

Our collaborative process was not dissimilar to the way the general public license was designed. The general public license is the open-source contract that gives away the author's copyrights so that others can modify and use the copyrighted software code. Twenty-one of the largest technology vendors worked on the draft of the general public license every other week for a year and a half. Working in teams, they marked up and commented on the contract. There were meetings on every continent save Antarctica. In addition to technology firms, twenty-four of the largest open-source software users—including banks, government agencies, brokerage firms, and their lawyers—consulted weekly. (In)famous hackers with standing in the community also participated in forging that consensus.

Over the course of the development of Peer-to-Patent and even after the launch of the website in June 2007, more constituents began to join the planning process. Representatives of the financial and securities industries from such institutions as Goldman Sachs thought through the necessary adaptations to expand the project from software to include business method patents. Interested computer programmers weighed in by e-mail. Peer-to-Patent reviewers and inventors who had participated in the project started to propose improvements.

At each workshop, the lawyers asked why anyone would share expertise online. After all, a good litigator knows to hold on to information relevant to a competitor's patent until it can do the most damage in litigation. The government professionals, reared in the philosophy of centralized, bureaucratic expertise, were likewise unclear on the concept. Asking for help reveals what one does not know. The technologists and activists laughed. Why would anyone *not* want to distinguish herself by sharing expertise online—and potentially preventing a bad patent from being granted in the first place? After all, a good technologist knows that better code comes from sharing, not hoarding, information about bugs. Despite the cultural differences, the rancor or mistrust often characteristic of public lawmaking did not plague the Peer-to-Patent community.

Other issues did generate concern and fierce debate. An early fear was that no one would participate. USPTO representatives helped resolve this problem by devising incentives for participating inventors, proposing that they would have their applications reviewed first and jump the million-application waiting line. Or given these incentives, perhaps eager inventors would storm the gates, deluging the Patent Office with more requests to join the pilot than it could accommodate. Worse than concerns about inventors were those about the public peer reviewers. Who would participate? Would those with competitive interests overwhelm the process? Would those with a stake in the patent application itself submit misleading information to distract the community, enervate the examiner, and defeat the process? Even those without malicious or competitive intent might have trouble recognizing prior art and submit poor-quality information. Alternatively, the abstruse quality of patents might depress participation to zero. The safeguards built into the granular, group-based, and reputation-backed process may be part of the reason that none of these outcomes came to pass.

We wanted those with constructive and critical expertise—professors with flyaway hair, youthful computer geeks dressed as if they were still breaking boundaries in high school, and sartorially splendid lawyers—to help design the process. Because this was a pilot that would generate empirically ascertainable results, there was also no urgent need for representative participation by stakeholders. If by representative we had understood anyone with an interest in patents, we would have had to include even those wishing to torpedo the endeavor, and we would not have invited the techies. Instead, we brought together those willing to contribute productive, creative, original, visionary thinking about how to test a set of ideas.

The process was transparent. Every mock-up of the website, Power-Point presentation, and use-case scenario went up on the public project planning website (http://dotank.nyls.edu/communitypatent). Post-launch, the project team posted the data about inventor and public participation. The students at New York Law School collaborated with interested volunteers around the country to calculate everything from the time to first office action from the USPTO to the number of discussion comments to the frequency of nonpatent prior art literature submitted by the public compared to the disclosures made by the inventor. There was a project listserv with sporadic announcements, imploring those who had signed up to get involved. That general listserv was the kiddy table in comparison to the technical listserv, a web-based message board for the technologists who contributed to choosing the technical architecture and coding strategies.

The planning was not without its share of bureaucracy: countless USPTO officials, including the examiners' union, had to vet decisions, and at one point the government wanted the law school to indemnify it for patent infringement in the unlikely event someone would sue the USPTO for infringing a patent on public participation in patent examination (who would sue the USPTO for patent infringement?). But the cooperation proceeded smoothly, with regular communication among the Patent Office, corporate lawyers, academic advisers, technologists, and designers. Everyone gave generously of time and resources. The conversation reinforced mutual trust and goodwill, enabling all involved to take a collective deep breath, make the first step (which included many missteps, false starts, and a path yet untaken), and see what happened.

Perhaps surprisingly, the collaborative nature of the process—because it was focused on a concrete outcome—did not lead to a protracted schedule. The idea of interdisciplinary collaboration among lawyers, technologists, and policymakers might seem like a self-evident good, yet it is rarely practiced in government. There are several councils (such as the CIO Council and the Webmasters Council) but they convene all too infrequently and are not expressly interdisciplinary. There are cross-agency projects like e-rulemaking; but the working group represents different agencies, not unique functional specialties. There are no social networking sites (yet) in government to connect communities of practice or identify ideas and innovations lurking in the "basements" of agencies. An ABA blue-ribbon commission on Internet and agency rulemaking, which proposed improvements to the e-rulemaking website, was overwhelmingly populated by lawyers.[52] An NSF-funded international working group on citizen participation convened political and social scientists, in addition to lawyers, but invited no techies.[53] The New York City Commission on Public Information and Communication has no members who know technology well enough to speak to how it might be used to achieve the commission's goals (as of this writing, it does not even have a website). Yet too often technologists make important decisions about the design of the technology that underlies practices of participation and engagement without the insight of those who understand and could change them. (Hence it was a revelatory and uplifting experience during the Obama-Biden Transition Project to convene technologists, social theorists, policy wonks, privacy lawyers, and civil service experts to design some of the collaborative tools now in use in government and even on the White House website.)

EARLY RESULTS

The Peer-to-Patent pilot was intended to test the hypothesis that groups of distributed, self-selected, nongovernment experts, coming together via the web, could produce expertise to assist the Patent Office with decisionmaking. In a little more than a year, the pilot attracted 2,300 volunteer reviewers, working on eighty-four applications. Of the volunteers at least 365 were actively participating reviewers who posted prior art, participated in discussions, and rated each other's submissions. The public has proffered 255 pieces of prior art and 46 research suggestions. They have posted close to 500 discussion comments and put 232 tags on patent applications.

The early benefits of Peer-to-Patent can be measured in two ways: through the objective evidence provided by the patent examiners' invocation of prior art and through the subjective evidence generated by an anonymous survey of examiners. Of the first forty-six applications examined by the USPTO, the examiner used publicly submitted Peer-to-Patent prior art to determine the rejection of an application in thirteen cases. In another two cases the public guided the Patent Office in its research to find a reference to apply in support of her decision. When one compares information submitted by the inventor with the application to the public submissions, the USPTO is more than twice as likely to use a Peer-to-Patent submission.

Take for example the HP application "Tuning core voltages of processors," which went through Peer-to-Patent review.[54] The application describes a method, apparatus, and system for tuning the core voltages of processors in order to avoid failures—a critical requirement for reliable, fault-tolerant computing in mission-critical computer systems, such as those used in banking, telecommunications, and stock markets. The Peer-to-Patent team cited three print publications in connection with this application, while the applicant cited ten with the original application. The examiner used one reference each from the Peer-to-Patent project and the applicant in rejecting the claims for lack of novelty and nonobviousness. In the case of the "User-selectable, management-alert format," the public cited nine references, while the applicant cited twenty-two.[55] The examiner used one of the documents submitted through Peer-to-Patent.

In addition to this "objective" feedback, the USPTO surveyed examiners on the usefulness and expertise of public participation. A thirty-two-question, web-based questionnaire, which was coordinated with the patent examiners' union to ensure confidentiality and compliance with union workplace procedures, elicited supportive feedback for public participation.[56] Fifty-nine percent of examiners thought that prior art submitted by peer review was helpful, with many commenting along the lines of, "The art was much better than what I would see in a normal [inventor's disclosure]." The Patent Office usefully agreed to have an examiner "control group" in which, in one out of every five cases, the examiners would do a complete search and write-up before reading the public submission rather than after. Of the examiners queried, four of five had done her initial examination before reading the public submissions. Of those, 54 percent indicated that the submission assisted in their search. Another 24 percent of examiners reported that information provided by Peer-to-Patent did not turn up in their own search, while 21 percent stated that prior art from Peer-to-Patent was not even available to examiners through USPTO sources.[57] Their comments included statements like, "Some nonpatent literature art that was submitted would not be easily found using the USPTO resources," and "It would have taken much longer to find such art." Eighty-nine percent of examiners felt that the presentation of prior art submitted by Peer-to-Patent was clear and well formulated. "There was a good description of the prior art and how it could be useful," said one.

The strategy of having members of the community assess their own and each other's submissions met with a particularly positive response from the examiner corps. In response to an anonymous questionnaire circulated to the participating examiners eight months into the pilot, participating USPTO examiners offered several reflections on the work of the Peer-to-Patent group process and the website: "It was nice to see that the art submitted could be evaluated, given thumbs up or thumbs down." Another examiner responded, "I thought the annotations were helpful to see how the public mapped the art. It was in a way like asking another examiner how they interpreted a claim." Another said, "The discussions gave me an insight as to how peers view patent claims and how they interpret references. Once seeing the references, it helped focus on another search." Yet another examiner replied, "Even though the claims were not explicitly mapped to the prior art, the discussion on what the peers thought gives an insight on how others interpret the claim and prior art."

Inevitably, there were disappointments. While the results were favorable, the numbers were small. Notably, we did not attract as much participation in the first year as I would have liked. The part of me socialized in an earlier technological era of television and the early web days of mass-appeal websites wanted armies of amateur reviewers. Two thousand participants (a large fraction—about 18 percent—of whom worked for IBM) was not yet a social movement to revolutionize the patent system.

Peer-to-Patent project team members had to do a fair share of hawking—standing on the virtual sidewalk shouting to bloggers and their audiences to come in. In truth, we had not budgeted enough (nothing, really) for systematic "marketing." The USPTO transitioned to a new director of its communications office and did not end up doing any mailings about the project in the first year of the pilot. And we were faced with the unanticipated challenge that the inventions that formed the subject matter of the applications were too different, meaning that a wind-farming application from General Electric did not appeal to the same audience as an invention about social networking from Microsoft.[58] It was as if each application was its own website, its own community. Patents prove the "long tail" idea: there are many distinct inventions for which there is a small market of participants. We tried to raise awareness and excitement on various blogs, surfing the web for experts on wind farming. A search for blogs about wind farming and a few e-mails to those bloggers did yield sixteen reviewers in one day. But this kind of "manual" recruiting of peer reviewers is not practical at scale as a way to enlarge the community of participating inventors and reviewers.

The results have been promising enough to prompt the USPTO to expand and extend the pilot to cover business methods as well as high technology and to try out the process for another year. The chancellor of the exchequer in the United Kingdom, Andrew Gowers, issued a report specifically calling for the adoption of Peer-to-Patent: "The Patent Office should conduct a pilot of Beth Noveck's Community Patent Review in 2007 in U.K. to determine whether this would have a positive impact on the quality of the patent stock" (cringe).[59] The United Kingdom began implementation of Peer-to-Patent in 2009. The Japan Patent Office launched its own, closed-door, alpha test of outside participation in patent examination and is considering full-scale adoption of Peer-to-Patent.[60]

Eventually, the hope is that we can transition from a citizen-participation project brokered by an academic institution on a pilot basis to a more permanent, institutionalized process of public participation in agency decisionmaking (as called for by President Obama). As the project develops over time, there will be more data to inform us about how to improve the process. For example, we might eliminate registration altogether and allow the community to grow faster. We might invite those with the best reputation to serve as a citizen jury overseeing the work of the examiner as the application proceeds through its multiple stages of review. With legislative reform to allow the agency to invite third-party commentary without inventor consent, it might then become possible for the examiner to join in the peer review process and invoke public participation only in the cases where she has trouble finding prior art. Embedding the social practices of participation in software, we can then change them more easily, trying different techniques to reflect a strong sense of both the physics and the culture through the interface.

Virtual reality expert and visual artist Jaron Lanier may be right, that "human cognition was designed to function in 3-D, and our computation eventually has to have a 3-D interface to maximize the match-up with the human brain as it evolved."[61] But for now, *visual* need not imply high-end graphics. Whether it be a website or a cell phone, any technology that enables us to perceive ourselves as a group and to make our collaborative workings more intelligible can produce more visual deliberation. Peer-to-Patent used the interface to communicate a sense of the group by displaying the activity level on the home page, showing the number of comments, the submissions of prior art, and the annotations of that art by the community as a whole and by each group working on a specific application. We wanted to create a sense of togetherness even where none existed among distributed strangers joining the website. The design endeavors to forge a sense of belonging to a group and to demonstrate specific tasks.

Technology can play a significant role in framing and influencing the choices people make about which groups to join and what those groups will accomplish. Institutions can now design the tools—paying special attention to the screens that make those choices intelligible—to ensure that both institutional and volunteer participants in the decisionmaking process can take action together.

PART THREE

THINKING IN WIKI

CHAPTER FIVE

SOCIAL LIFE OF INFORMATION

Never doubt that a small group of thoughtful, committed citizens can change the world. Indeed, it is the only thing that ever has.

—MARGARET MEAD

IN CHAPTER 4 I focus on how technology can be designed to reflect the work of a group back to itself and, in so doing, create an impetus toward successful collaboration. In this chapter, I continue to explore the role of information technology in fostering collaborative democracy by examining the ways in which groups can enrich the quality of information used for decisionmaking and problem solving. The technique of visual deliberation that exploits the screen to convey specific tasks and roles can also reduce the coordination costs for teams to source, evaluate, and use information (if the data are available, in the first place) meaningfully. The screen is an excellent device for making information intelligible to groups to enable collaboration and, at the same time, for enlisting the work of groups to mash up and make use of raw information about the economy, the environment, or education. So even though the patent system is unique in many ways, what we're learning from Peer-to-Patent about how to design the technology in relationship to groups and information has relevance to other areas of policymaking. Distributed groups working together mediated by a screen that mirrors their work back to them can improve governance in helpful and unexpected ways that have not counted before as traditional political participation.

The goal of this chapter is to focus on the role of information as a catalyst for group participation and, in so doing, to make the case for an information policy that goes beyond mere data transparency to ensure that groups can make use of public information, thereby producing better informed and more accountable decisions as well as creating new, collaborative approaches to addressing issues and solving problems.

BEYOND TRANSPARENCY

Peer-to-Patent demonstrates that groups are good at sourcing information collectively, but this need not be limited to the patent domain: every policy arena has issues that can be addressed with better data, and people are often in a position to obtain and evaluate that information because of their professional training and expertise or because of their unique experience and circumstances. For example, the CIA famously set up the Intellipedia (nicknamed Spypedia) wiki for internal collaboration and information sharing about intelligence.

Data gathered by a network can complement expertise and inform authority. "Imagine being able to pinpoint environmental hazards in real time at the neighborhood level, draw detailed comparisons among health care providers or measure the effectiveness of teacher preparation programs across school districts," comments Reece Rushing, director of regulatory and information policy for the Center for the American Progress.[1] Such data-driven policymaking can lead to lower costs and better performance-based outcomes. In health care it can even save lives.[2] The Commonwealth of Virginia has launched a website, Virginia Performs, to show how the government is meeting performance benchmarks based on data. The collection and evaluation of such information can be accomplished most efficiently through collaboration with those people in the best position to gather, evaluate, or understand the data.

Traditionally, the democratic mandate under the Freedom of Information Act has focused on ensuring openness of information. For example, the Patent Office nominally publishes most applications online in a web-based database. But people must already be familiar with the patent system and its workings to know how to search the website. Only a few search criteria are allowed. (Peer-to-Patent has to repost eligible patent applications on its own website to enable users to comment on the applications. The USPTO scans documents with an optical character recognition system. Peer-to-Patent documents that started out as electronic files therefore become less usable than they were before.) Transparency activists want to ensure that information is published rapidly online. But transparency for its own sake—mere publication of data—does less than it ought to engender openness and participation.

Sunlight may be a disinfectant but the best way to ensure openness is to think about every piece of information as a potential community. The District of Columbia's chief technology officer, Vivek Kundra, requires every D.C. agency to make "feeds"—subscriptions to updates of government data—available from a central website. Residents can find crime statistics, school data, and other information collected by the District online. But Kundra does more than provide raw information; he conceives of his role as building a digital public square. Because he sees data in relationship to the groups who use them, he launched Apps for Democracy, a contest that challenged citizens, nongovernmental organizations, and the private sector to develop new software applications to make the government's data more accessible and useful for the general public and the government and, in so doing, to be "co-creators of government."[3]

The winning entry in Apps for Democracy was iLiveAt. This application mashes up a wide range of local data to provide a picture of life at any given address in D.C. The various categories of data include Errands (the nearest shopping center, post office, and convenience store), Crime (recently reported offenses), and People (colored pie charts giving information on age range, ethnicity, and marital status). Another winning entry, Stumble Safely, offers a visual, dynamic map of local bars and the safest routes to stumble home, plotted against crime and policing data. The D.C. project is inspiring federal government efforts to create a central repository where the public can find and subscribe to federal department and agency data feeds. The Sunlight Foundation has launched Apps for America, which invites the public to create helpful consumer tools using those data.

The D.C. approach is not simply about transparency for its own sake but about creating an ongoing collaboration between government and citizens. Imagine how this could redound to the benefit and protection of the public. Given the instruction to design new collaborative strategies for cocreating government, a group of my students at Stanford designed a new website for the public and the Consumer Product Safety Commission to police dangerous toys more effectively together. Consumers call in to complain about malfunctioning cribs, self-decapitating dolls, and flammable baby blankets. The agency then has to research the claims on its own and, as a result, can investigate only 1 percent of the complaints it receives. Working alone, the agency misses opportunities to protect children. It might, instead, share its database and invite the public to upload information about its own experiences with dangerous toys, sharing text, video, and audio to inform the work of the agency and help the commission identify opportunities for enforcement.[4]

But individual responses provide little insight as to the qualitative or quantitative scope of the problem. Instead, the commission might design an information-gathering process geared toward a community, rather than individuals. This is the difference between posting a complaint that no one else can read and enabling members of the public to compare information with one another and provide a more nuanced picture of the danger posed in order for the agency to prioritize the most critical public complaints. Designing information for use by groups also suggests a strategy of making the data exportable for use by organizations like Consumers Union. A group-based strategy for managing information—both the inputs and the outputs—might lift some of the burden off the agency by mobilizing the public to launch its own boycott campaigns, providing the impetus to organizations to create maps showing where dangerous toys are being sold, and encouraging the toy industry to begin collaborating with the commission and consumers to promote safer toys.

BEYOND CROWDSOURCING

When groups interact with information, their members can leverage diverse skills to transform raw data into useful knowledge. While agency decisionmakers are usually policy professionals (and the information technology staff is busy with its own operations), third parties with the right tools and sufficient enthusiasm can bring technical, design, and statistical acumen to a project and make information meaningful. In addition to convening people of diverse skills, data-driven projects could be designed to bring together those with diverse roles, like government authorities, nongovernmental and corporate organizations, the media, and the general public.

Bringing diversity to data can have life-saving effects. In the spate of fires that struck San Diego, California, in 2007, private citizens in collaboration with public media collected fire and police reports and eyewitness accounts submitted via cell phone, camera phone, e-mail, and other media. They aggregated these with accounts from traditional broadcast outlets to create up-to-date Google Maps to assist residents and first responders. Afterward, one of the participants in this mashup effort wrote that working in a team meant that the volunteers could "aggregate data into multiple methods of consumption like Google Maps, Google Earth overlays, video streaming, audio streaming, photographs, etc. Not one of those methods is out of reach of a small team of technophiles and eyewitnesses."[5] But imagine how much more effective a system to help first responders would be if volunteers were connected to government, if government agencies were speaking to each other, and if those with technical know-how worked with those with policy expertise.

One of the first assignments Alabama Governor Bob Riley gave the Alabama Department of Homeland Security when it was established was to ascertain what data the state possessed that might be useful in the event of a crisis, where those data were located, and why they weren't being shared. In 2005, when Alabama was hit by the worst hurricane in U.S. history, agencies were crippled by an inability to access information about the conditions on the ground.

To solve the problem, Alabama purchased a private and secure installation of Google Earth in order to collect, map, and share critical data about Alabama's infrastructure. Information would be shared in a common "cloud" (servers connected to the Internet) rather than in localized databases that cannot easily be shared. Because the data and software are stored in the cloud, relatively cheap devices can access information quickly.[6] Now within two hours of a storm all officials from police and fire to homeland security can access aerial photography of the disaster area, full damage assessments, and real-time tracking of resource deployments across every level of government. This Virtual Alabama platform enables sharing of three-dimensional building models, real-time location of emergency vehicles, property data, and more.[7]

Designed for emergency management at a cost of a mere $150,000 (and set up in fewer than ten days), Virtual Alabama is now being used for information sharing in areas as diverse as education, law enforcement, and environmental management. The ability to collect and share data collaboratively is, in turn, driving important new cross-institutional projects. Since its launch, Virtual Alabama has grown to more than 2,100 users, representing over 550 agencies across the state. Could a Virtual USA platform, established by the federal government, be the next step?

MAKING INFORMATION VISUAL

In the physical world, information comes in many forms. We order sensory inputs by size, shape, color, sound, intensity, and location. We form patterns in our mind's eye that help us process what we are learning. But in the web world, text-based web pages are two-dimensional.

The Community Reinvestment Act, the law intended to encourage banks to do business in underserved communities, mandates data collection about bank practices. But the mass of cognitively overwhelming charts and tables are, for all intents and purposes, unreadable. This lack of functional transparency may have helped to produce the economic meltdown in the banking industry in the fall of 2008.[8] The science of information visualization focuses precisely on trying to render information more intelligible by making it graphic and visual. Visual strategies for information make it easier to intuit complex information. Were banking data to be plotted visually, the redlining and lending practices of banks and how they affect specific communities might become more accessible to consumers and enable them to make better choices among financial institutions. They might also enable everyone to spot dangerous trends. This is one reason that economic recovery legislation in 2009 called for creating Recovery.gov, a website with user friendly visual presentations to enhance public awareness of the use of funds.

Information visualization has proliferated recently, from newspapers' increasing use of visual diagrams to explain complex political phenomena like voting patterns, to the greater use of interactive, three-dimensional network diagrams to show the Internet's growth, to the explosion of interest in Google Earth, Google Maps, and other ways of seeing information in relation to geography. Even the august *New York Times* now has a visual op-ed columnist responsible for "op-charts" instead of articles.[9] Information visualization marries the latest technology to techniques for mapping data and rendering information more intelligible by means of pictures. The noted information designer Edward Tufte decries that the "world portrayed on our information displays is caught up in the two-dimensionality of the endless flatlands of paper and video screen. . . . Escaping this flatland is the essential task of envisioning information—for all the interesting worlds (physical, biological, imaginary, human) that we seek to understand are inevitably and happily multivariate in nature. Not flatlands."[10]

Tools like the activity maps on Peer-to-Patent help us to escape the flatlands of paper-based, chronological representations of information toward the representation of information in physical and graphic form. During an election year, especially, news organizations make great use of maplike blue and red state graphics to convey complex electoral trends in digestible format.

An experiment by government researchers in Washington State enabled people to visualize their energy consumption via the computer screen. The pilot program installed 112 digital controllers that connected devices like water heaters and clothes dryers to the Internet for families living in the Olympic Peninsula. The devices enabled homeowners to monitor their own usage to see and understand their electricity use and therefore to adjust their consumption via a web interface and "become active participants in managing the load on the utility grid and their own bills."[11]

Newsmap, for example, is a tree-map visualization (like Peer-to-Patent activity maps) that displays on screen the stories from the Google News website aggregated by country in a compact way. Tree maps use size and color coding to visualize directory tree (hierarchical information) structures. Newsmap divides the news into color-coded bands on this planar map. The color connotes type of news, the size, and number of stories. Tabs offer visualizations of news patterns in the United States, Canada, Australia, and several European countries. C-SPAN devised a tree map that displays the frequency of use of various keywords mentioned during the four presidential debates of 2008. The graphic makes it possible to know at a glance how many times each candidate used the words *taxes, war, economy,* or *energy.*[12]

Perhaps the computer scientist J. C. R. Licklider, who wrote the seminal 1968 article "The Computer as Communication Device," best captures why visualizing information can be so important:

When people communicate face to face, they externalize their models so they can be sure they are talking about the same thing. Even such a simple externalized model as a flow diagram or an outline—because it can be seen by all the communicators—serves as a focus for discussion. It changes the nature of communication: When communicators have no such common framework, they merely make speeches at each other; but when they have a manipulable model before them, they utter a few words, point, sketch, nod, or object. The dynamics of such communication are so model-centered as to suggest an important conclusion: Perhaps the reason present-day two-way telecommunication falls so far short of face-to-face communication is simply that it fails to provide facilities for externalizing models.[13]

The ability to give information physical form may make it more likely that people will perceive it.[14] It is when we can see the information that we can make use of it as a group. The science historian Arnold Pacey describes the history of technology as the story of an evolution toward visual thinking and representations that render human understanding more visible.[15] Just as microscopes, cameras, and other devices once helped us make sense of the world, now modeling tools, mapping technologies, and visual techniques also help to transform mere information into meaningful knowledge.[16]

MAKING INFORMATION VISUAL TOGETHER

Visual presentations of information channel the focus of a group's attention to the "golden calf"—the visual representation and embodiment that is easier to intuit than ineffable concepts and abstruse data. But visualizations also present a vehicle for groups to *create* data together. The idea of a group making complex visualizations for itself merits a brief additional discussion.

The Visual Communication Lab at IBM's Collaborative User Experience research group is built on the idea that "human visual intelligence" sparks collective insight about data. The Many Eyes project attempts to "democratize" visualization by enabling people to look at data together, in groups and communities, to make sense of what they are seeing. The Many Eyes website declares: "It is that magical moment we live for: an unwieldy, unyielding data set is transformed into an image on the screen, and suddenly the user can perceive an unexpected pattern."[17] The strategy is the right one: namely, take advantage of the ability of groups to understand, collaborate, coordinate, see connections, and take action using information.

But Many Eyes also goes the next step by offering tools for people to create and share complex visualizations. Similarly, Swivel, a web project founded in California in 2006, offers a forum for people to collaborate on the analysis of maps and data.[18] With Swivel users can create data groups to sort, filter, plot, and map data publicly and then blog about it. Swivel groups aggregate data on subjects as diverse as death row and *American Idol*. Sense.us, like Swivel and Many Eyes, is a visualization system for annotating and making sense of census data collectively. The design of its screens helps to coordinate and channel comments to the right places by labeling where annotations belong. The interesting points on each graph are prelabeled alphabetically (A, B, C, D, and so on) so that annotations can be coordinated and sorted faster. According to Tufte the "high-density" display of visual information allows "viewers to select, to narrate, to recast and personalize data for their own uses. Thus control of information is given over to viewers, not to editors, designers, or decorators."[19]

Even government agencies are beginning to use visual techniques to enable people to work together to create visual information. The EPA launched the AIRNow website, which offers transparent and visualizable air quality data.[20] Built with Google Earth technology, AIRNow allows users to combine detailed mapping with environmental data and, in turn, to mash up the data and display air quality layered on top of property listings or touristic information, three-dimensionally.

MAKING INFORMATION INTELLIGIBLE

Another advantage to a visual approach to information is that it makes it easier to design a process that focuses the attention of the group on spotting and filling in gaps in knowledge. With a map or a graphic, more so than with a list or chart, it is perhaps easier to spot what is missing. The Sunlight Foundation's *Where Are They Now?* project, a distributed research project for identifying the whereabouts of former congresspersons and congressional staffers to determine if they have become lobbyists, has a very clean and clear screen design, which communicates to users what the organization already knows and where work is needed.

In addition, the web-based Tunisian Prison Map project coordinates the information of an anonymous, distributed network, sharing data about the location of sometimes-secret prison facilities in Tunisia.[21] The map depicting the locations is a mashup: maps from Google Maps layered with data from human rights nongovernmental organizations concerned with abuses in Tunisia. This innovative strategy enables online groups to pool their knowledge and resources to create informative visuals that prick the public's conscience. The Tunisian Prison Map website provides a framework for identifying the gaps in information that need to be filled, allowing people to recognize the need and assume a task as part of the larger project.

Freebase, the open-database project launched by the artificial intelligence pioneer Danny Hillis, contains structured information on a growing range of topics.[22] It pulls information from large, open-data sets such as Wikipedia or the U.S. Securities and Exchange Commission archives and adds structure to it by moving the data into specific fields. Where Wikipedia organizes information into articles, Freebase sorts knowledge by facts. In other words, from a biography of a famous person in Wikipedia, Freebase sorts the information into categories (name, date of birth, place of birth, spouse, hometown) so that the fields can be searched more easily. While the software does some of the work by structuring the knowledge automatically, the user community works together to add and organize information and fill in missing facts. Because Freebase adds a common set of fields to the entry for every person, it makes clear to people where they can do the work of filling in the holes. Incidentally, Freebase is amassing a collection of data about patents as well, creating interesting possibilities for seeing the linkages between them and the prior art they cite.

This ability to recognize patterns can lead to powerful results. The Ashoka Foundation holds a competition each year to solicit strategies for solving "pressing social problems." Social entrepreneurs—innovative activists devising their own solutions rather than turning to government or business to address a need—submit proposals for funding. These "changemakers," as Ashoka calls them, are asked to situate themselves in a mosaic of solutions, revealing where they lie in relationship to other possible ways of solving that type of problem. Ashoka claims that between 49 percent and 60 percent of those selected will have changed national policy within five years. Observers credit this to the mosaic process.

The mosaic outlines the key barriers and principles framing the competition topic, utilizing a matrix to map visually an initial set of innovations and innovation gaps. The mosaic-building process is crucial for understanding the field in its entirety and for setting the focus for the collaborative competition.[23] By focusing attention on what's missing, the design can help to demonstrate with clarity why particular information is sought.

Bringing Experts and Expertise Together

Members of groups can aggregate information from disparate sources, but they can also serve as a source of data and expertise themselves, bringing experience and expertise to bear from a distance. New specialty social networking sites, like Academici and Edutopia for professors and Legal OnRamp for lawyers, spring up to complement such general social software platforms as Facebook and MySpace.

A new search engine called Delver claims to allow people to search the web through the prism of their "social graph"—their connections and relationships. A person begins a search at Delver by typing in her name; Delver builds and visualizes a network of associated institutions and individuals based on information about the person in social networking sites such as Linked In and Facebook.[24] When the user enters a search query, results related to, produced, or tagged by members of her social network are given priority. Social searching points to the idea that information is sometimes more valuable in the context of a group and that the technology may be emerging to help groups make sense of more information faster. I may not want to search my own social network for the answer to a question about astrophysics, but I do want to tap into the expertise of the network of astrophysics experts.

Naver, the number-one search portal in South Korea, pioneered a service called Knowledge Search in 2002, in which users pose questions and select among answers provided by other users, awarding points to those who offer the best responses. Over 4.5 million people use the service, with 40,000 people posting questions daily. This database of community-created content exceeds 60 million pages.[25] Other expert websites have been emerging, such as WikiHow, an online manual of "how to do just about anything," to enable people to share expertise with one another directly about how to do everything from making coffee granita to tiling a shower. Commercial projects like Yahoo! Answers and Google Answers and Witkey in China connect people with questions to people with answers (sometimes for a fee).

The IBM Social Computing Group has developed the Atlas project, which uses the data available about company employees—job descriptions and information in the corporate directory, blog tags, bookmarks, and group memberships—to create visual representations of relationships in the firm.[26] Atlas's four features are Find, Reach, Net, and My Net. Find and Reach are for locating experts in particular fields. Through Find, a user enters search terms and receives a list of experts, ranked on the basis of information gleaned from social data, the level of the expert's activity in the community, and any connections he may have to trusted associates of the user. Reach then helps the user plot the shortest path to make the connection to the expert, suggesting people the user already knows who could put him in touch. Net and My Net are primarily meant to help people analyze their existing networks.

Unlike a typical social networking site, however, Atlas shows patterns of relationships within particular topic areas at a companywide level. For example, Atlas's Net feature might analyze data on people interested in social computing and produce a map of how those people connect with each other through blog readership and community involvement. It's not dissimilar to a project that Sun Labs at Sun Microsystems created called *Constellations,* which visualizes relationships between experts and novices in an organization on a given topic area, thus creating a visual corporate directory.[27] It is not a far leap to imagine the idea of Atlas and Constellations applied in government to connect federal, state, and local officials to answer questions and solve problems collaboratively. Such a best-practices social networking site might link up all procurement officials to address the best and worst ways to acquire open-source technologies or recyclable office supplies. It could help break down functional barriers and create effective, cross-cutting, virtual work teams with the necessary skills to work on such complex social and economic problems as climate change and clean energy. This kind of social technology can cut through red tape and bureaucratic hierarchy to invite proposals for new ideas and innovations from those in the far-flung corners of the enormous organization.

SPACE, PLACE, GROUPS, AND INFORMATION

The shift toward the visual may have another advantage: it may help to recreate some of the social cohesion that groups experience in "real" space. The ritual of breaking bread as a way to cultivate solidarity does not exist in cyberspace; there has been no substitute online for the fellowship of the Kaffeehaus, because virtual space did away with physical place, physical embodiment, and the concepts of proximity and contiguity.

We not only lost the civility that comes from face-to-face interaction, we lost the idea of place, which has been central to having a sense of the group. The decoupling of cyberspace from geography gives rise to encounters with new people, but at the same time it impedes the purposive interaction that fosters belonging and friendship and allows groups to cohere. Although we have a sense of being somewhere when we visit a website, the absence of place makes it harder to create the connections for the body politic.

Through visual and graphical representation, however, new technology enables groups to form around new, three-dimensional, social spaces online. Virtual worlds like Second Life and There.com, and video games like World of Warcraft, are spatially oriented with their own sense of place. In virtual worlds, for example, groups develop their own themed spaces, where they congregate. In Second Life, the popular commercial virtual world, there are areas for World War II fanatics and for skydiving enthusiasts. I can occupy a plot of land, build a house, invite people over for drinks, stage rallies and protests, and invite people to cohere around specific locations defined by space.

It is possible to imagine virtual world spaces for citizen participation and the formation of policy communities, too—a kind of town hall or public forum in cyberspace.[28] At least one government agency, the National Oceanic and Atmospheric Administration, has a presence in the Second Life virtual world. Newer technologies such as Microsoft's Photosynth software, which assembles photographs of the same location taken by disparate people with different cameras and from different angles into a single picture, make it simple to erect three-dimensional simulations. Photosynth also allows many people to participate in making those shared photos by contributing their own snapshots. Google Earth and Google Local also provide new ways to navigate simulations of real spaces online.

That sense of belonging to the group and participating in the shared accomplishment of goals does not require the simulation of space so long as the screen is designed in ways that encourage belonging. By displaying the teams obviously and visually, Peer-to-Patent makes it easier for potential reviewers to know which groups are available to join. One can imagine how much easier it would be to sign up for a project—be it a PTA picnic, an EPA cleanup, or a MoveOn.org protest—when such opportunities are clearly labeled and the roles and tasks well defined. Open Congress offers a defined place for people to discuss pending legislation. Through graphic representation, people can see themselves and others through the screen and perceive the groups they have joined and the role they have assumed in relation to the task at hand.

LINKING INFORMATION AND ACTION

When we can visualize together, whether by putting a pushpin on a map in real space or on a Google Map in virtual space, we also begin to communicate collectively as a group. The cyberlandscape is filling up with graphic information objects—images on the screen—created by groups and communities. When we create such information together, it not only focuses attention on the question—"externalizing the model," as Licklider says—but it causes us to speak as a collaborating community responsible to one another, strengthening the sense of belonging to a team. As the cyberlaw scholar David Johnson points out:

> The development of graphical interfaces has enabled a new form of "writing," which involves decisions by users to place particular graphical elements in particular locations within a larger graphic environment. This "semantic placement" has the potential to give us a new form of asynchronous group communication. The key point is that graphical objects can stand for ideas or people or things and that the placement of such objects against a background (or in effect in a location in a particular online place) can communicate the relationship between such persons or things (or the view of such persons or things or ideas held by the person doing the placing).[29]

All of the new collaborative editing technologies that allow us to create content together are really ways of speaking and communicating as a group. So, too, the images on the computer screen reinforce the connection between members and a cause. Activist websites now encourage users to take and then post pictures of their face-to-face get-togethers or to create simple online maps showing where members live, in order to give the community a sense of itself. In the run-up to the election of

2008, the TechPresident web log, which tracks the use of technology in presidential campaigns, overlaid the list of events planned by supporters of Barack Obama on the Google Earth map of the United States. This mashup transformed a list of get-togethers into a social movement illuminated by push-pins. The ability to see oneself visually as part of a larger happening has the same persuasive power as being in the midst of a crowd.[30]

Aimed at preventing voter fraud and abuse and celebrating the democratic experience, Video Your Vote enabled people to visually document and share their election experiences (along with any problems they encountered—long lines, aggressive challenges, unexpected procedural hoops).[31] The hope was that citizens would capture violations of voting rights and upload them instantly for the world to see. "Show me the money" is an adage with real currency when it comes to online action; such visualizations increase the rate of voluntarism.

INFORMATION TRANSPARENCY

To take advantage of the ability of groups to aggregate information and make it more intelligible and visual, there is an essential precondition. Information must be transparent: accessible, searchable, and usable. These are distinct requirements, each of which demands attention and investment.

MAKING INFORMATION ACCESSIBLE

By disinfecting corrupt practices with the light of sunshine, government transparency policies endeavor to "liberate" more data online and thereby create greater accountability to the public.[32] Before private individuals can seek to influence policy decisions, they need to know which decisions are being made.[33] But accountability does not by itself induce better participation or stronger democracy.

Despite forty years of the Freedom of Information Act, which mandates the disclosure and publication (with exceptions) of information controlled by the U.S. government, not all government information is available to the public.[34] Despite over a decade of the Paperwork Reduction Act, which is supposed to "maximize the utility of information created, collected, maintained, used, shared, and disseminated by or for the Federal Government" by requiring online publication of documents, data are not all online or web-accessible.[35] Darrell West, the leading social scientist studying the introduction of technology into government, finds that "global electronic government is not producing a major transformation of the public sector."[36]

For example, the Consumer Product Safety Commission's database of dangerous products is not available to the public online (yet).[37] Ironically, filings of ethics disclosures by members of Congress with the clerk of the House and Senate, as well as disclosures by senior officials to the Office of Ethics, are not publicly available via the Internet (yet).[38]

The advance of information technologies has created momentum and new opportunities to digitize information. Now activists want to see even more progress toward disclosure.[39] They want the president and other government leaders to mandate proactive publication that would make publication of government information the default rule. Government must set technical requirements and guidance to ensure publication in formats that enable manipulation as well as reading. Transparency activists like Carl Malamud of Publicresource.org are crusading to make more government information available online. Malamud has hatched the brilliant and devious idea of getting people to buy public information (ironically only available for a fee) and then post it for free on the web.[40]

When the SEC claimed that putting EDGAR on the Internet was not technically possible and would hinder the efforts of information retailers to sell the data, Malamud got a small grant from the National Science Foundation and went into competition with the retailers. He purchased all the EDGAR data at wholesale, posted it on the Internet (first in Gopher, then in http, then as one of the world's largest WAIS databases). He ran the service for two years, built up a large user base, then persuaded the SEC that it was their job to take it over after giving them a sixty-day deadline. When they complained that they wanted to take over the system but couldn't do it in sixty days, Malamud explains, he loaned them equipment and configured their Internet line so that they could get up and running.[41]

A 2008 white paper on access to government information by James Grimmelmann at New York Law School calls for governments on all levels to share law freely on the net and avoid using intellectual property restrictions to tie up access to public information.[42] Not all governments do. The state of Oregon, for example, endeavored to use copyright law to prevent another website from posting Oregon's statutes. In 2007 another group of open-government theorists convened in a national conference under the auspices of Tim O'Reilly, the technical publisher, and articulated a set of eight principles relating to government data, including ensuring that all data are published in a complete and timely manner without restrictions imposed by copyright law.[43]

A contemporaneous report from Princeton University's Center for Information Technology Policy called for the executive branch to create the infrastructure to provide all government information openly. The report charges that the federal government focuses too much on its role as a website publisher and not enough on finding better ways to make the underlying data it creates available. Counterintuively, the authors argue that the federal government ought to reduce its role in presenting government information to citizens and, instead, "focus on creating a simple, reliable, and publicly accessible infrastructure that 'exposes' the underlying data."[44] Considering the investment it takes to comply with twenty-four applicable regulatory regimes with which all government websites must contend (none of which relate to participation), focusing on data and ensuring their availability would cost less and allow others to mash data up and make good use of them.[45] With data feeds—the ability to subscribe to receive notification of new information posted online via e-mail or newsreader—the public can find information more easily.[46]

MAKING INFORMATION SEARCHABLE

Information also has to be searchable. While the regulations.gov website provides electronic access to pending regulations from 180 government agencies, it lacks a good search mechanism, without which it is all but impossible for even the avid activist to locate and comment on pending proposals. Regulations.gov offers no full-text search, only the ability to look by title or keyword.

According to the Congressional Research Service, there are serious problems with "the general navigability of the website, the consistency and completeness of the data, [and] whether the system allows users to adequately search existing dockets."[47] The situation is so problematical as to have given rise to two blue-ribbon commissions to study the shortcomings of the electronic rulemaking website. But the absence of search opportunities extends far beyond this one portal. Far too many government databases offer only limited search capability.

It is hard to know the extent of the problem, because there has never been a comprehensive assessment of federal websites or data warehouses. Major search engines like Google or Yahoo do not index much or even most government information. Documents are scanned and uploaded as images and are therefore not findable. During the presidential campaign of 2008, President Obama called for the creation of a Google for Government, which would make it easier to sort through the morass of data about everything from environmental toxins to road safety conditions. The USA.gov federal government web portal offers a search mechanism. But we are just at the beginning of identifying ways to make government information—reports, laws, data—searchable by USA.gov and commercial search engines.

MAKING INFORMATION USABLE

More data does not always mean more usable data. While it is important that the operations of government be open and that hearings and other meetings be broadcast, it is insufficient to share information for purely passive consumption instead of releasing data in open, structured, machine-readable formats that make it possible for third parties to reuse, manipulate, and visualize the data.[48]

The EPA's Geospatial Data Access Project, designed by a private sector consultancy and launched in early 2007, posts 60,000 environment records but offers no facility to discuss the data collectively and send insights back to the agency.[49] The Urban Institute's National Neighborhood Indicators Partnership offers via the web a welter of facts and figures about conditions in thirty cities—ranging from Des Moines, Iowa, to Camden, New Jersey. But those data are all top-down. The statistics cannot be annotated, commented upon, mashed up, or contributed to by those who might read them.[50] Multiple levels of password controls are required to even access any of this public information, let alone use it.

The *Federal Register,* the official journal of the U.S. Government that publishes all agency notices, comes to 70,000 pages each year. Such documents are harder to interpret, especially when they contain complex government data like patent applications. Whereas data in the *Federal Register* are being put online consistent with statutory publication requirements, the right of transparency is eviscerated by the practical inability for all but a handful of professionals to make sense of such information.

Mere digitization must be distinguished from visualization. In cyber-space government is typically posting paper-based information in electronic form (usually pdf files), without enough consideration of how the design might encourage others to make use of it. In many cases, the proverbial file cabinet is simply being dragged into cyberspace without creating any community connected to that information. Consistent with the familiar metaphor of the file cabinet common to the computer operating systems we know, the legalistic approach to information is to determine how to label the files and who has the right to look at them.

But if we abjure the focus on paper and, instead, look at the interrelationship between information and the larger sociolegal context for how that information is used, we would think of new ways to design the storage, collection, and distribution of information so as to make it useful within the context of the decisionmaking system. We would be looking at how people—not just individual users but groups within the process—translate information into knowledge. Instead of a voluminous electronic pile of papers, the *Federal Register* might instead be transformed into the centerpiece of a government community in which officials and others might tag each entry, annotate the publication, translate text into visuals, and show links between past and present notices. The Government Printing Office would offer effective search and communications tools, including data feeds, so that interested users could subscribe to read new notices in the *Register.*

Sometimes the responsible designers have not thought through the consequences of opening a channel of communication at all. The U.S. General Services Administration posted a searchable version of its 1,700-page semiannual regulatory agenda online, including the administration's proposal to set standards for a "retirement home for chimpanzees used in federal research" and recent rules "to determine whether passengers on small planes should get compensation when they are bumped from a flight on which they have reservations."[51] But the agenda is listed by agency and not by subject matter. There is no indication of the level of priority of any item, what has already been accomplished, or what the impact of different proposed rules might be. Although people may comment on the pending rules, the information, for all its breadth, is next to useless to others.

Agencies are disseminating more information online than before and "liberating" more information from government *to* citizens. This does not mean that they are doing enough to solicit information *from* citizens or to disseminate it *among* citizens.[52] The EPA is developing Puget Sound Wiki, whereby citizens collaborate to envision the future for the Sound. The EPA also enlisted 320 residents to review data and information to identify and reduce local toxins in Pacoima, California.[53]

Engaging outsiders in the process also helps to ensure that data, once posted, cannot later be sequestered and taken down, as was done with numerous databases under the Bush administration. To do so now would result in a public outcry from those involved in creating the repositories in the first place.

BUILDING TOWARD COLLABORATION

The history of citizen participation, investigated in the next chapter, explains why there is so little focus on opportunities for collaboration around information. There are exceptions, of course: Safercar.gov, for example, compiles information from various sources to offer a helpful consumer website about automotive safety. It is a cross-department collaboration among the National Highway Traffic and Safety Administration, the Department of Transportation, and the Office of Citizen Services and Communications. We can only anticipate more widespread use of such visual and social technologies to unleash collaborative approaches to data-driven policymaking. Just as the screen can make it possible to reflect the physics and culture of the group back to itself, participation practices can take advantage of new tools to strengthen the ability of a participating group to help the agency and to take action for itself.

The John D. and Catherine T. MacArthur Foundation, the $6.4 billion philanthropy, recently invested $2.55 million in an initiative called the U.S. Fiscal Future and American Society. The foundation commissioned the National Academy of Sciences and the National Academy of Public Administration to establish an expert committee to develop a fact base that can assist in public discussion of ways to address the country's projected deficit. The money goes to fund a report and a set of policy scenarios by these two Washington-based nongovernmental organizations. The goal of the project is to contribute to increased awareness of the issue, educate citizens about the facts, inform a discussion about the values involved in the trade-offs that will need to be made over budgetary choices, and enable citizens to feel as though they, individually and collectively, can take actions to help improve the nation's fiscal future.

But imagine if next time MacArthur funds such a project it also funds a project to map information about the fiscal future on the screen and to build a community around it. Imagine if both the government and Beltway nongovernmental organizations (NGOs) posted their data in formats that allowed others to make them visual by mapping, mashing up, running simulations, and showing us the complex information on the screen.

Or what if Freebase absorbed these interesting data about the budget into its structured database, where facts and figures might easily be compared? Imagine if interested communities then put these data on Swivel or Many Eyes to make sense of them collectively with a far greater range of participants. Imagine if such a project clearly communicated what the NGOs didn't know and couldn't find, allowing others to use the screen to fill in gaps in knowledge. Imagine if the interface communicated projects and tasks to be taken on by communities and groups of people, including other organizations as well as individuals. They could use the screen to self-select to take on different pieces of this complex puzzle, diving into specific areas, such as environmental budgeting or accounting methods or strategies for outreach in depth.

If we use the computer screen as a looking glass—a mirror to reflect the work of the group back to itself—we may be able to help people to form groups. "Seeing" reduces the cost to a person of deciding which groups to join and where to invest time and expertise. By making information more visual, we make it easier to understand. By enabling people to collaborate, coordinate, see connections, and speak together around a specific problem, we also create opportunity for collective action.

CHAPTER SIX

HISTORY OF CITIZEN PARTICIPATION

Other states indicate themselves in their deputies . . . but the genius
of the United States is not best or most in its executives or legislatures,
nor in its ambassadors or authors or colleges or churches or parlors nor
even in its newspapers or inventors . . . but always most in the common
people.

—WALT WHITMAN

WHILE INNOVATIVE IN APPROACH and design, Peer-to-Patent is hardly the
first effort to involve citizens in government decisionmaking in the
United States.[1] This chapter situates Peer-to-Patent in the history of citizen participation since the New Deal, a history that includes attempts to
create greater openness and transparency about the workings of government as well as practices designed for citizen comment. It is not a comprehensive chronology of administrative law but rather a look at some
of the approaches to soliciting information from sources outside government before and since the advent of the Internet. Of course, specific
statutes and methods for engaging the public differ across agencies; for
example, increased public involvement is mandated by most environmental legislation. But I look, in general, at the ideal types of notice-and-comment rulemaking, negotiated rulemaking, traditional peer review
practices, and such innovations as prediction markets. (I do not examine
after-the-fact forms of participation, like citizen suits.)

To know where to go from here in a new digital age, we have to
understand the institutional experience and how far it differs from the
theory and practice of collaborative democracy. Just as transparency
policies, which focus on "liberating" more paper in electronic form, are
not producing access to searchable, usable information designed for

groups, outmoded conceptions of expertise dog efforts to make participation practices effective and efficient. Most methods by which agencies
consult with citizens are still rooted in the notion that government
knows best and that either individual and attenuated, mass-based participation (rulemaking) or face-to-face, small-group participation (federal
advisory committees) are the norm. These methods predate the understanding that people working together can accomplish more. They surely
do not contemplate solving problems outside the framework of agency
decisionmaking. Without the conviction that there is room for improvement when a group of people with diverse talents and abilities convene
to help the decisionmaker, the practices of participation will continue to
be designed to thwart effective collaboration.

FAILURE OF PUBLIC CONSULTATION

The modern administrative state secures a legal right for the individual
to participate, but in practice public engagement is limited and ineffective. Traditional theories of representative government continue to separate its official functions from citizenship. This is unnecessary. Indeed,
our early notions of democracy in Athens involved obligations on the
part of every citizen to play a politically active role. Every free adult male
participated in the deliberations on the Pnyx, the hill west of the Acrop-
olis. In our complex and geographically distant society, this ideal of participatory democracy has all but vanished.

In the 1930s the Great Depression and the resulting New Deal ush-
ered in an era of top-down regulatory centralization and control over
economic and social life at the national level. Bolstered by adherence to
philosophical and scientific pragmatism, the New Deal came in response
to the dislocations of economic depression. The demand for relief and
recovery gave rise to the modern administrative state, and the number,
size, and scope of expert regulatory agencies exploded. The public interest, according to the emerging theory of administration, demanded that
these expert institutions solve problems in ways more technocratic than
democratic.

The centralized specialization of the agencies was regarded as the
source of dispassionate and incorruptible legitimacy. As the noted legal
scholar James Freedman writes, "The New Deal believed in experts."[2] The
common law evolved in response, and courts articulated the principle of

judicial deference to the agency's decisions. Even as dissatisfaction with agency performance grew, what the administrative scholar Gerald Frug calls the "expertocratic" view of the rational function of government agencies remained strong.[3]

To create a democratic check on the work of unelected and largely unaccountable agencies, the Administrative Procedure Act of 1946 (APA) provides for citizen consultation in connection with all agency rulemaking activities.[4] While Congress passes a few hundred general pieces of legislation each year, the agencies of the U.S. government annually enact 4,000 to 8,000 regulations that govern every aspect of our lives, from the quality of our air and water to the width of doorways in new homes to the rules regarding the transport of dry cleaning chemicals to the number of peanuts in peanut butter and holes in Swiss cheese.[5] American University scholar and president Neil Kerwin calls rulemaking "the most complex and important form of political action in the contemporary American political system."[6] There is no aspect of life that is not touched by the rulemaking process.

Whenever an agency promulgates a proposed rule, it is required under the APA to give notice to the public and to "give interested persons an opportunity to participate in the rulemaking through submission of written data, views, or arguments with or without opportunity for oral presentation."[7] Public consultation under the APA generally takes the form of either hearings or written comments mailed to the agency or, in recent years, submitted electronically via either fax, e-mail, the agency website, or the regulations.gov website (the clearinghouse where most agency rulemakings are also published).

Several rationales have justified mandating public submissions. Consultation shines the light of public scrutiny on rulemaking, which would otherwise be subject to few democratic controls. Asking the public to comment on draft rules is also designed to evince objections that will inform the regulator of potential litigation and hurdles to implementation. Public participation also "breeds" citizenship by offering an avenue for active participation in the life of the polity. Thomas Jefferson said that "making every citizen an acting member of the government, and in the offices nearest and most interesting to him, will attach him by his strongest feelings to the independence of his country, and its republican constitution."[8]

While the APA enshrines the right to participate in law, actual consultative practice has enjoyed less success. In a study of more than 1,500 comments filed in about two dozen rulemaking proceedings at the U.S. Environmental Protection Agency (EPA), individual members of the public submitted fewer than 6 percent of the comments, in contrast to 60 percent by corporations and industry groups and 25 percent by government authorities.[9] In another study of eleven rulemakings, not a single "ordinary person" filed a comment in a process dominated by professional interest groups or government agencies.[10] Even among legal professionals, there is limited awareness of or attention to regulatory rulemaking. In 2004 the American Bar Association reported that 55 percent of the 320 administrative lawyers who responded to the survey had not filed a comment in the past three years.[11]

Equally important, the quality of participation in response to notice-and-comment rulemaking tends to be low. Critics complain of a range of defects, from regulatory capture (as political scientists call excessive influence on regulators by those stakeholders whom they regulate)—of the consultation process by large organizations and lobbyists—to excessive participation by individuals who carp but offer little useful information. Because the playing field for participation is not level but biased toward legal and interest group professionals, the agency often receives comments only from interested parties "inside the Beltway." When ordinary citizens get involved, they often overburden the regulator with postcard comments, written and duplicated by an interest group that offers no new information. The EPA received over a half million comments in response to its clean air rulemaking on mercury in 2004.[12] Only 4,500 of these were unique. Postcard comments help groups mine for data and donations from potential members more than they inform policymakers.

When many comments are submitted, agency officials do not have the resources to consider the merits of each and formulate considered replies. In some agencies, the review of comments has to be outsourced. The Fish and Wildlife Service conducted a notice of proposed rulemaking about endangered species. It deliberately vetoed electronic commenting, seeking to stave off the onslaught of comments. This only provoked environmental groups to solicit electronic comments from members, print them out, and deliver them by hand. The agency, eager to conclude the process, announced that it would review 200,000 public comments in a mere thirty-two hours (or nine seconds per comment).[13] Agency officials complain of overwork and a high noise-to-signal ratio. Either they receive no response; or there is an avalanche of identical postcard comments; or voluminous comments akin to legal briefs deluge the office. In many cases, prolix comments arrive at the eleventh hour, hand-delivered minutes before the deadline to thwart access by corporate rivals.

In an attempt to overcome some of these shortcomings of public consultation and to drive more directed expertise to the agency, Congress passed the Federal Advisory Committee Act in 1972. Under this legislation, Congress in authorizing legislation, the president by executive order, or an agency head by official notice can convene a committee to advise the agency on a specific issue (though Congress has directed that the number of these be kept to a minimum). The General Services Administration oversees the work of more than a thousand federal advisory committees. These small teams are advisory and may play no role in decisionmaking. That said, they are still vulnerable to political bias. Participants are handpicked by agency officials, not self-selected, which increases the opportunity for political litmus testing. Members have conflicts of interest and often favor the corporate rather than the public interest. Even when the selection produces more balance in the composition, there is a limit to the range of skills and know-how that such a small and relatively unchanging group will leverage. A small group of economic advisers, for example, can barely cover classical economic viewpoints let alone bring in thinking from neuroeconomics, complexity science, or other law and economics disciplines.

Agency staff also meet with industry and interest group stakeholders; they also conduct public workshops and public hearings. But these face-to-face methodologies take place after the fact, once the agency has already devised the rule and its proposed approach, affording little opportunity for genuine input or exchange of information.[14] Agencies also differ widely in the transparency they apply to reporting on the work of advisory committees or other consultations.

Negotiated rulemaking (reg-neg)—another face-to-face consultative practice—suffers from similar problems. In 1990 Congress passed the Negotiated Rulemaking Act as an amendment to the APA. Started in the 1980s to elicit expertise from outside of the agency, reg-neg is a discretionary methodology that any agency can use when consulting the public. The aim is to convene a small group of affected stakeholders to negotiate consensual solutions to regulatory problems.[15] Agency officials choose who is included in the reg-neg small-group discussion and, by extension, who is excluded.[16] These consensual deliberations do not involve amateurs, only institutional regulars. Reg-neg demands that agencies handpick participants and meet face to face, which can be undertaken only in very limited circumstances. While reg-neg has fared better than traditional rulemaking in participant satisfaction, running these groups is expensive and time-consuming, and the resulting outcomes are not appreciably better.[17] Initial enthusiasm for the innovation among administrative scholars has been dampened by the reality of plus ça change.[18]

In sum, despite more than half a century of the right to participate in rulemaking, the practices of public participation are neither well developed nor widespread. Few people know they even have such a right, let alone ever exercise it. Despite the potential benefits of consultation, many government officials, whether in agencies or other branches of government, believe at some level that the public is an irritant—the pea to the administrative princess—unduly influencing and burdening the expert who alone possesses the knowledge and dispassion to make decisions in the public interest. Because agencies deal with increasingly complex decisions about public and planetary health and safety that depend upon scientific and technical information, there is a persistent belief, despite the APA (or perhaps because it offers so little specific guidance about how to consult), that public participation cannot work well.

GOVERNMENT ACCESS TO INFORMATION

One important consequence of the shortcomings of public consultation is a reduction in the quality of the data used to make government decisions. Despite transparency and participation legislation, the current paradigm for regulatory decisionmaking remains highly vulnerable to ideological bias and manipulation. The Bush administration, by imposing an ideological litmus test on scientific advisers, eliminating advisory panels, and selectively editing reports on environmental hazards and endangered species, represented the peak of the abuse against scientific truth in policymaking that began with President Nixon.[19]

Some of this "science bending" can be discounted as the outcome of inevitable and perhaps even desirable political disagreement.[20] Yet the practices by which government gathers, analyzes, and distributes expertise open the door to political abuse and manipulation; even in the absence of bad intentions, these practices limit access to good information and good science. In a 2006 survey of environmental lawyers conducted by law professors J. B. Ruhl and James Salzman, a mere 2 percent felt that agencies give appropriate recognition to conflicting data, while 70 percent disagreed.[21] The statement "Agencies usually employ adequate scientific analysis when using the data they present as supporting their final conclusions" drew a mere 6 percent yeas but 56 percent nays.[22]

The consequences of this failure can be very real. Take, for example, the *Challenger* disaster. In 1986 the Rogers Commission, which investigated the explosion of the spacecraft, in part blamed NASA's decision-making processes for not taking action on the warnings of engineers, thereby contributing to the accident. The physicist Richard Feynman famously criticized NASA management for promulgating estimates of reliability that differed from the scientific information a thousandfold.[23]

Among the techniques for bridging the gap between politics and science is peer review. Harvard Kennedy School expert Sheila Jasanoff writes that such "refereeing procedures have come to be regarded as the most effective method of validating science in two quite different spheres of professional activity: prepublication review of journal articles and screening of applications by federal research sponsoring agencies. There is thus an appealing logic to the syllogism that links peer review to 'good science' in the regulatory process."[24] Through peer review, researchers allow other experts to examine, criticize, and improve their work. This enhances the quality of science and innovation while maximizing the efficient use of the scarce resource of time. Peer review allows colleagues to evaluate each other and in so doing to "certify the correctness of procedures, establish the plausibility of results, and allocate resources."[25]

Peer review is in common use in government.[26] The National Science Foundation and the National Institutes of Health use peer reviewers to determine if research is novel and represents a contribution to its field. The National Science Foundation relies on a network of over 50,000 reviewers. The National Institutes of Health uses outside review groups and advisory councils from the scientific community to review over 70 percent of its applications. The EPA grant selection process depends upon science review panels, which are peer review groups chosen and managed by an outside scientist.[27]

Typically, a professional elite within a given scientific discipline conducts the review, which opines on a given work product. Government peer review is not as far-ranging as in academia. Agencies use industry and academic peer reviewers to vet grant proposals and conduct site visits to university labs. According to the Government Accountability Office (GAO), agencies also rely on peer review to assess the merit of competitive and noncompetitive research proposals, to determine whether to continue or renew research projects, to evaluate the results of the research before publication of those results, to establish annual budget priorities for research programs, and to evaluate program and scientist performance.[28]

The methods for conducting peer reviews vary among and within the agencies. For example, agencies select peer reviewers from academia, private industry, and government and obtain review comments not only in person during site visits but also by mail, in workshops, or via a combination of methods. Scientific peer reviewers, however, do not decide policy, and as a general matter they do not set budget priorities or allocate resources. EPA peer reviewers oversee the scientific research conducted by outside groups for the agency under its Office of Research and Development's $541 million research budget.[29] They do not necessarily have a voice in decisionmaking. In no instance is an agency accountable to the scientific community.

Congress has tried to increase agencies' use of peer review (even as it mandates that agencies reduce the number of federal advisory committees) to improve the quality of information they use. The Safe Water Drinking Act of 1974 directs the EPA to promulgate drinking water standards based on peer-reviewed science. The 2001 Data Quality Act, known also as the Information Quality Act, requires federal agencies to "issue guidelines ensuring and maximizing the quality, objectivity, utility, and integrity of information (including statistical information) disseminated by the agency."[30]

While Congress does not specify this, OMB's interpretive guidelines say that data will be of sufficient quality if they are subjected to independent peer review. According to the OMB good peer review focuses on timing of peer reviews, selection of reviewers, transparency of reviews, and opportunities for public participation. Data-quality legislation establishes the right for "affected persons to seek and obtain correction of information maintained and disseminated by the agency" that does not comply with the agency's own standards, thereby creating greater impetus to conduct peer review.[31] Many believe that this data-quality law does little to improve access to information and, instead, helps large corporations forestall regulation by contesting its scientific basis.[32] In fact critics complain that this legislation, sponsored by the Philip Morris (now Altria) tobacco company, was intended to create "an unprecedented and cumbersome process by which government agencies must field complaints over the data, studies, and reports they release to the public. It is a science abuser's dream come true."[33] While the Information Quality Act, on its face, ensures transparency and objectivity of government information, in practice it gives business an opportunity to tie up regulatory rulemaking activities by challenging rulemaking processes and staging a science fight.

At first glance, it would seem that peer review is a fairly conservative means to resolve the information-quality problem and provide oversight and accountability by means of an improved administrative process—at least for scientific settings. It is a collaborative, group-based process. But as a practice, traditional peer review is fraught with problems that undermine its credibility.[34] The biases of participants selected for peer review inevitably skew the process. There is no assurance of transparency in the selection of participants. Peer review notoriously produces a buddy system, in which insiders reward friends and punish enemies. And the high cost of having to select peers and administer reviews means that the machinery can be wound into gear only on limited occasions. It is an elite, closed process and therefore subject to manipulation and bias (closed not necessarily in the sense of secretive but in the sense that agency peer review groups are empaneled—not self-selected). It is therefore possible to stack the deck with ideologues. This can contribute to corporate and political corruption. But even without corruption, the scientific community has no say over who participates in peer review.

Typically, only certain kinds of industry and academic experts will be invited to participate in peer review processes. Those limitations need not be based on politics—though a political litmus test is sometimes imposed—but may be based on profession and thereby foreclose diversity. There is no room in such closed processes for disciplinary or dispositional diversity. A policy discussion about energy, for example, should include experts on foreign policy, the environment, and technology. Web 1.0 policy people should be combined with web 2.0 collaboration experts. Those who are good at brainstorming ought to sit down with those who are constructive critics and those who are successful synthesizers.

Also there are those who possess a great deal of expertise but do not necessarily have the "right" credentials and are not being invited to consult. As an academic, I know all too well that it is often the same academics from the same prestigious institutions (and I am sometimes one of them) who get invited to speak at conferences or write for journals, often to the exclusion of equally capable individuals who may be less advanced on the academic tenure track or still graduate students. Realistically, those with the closest ties to the publishing industry, not necessarily the best writers, receive the book contracts and marketing deals. Venture capitalists may invest in innovative ideas, but they hire known management teams to carry them out. Scientists working on the most popular or least controversial topics get big grants, which translate into bigger labs, fancier titles, and more prestigious appointments. Nonminorities enjoy professional advantages. Although it is true that open practices may attract those wishing to derail the process, closed practices are at risk of engendering abuse.

Because there is no single set of procedures that define peer review and no required mechanisms to ensure transparency in the work of agency peer reviewers, the mere fact that these panels share the name *peer review* with their rigorous academic counterparts does not ensure rigor on their part. There are no guarantees that what they do is based on good science rather than political prejudice. The GAO has found that "further improvements are needed to expand the scope of peer reviews [at EPA] and make them more independent" and that the implementation of EPA's peer review policy has been "uneven."[35] Even OMB's own peer review practice has no "internal guidelines, no conflict of interest disclosure requirements, repeatedly uses the same reviewers, and has no requirement of balance." There is also no guarantee that suggestions made by peer review panels will be followed or lead to any outcomes.

Peer review is also time consuming to organize and run. Because the group has to be selected, vetted, and approved and because fights can arise over membership, it is a difficult process. Conflicts of interest have to be identified and sorted out. Participants have to be convinced to join. And there is a well-established culture of peer review only in the sciences, not in other policy domains. It is, perhaps, in part because of the work that must go into maintaining a peer review system that review generally happens late—too late in the process to have a maximum impact on regulatory decisionmaking. Agencies ask for public comment once a rule is already written, often allotting the public a short period in which to provide feedback, leaving little room for meaningful change. If a peer review team rejects research findings, for example, it is not set up to put anything positive, productive, and informative in their place.

Alan Daul and Julie Dwyer write in an article on science in the regulatory process:

> In many cases, end-of-the-line review cannot repair mistakes or omissions made early in the regulatory development process or fill data gaps. Back-end inspection may be able to identify scientific uncertainties, but rarely can it reduce them. The benefits of regulatory science quality control must also be balanced against the potential for peer reviewers to intrude on the policy domain. If determining whether the data and analysis are adequate for regulatory decisionmaking is the problem, then peer review does not solve the problem. It shifts the problem from decisionmakers to reviewers.[36]

THE INTERNET AGE AND PARTICIPATORY PRACTICES

Just as information technologies support greater access to government information, they also enable online citizen participation practices. Until the Internet era, the basic communicative practice of gathering information required consulting with known and invited individuals through peer review, reg-neg, town hall meetings, and hearings. In the E-Government Act, Congress legislated e-rulemaking to put the APA public comment process online to "improve the quality of federal rulemaking decisions."[37] While thirty agencies were already using the web to put notice of rulemaking activity on the Internet and to make relevant documents available in electronic form, e-rulemaking consolidated activity and spending (and therefore power) around one centralized website (www.regulations.gov) under the control of the Office of Management and Budget. But the digitization of citizen participation practices has not worked well. Centralization into one website but without common standards has produced the lowest quality common denominator in the design. The website merely lists a draft rule and provides a box and a button to "click here for comment." Online participation has thus evolved into "notice and spam" rather than notice and comment.[38]

As the Yale environmental scholar Dan Esty writes,

The promise of cyberdemocracy with a fully informed and engaged populace could give way to spam, misinformation, and dialogue among the uninformed that diminishes thoughtful deliberation. More opinions being heard may lead to chaos and breakdown rather than higher quality decisions. Even if some participants in the policy process stay engaged, a flood of information could lead to narrowly focused decisionmaking with little consideration given to the broader context of a policy choice.[39]

The web has made it easier for machines, or bots—rather than people—to send electronic postcards, further deluging the agencies with unusable information. The FCC received a million comments in response to its proposed rule weakening the standards for cross-ownership of broadcasting outlets. Half a million missives flooded the EPA for its mercury rulemaking, and hundreds of thousands of responses went to the U.S. Forest Service after its rulemaking on road construction in wilderness areas (this despite the fact that the Forest Service has a promising injunction to provide opportunities for the pubic to collaborate and participate openly).[40] In a 2003 study of regulations.gov, the Government Accountability Office found that the website did not generate a more steady stream of usable comments.[41] The introduction of new technology had not changed commenting patterns.[42] Perhaps surprisingly, the advent of e-commenting has increased paper submissions. Some believe that taking up space on the regulator's desk will increase the likelihood of being heard.

While e-commenting makes commenting easier, the farrago of comments on regulations.gov is neither organized nor sorted by any meaningful search criteria. Comments are not deliberative; they do not respond to one another (in most cases commenters cannot see one another's online comments) but are one-off communiqués between submitter and agency. Nothing in the design of the process encourages better informed participation or greater representation of those who are not participating in the process.

The Obama administration has enacted reforms to bring greater efficiency and effectiveness to the processes of regulatory rulemaking. Outside government—especially in the academy—innovative proposals for rethinking regulation proliferate, leading some to speak of a new New Deal.[43] Yet even this scholarship typically gives short shrift to the role that technology can play in bringing about reform, notably by creating new avenues for the sharing of citizen expertise.

David Schoenbrod, a pioneer in the field of environmental law and justice who argues against excessive federal regulation of the environment, exemplifies the traditional nontechnological approach to reform. Like a modern-day Thoreau, from a farm in upstate New York he pens books, op-eds, and other philippics attacking EPA policy.[44] Perhaps because of years of impassioned litigation experience with the National Resources Defense Council, Schoenbrod knows how to tell a persuasive story about upstate apple farmers and cider pressers, western factory workers, or even Washington bureaucrats to make a powerful point about the need for environmental reform. With colleagues, Schoenbrod launched a bipartisan initiative called *Breaking the Logjam: An Environmental Law for the 21st Century.*[45]

Breaking the Logjam is a series of proposals (and a conference and a book). The proposals call for razing institutional boundaries that limit cross-cutting regulatory approaches and for reassigning regulatory authority to the level (federal, state, or local) at which each environmental problem is best addressed. In addition, they call for increased reliance on market mechanisms, such as the use of a cap-and-trade system to curb water pollution from farms. But what many of these proposals do not consider is a new, enhanced role for citizen experts in the environmental policy process.

Similarly, the environmental law experts Angus Macbeth and Gary Marchant propose that the EPA shore up its information deficit with a Scientific and Engineering Investigation Board and an Institute for Scientific Assessments.[46] These new administrative bodies would, in their view, be preferable to the EPA's science advisory boards, which currently review agency science after proposals have been drafted. Macbeth and Marchant want to see scientists involved earlier in the process, funneling more scientific information about air and water, fish and wildlife, toxins and pesticides, flora and fauna before rather than at the end of the EPA decisionmaking cycle. While earlier access to information can only be good, setting up another agency to conduct scientific assessments overlooks the existing problems with peer review, reg-neg, and traditional consultation. Macbeth and Marchant would be replicating the same kinds of closed-door processes that now limit participation to only a handful of members of the scientific community, rather than empowering more experts to get involved.

Cass Sunstein, in contrast, embraces the role that technology might play in regulatory reform. In *Infotopia,* Sunstein suggests that politics adapt "prediction markets" to decision markets.[47] Unlike traditional voting or polling, such markets require participants to back up their guesses with bets (usually using fake currency or points).[48] These probabilistic mechanisms are not always accurate, and we are still learning when they work, but they are one way of aggregating answers from a large number of people to inform decisions at scale. Such predictive mechanisms can also help spur collaboration and communication by involving distributed employees, customers, and others in the guessing.[49] Businesses are turning to online predictive mechanisms to aggregate private information to inform decisionmaking. The Iowa Electronic Markets, for example, have been successful at guessing the results of presidential elections, while the Hollywood Stock Exchange does remarkably well at predicting Oscar winners.[50] Simon and Schuster's MediaPredict project is a prediction market in which readers guess which manuscripts will become best sellers.[51] A site called Kluster allows users not only to set up projects but also to "invest in" and bet on the success of those projects—in other words, to guess at their likely success and thereby establish a futures market to drive good ideas.[52]

With a prediction market applied to regulatory policymaking, citizens would guess at the likelihood or risk of certain events; agencies would then use those aggregated probabilities to guide their policy choices. Mathematically, these betting markets are at least as accurate as other mechanisms for predicting outcomes (especially when we consider the findings of the social psychologist Philip Tetlock: that political professionals are not very good at making such predictions).[53] Betting markets tend to work well for reducing uncertainty in deciding between specific outcomes. That is, they can be used to identify big mistakes.

The Breaking the Logjam group and Cass Sunstein, among others, offer flexible, practical strategies for addressing the shortcomings of consultative practice. Many of their suggestions would lead to a vast improvement over current policies. But these innovations, which focus on institutional legal solutions, do not address the use of technology to connect the specific expertise of individuals to agencies or to coordinate private action by networks driven by government priorities but evolving new ideas for solutions outside government. They do not account for the expertise that could be unleashed for the benefit of the agency. Prediction markets envision the role of citizen as push-button predictor without specially situated knowledge. She can react but not act; criticize but not innovate.

These and other new New Deal innovators propose interesting market-based solutions, but their view of the role of the agency perpetuates the expertocratic vision and limits citizen participation either to closed-door, small-group processes or to mass-based consultation. Even reformers adhere to what the political philosopher Roberto Unger terms "institutional fetishism" because of a belief that only selected and known "experts" can assess science, while "citizens" can only express values and opinions.[54] "Perhaps the best we can hope for," writes another commentator, "is a benign paternalism that spoonfeeds the public a dumbed-down version of solutions achieved by qualified scientists after the fact of their achievement."[55]

Would-be reformers fail to account for the fact that amateurs possess extraordinary expertise. The nongovernment public includes "experts," and that expertise comes in a variety of forms—including scientific, economic, mathematical—that can produce and vet information in the decisionmaking process in a timely fashion. The reformers seem to assume that "there are a great many scientific findings that educated laymen do not have the background to critique or judge."[56] But the Internet can help an agency manage a process that empowers experts to participate usefully. These same ideas could be made more effective and powerful with the incorporation of technology. Innocentive, a company that farms out pharmaceutical and biochemical problems to an online network of solvers, has now started doing the same with public sector problems, attracting a wide array of experts.

IMAGINE THE ALTERNATIVE: POKING OUR WAY TO PARTICIPATION

Under the Clean Air Act, the EPA has to draft an air quality criteria document—a preliminary assessment of air quality—before setting national ambient air quality standards. Instead of turning to seven agency-selected experts for help, as it does now, it could consult a network of self-selected as well as invited online advisers. In developing its assessment, the EPA could put relevant queries to the scientific community.

Experts could invite other experts. The consultation could take place both early in the process and again, once the document is drafted.

Law professors Josh Eagle, James N. Sanchirico, and Barton H. Thompson Jr., participants in Breaking the Logjam, suggest that to mitigate problems of overfishing, damage to marine habitats, accidental mortality of nonfished species, and other challenges to the health of our seas, the U.S. Ocean Commission institute a program of comprehensive ocean zoning.[57] In this plan, commercial fisheries, recreational fishermen, conservationists, and other stakeholder groups would assume responsibility for different ocean zones. Now imagine that we apply a collaborative approach to this interesting proposal as well. The U.S. Ocean Commission might usefully set up a process and online platform for each of these stakeholder groups to develop policy, to solicit information and feedback, and thereby to take responsibility for managing its zone of the ocean in an informed, open, and expert fashion. (We explore innovations like these in chapter 7.)

In devising these practices, we have to remain open to all forms of technology, even those that initially seem trivial or irrelevant. Potentially, ubiquitous social networking technologies like Facebook and MySpace, in which participants "friend" and "poke" those in their personal networks, can teach us more about the idiom of participation than the legalistic practices in which so few of us actually participate. Social networking sites have not directly produced political action (any more than putting a political slogan on a bumper sticker does). Though candidates and interest groups have Facebook pages and even storefronts in Second Life, these are still window dressing. As the technology theorist Danah Boyd comments, "Typical [social networking site] participants are more invested in adding glitter to pages and SuperPoking their 'friends' than engaging in any form of civic-minded collective action."[58] But these technologies constitute a milestone in the history of citizen participation, because they make it easy to create and join a group. The organizers write up and post a short description of the group's goals and decide who will have the power to administer membership. They can set up a discussion board, send messages to the group, and post videos and other content at no cost. (Stephen Colbert's short-lived presidential bid, 1,000,000 Strong for Stephen Colbert, achieved its membership goal in nine days.)

Even though such groups are not designed for real group action, nonetheless, the individuals who use them are engaged in an unprecedented exploration of social interaction and learning. Members share knowledge and expertise. Because the screen displays social relationships among participants—sometimes called social graphing (*A* is friends with *B*)—participants are not only made aware of existing friendships but also use these connections to create new communities of affinity. Thus these sites are shifting the focus from individual to community and laying the groundwork for collaboration.

The social tools of web 2.0 are increasing the granularity and embeddedness of social groups. With today's technologies, I can join a group by putting a pushpin on a Google map. Instead of simply contributing money, I can give to a cause by tagging a patent, a photo, or a piece of text on the web. I can write an entry in Wikipedia and debate it on the discussion boards there. I can find prior art for the Patent Office and discuss it with other self-nominated experts. This variability of embeddedness is spilling over into the world of government institutions.

As we saw in the last chapter, the legislative framework for transparency, by itself, has not produced a transparent government. The introduction of new technology and new ways of thinking about information geared to groups may yield a more open administration. Similarly, the legal framework for participation has enshrined the right to participate in theory but not in practice. Now technology can be designed for a richer array of citizen participation than reformers have traditionally envisioned. And cultural changes are making it more likely that, if asked, the public will participate. People are increasingly accustomed to loose collaboration across a distance by means of social networking, video games, and other tools. Employment trends may also have an impact on the millennial generation's willingness to get involved. Arguably, because young people are accustomed to changing jobs, they will be more likely to join new groups. Of the jobs that workers began when they were ages eighteen to twenty-two, 72 percent of them ended in less than a year, and 94 percent ended in fewer than five years.[59] This mobility and flexibility combined with changes in technology will inevitably have an impact on the practices of government participation.

When asked to apply what he had learned about collaboration at IBM to improving England's National Health Service, Irving Wladawsky-Berger, the retired chief architect of IBM's Internet strategy, commented,

"The more I think about it, the more I have become convinced that the only counterbalance to physicians, politicians, payers, and other powerful institutions are properly organized communities of patients, their families, and care givers."[60] Unlike the new New Dealers, Wladawsky-Berger imagines that successful participation is possible as a means to solve the crises of the health care system. He goes on to reflect,

> A participatory governance model would have been very difficult to implement only a short time ago. Such a model requires that all those working together have access to the information they need to make decisions, as well as having an effective means of communicating with each other. The Internet and World Wide Web have changed all that. They have enabled the more distributed, collaborative governance style being embraced by leading-edge organizations.[61]

Despite the absence of universal success with citizen participation practices in government either before the Internet, when they were impractical, or since, when they continue to be hamstrung by the limited vision of what citizens can contribute, participation is both possible and desirable.

CHAPTER SEVEN

CITIZEN PARTICIPATION IN A COLLABORATIVE DEMOCRACY

Build a new model that makes the old model obsolete.

BUCKMINSTER FULLER

UNDER THE CURRENT LEGISLATIVE framework for participation even the availability of extraordinary technologies has not translated into a supply of strategies to improve consultation or collaboration. Drawing on the experience of the Peer-to-Patent project, in this chapter I sketch out what it might mean to reinvent consultation as collaborative governance in other arenas of policymaking. In so doing, the goal is to rescue the concept of participation from the assumption that it is unnecessary, time consuming, and ineffectual and, instead, to demonstrate that collaboration is essential for effective governance.

After brainstorming some of the ways to adapt the Peer-to-Patent model for the coproduction of data to environmental policy, I suggest new, collaborative, group-based innovations based on similar design principles. I focus on the "policy wiki" for collaborative drafting and, more radically, the "civic jury" for citizen oversight of official action. If there is to be real improvement in the quality of government and not only lip service to engagement, concrete and ready-to-implement experiments must be undertaken. This chapter outlines a half-dozen such experiments.

Peer-to-Patent is not a panacea. The design is not the right design for all forms of decisionmaking. This is because not all problems lend themselves to solving by a group. An institution must be able to articulate the challenge to which the wisdom of the crowd will be applied. For collaboration to be useful, the work has to lend itself to "chunking" (this is why brain surgery cannot be crowdsourced). And, as Scott Page explains, the institution "must also believe that people with relevant perspectives and heuristics exist who could be encouraged to think about the problem."[1] Hence the success of collaborative governance is, in large measure, a question of creating a culture that wants to move away from the single point of failure. Without such a dispositional shift, the fear of admitting "I don't know" and the need for outside help will be slow to come in government institutions.

For a group-based strategy to work, it also has to be customized to the problem at hand and creative strategies employed to improve the flow of expertise in the specific context. Some problems, like that of the information deficit in patent examination, require information gathering. In other cases, parsing large quantities of information, such as searching through draft statutes for hidden earmarks or Freedom of Information Act exemptions may be what is needed. At other times, collaborative drafting of a statute or regulation may be relevant. Yet others may require inventing new solutions based on partnerships among businesses, nonprofits, and individuals outside of government with a wide range of tasks to be performed.

While there has been a groundswell of attention to the problem of transparency in government and the need for government to release information that is accessible, searchable, and usable, there is no similarly widespread outcry for participation or collaboration. Perhaps because the ideal of citizen engagement in government—as distinct from civic life—seems so unattainable or because our experience with citizen participation has been so anemic or because neither government professionals nor the public has yet embraced the theory of shared and collaborative expertise, no blue-ribbon commissions have been convened to address what it might require to reengineer the role of the public in governance. Just as incumbent businesses are slow to rethink old business models, there does not seem to be a great deal of political will among professionals, who are understandably mired in the day-to-day, to use the newly available technology to develop more effective governance through collaboration.

Hence some of this chapter is devoted to addressing why collaborative democracy may happen and what government can do now to evolve its own institutions. As part of this discussion, I address the role of political leadership in driving technology-based innovation and reform in government institutions. The Obama administration named the country's first chief technology officer, a role that is specifically intended to lead change. Because every leader has an imperative today to apply innovative, technologically enabled approaches to solve problems on the policy agenda, there is not necessarily a special focus on how technology can also help to create twenty-first-century institutions of governance. Hence this chapter offers guidance—whether to a CTO or other leaders—for how to be an evangelist for the redesign of government institutions and the promotion of collaboration with companies, social entrepreneurs, universities, state and local governments, and civil society organizations through the use of open technology, open standards, and innovative practices. Government is not typically thought of as a locus for innovation. Leadership can change that.

BEYOND PEER-TO-PATENT:
IMPROVING CONSULTATION

The Clean Air Act tasks the Environmental Protection Agency, in cooperation with the states and relevant authorities, with handling the "growth in the amount and complexity of air pollution brought about by urbanization, industrial development, and the increasing use of motor vehicles [which have] resulted in mounting dangers to the public health and welfare, including injury to agricultural crops and livestock, damage to and the deterioration of property, and hazards to air and ground transportation."[2]

What does this mean in practice? To take one example, once an airborne toxin such as lead has been identified, the EPA administrator has one year to issue national ambient air quality standards indicating safe levels of that pollutant, based upon air quality criteria that "accurately reflect the latest scientific knowledge useful in indicating the kind and extent of all identifiable effects on public health or welfare which may be expected from the presence of such pollutant in the ambient air."[3]

To accomplish this work now, agency staff members compose an air quality criteria document, which is reviewed by the agency's seven-member Clean Air Science Advisory Committee, composed of "persons who are knowledgeable concerning air quality from the standpoint of health, welfare, economics or technology." The air quality criteria document includes a notice of proposed rulemaking, along with a proposed ambient air quality standard, all of which are published in the *Federal Register*. A traditional sixty- to ninety-day public comment period follows, in which interest groups and individuals can offer their input on the proposed standard, following which the standard is then adopted into law. These public comment periods typically attract the attention of environmental interest groups but not individual scientists, environmentalists, or concerned citizens (except in their capacity as the filers of electronic postcards).

Imagine improving on this chronology with a Peer-to-Patent-style pilot program that invites an open, peer review network of self-selecting clean air experts to work with the agency on researching the criteria document. There are many specific questions the agency needs to answer to do its work: What is the relationship between lead in the air and lead in children's bodies? What is the relationship between lead in children's bodies and their health? How should the agency assess the effect of specific levels of lead on populations like asthmatics and children? Such questions lend themselves to a well-delineated and "chunked" process that could elicit specific information.

By adopting a software platform like Peer-to-Patent, the EPA could pose these questions online and establish a process for having small teams of experts and enthusiasts offer and vet responses in a transparent and open fashion. To promote discussion, the agency would post any data it already has available in an accessible and manipulable format. As in Peer-to-Patent, people would invite each other to examine the data, leveraging connections within existing professional and social networks to attract more expert participation. Reputation and rating software could be employed to rate these participants and the information they submit.

Public consultation on an air quality criteria document could also go beyond Peer-to-Patent and generate ideas that help achieve the proposed ambient standard. The consultative software platform might be used to help people brainstorm creative ways to control emissions at both the national and local levels. Members of the network might be encouraged to form green businesses that help to attack the problem profitably. In this way, the EPA would begin to transform its advisory committee into a solution search panel. By creating opportunities for self-formed teams to solve problems that would otherwise fall to the agency to solve alone, the agency would open up access to a much wider ambit of know-how and action.

One expert might propose an eBay-like exchange for trading the right to emit air pollutants like lead. (Some cap-and-trade carbon emissions trading and sulfur trading already occur.) Another person might suggest an air quality seal of approval to be awarded to local businesses that reduce their lead emissions. The EPA could collaborate with a community of reformers, including academia and industry, to implement such innovations. The agency could then curate and showcase examples of successful work on its website and in the media. This would demonstrate progress, build trust in the institution, and create a feedback loop leading to greater innovation and more effective solutions to the problems the agency is tasked with addressing.

POLICY WIKIS

To take this process one step further, consider the potential of collaborative editing technologies, known as wikis (of which Wikipedia is the most famous example). These technologies make it possible for a distributed team of individuals to craft a document together. An online group could not only consult about the science involved in setting an air quality standard, but it could also help the EPA draft the air quality criteria document. Rather than invite participants to comment on an already drafted document or regulation after the fact, the agency could tap public expertise earlier in the process and give it more scope. Again, such experiments should eschew traditional closed-door practices in favor of new technologically enabled ways of working that allow people to self-select as participants on the basis of expertise and enthusiasm. As in Peer-to-Patent, such a process need not cede agency responsibility to the public but could significantly augment its access to good scientific research.

Some government authorities have caught the wiki bug and, often at the behest of consultants, have created internal shared drafting platforms. But not every participant can or should put pen to paper (or to pixel). In any case, many officials would feel discomfort (at least initially) with asking the public or even outside experts to take a hand at drafting regulations or legislation. Whether there is a (surmountable) concern that nonprofessionals do not know what to do or whether there is a worry that loss of control and secrecy might lead to criticisms from the press (after all, what if something goes wrong?), there might be understandable reluctance to share drafting responsibilities.

Still, drafting requires so much more than writing, and there are numerous roles for people to assume beyond working on the actual text. Hence a policy wiki should not simply be a way for everyone to *write* together. Instead, it should be a website where the goal, such as drafting an air quality criteria document, is described and broken down into specific tasks, which small groups of people can elect to undertake—experts and nonexperts alike. Besides writing, such work might involve:

Drafting and posting background research materials relevant to determining the air quality standard.

Inviting experts and other participants to join an advisory network to take part in vetting the standard once drafted.

Researching the claims in the document to identify their environmental impact and to raise awareness of unintended consequences.

Commenting on and editing particular provisions already drafted.

Vetting, evaluating, and rating the comments of others.

Summarizing and translating texts into plain English.

Analyzing positions of stakeholders and interested parties.

Creating visualizations (diagrams, charts, and illustrations) to reflect and represent the draft.

Identifying abuses, inaccuracies, and corruption, when such problems arise.

Moderating discussions.

Promoting the effort to other weblogs and websites, helping to get the word out, and prompting grassroots mobilization.

Displaying an electronic "bumper sticker"—an icon or button—on one's own website to show support for and encourage others to get involved in the effort (the Mozilla Foundation encourages its users to post a Firefox button as a way to encourage others to download the software).

By splitting the overall task into many smaller fact-gathering and decisionmaking exercises for members of a network while preserving the authority and oversight of the government official, the software platform can make it significantly harder for a small group of people to control and corrupt the process. It can also facilitate collaboration, as in Peer-to-Patent, by representing the "physics" of the process on the computer screen—that is, by showing people the roles and tasks they have taken on as part of an air quality drafting committee and the rules of engagement. By using visualizations to show the group back to itself and make its goals and tasks intelligible, the software can help strengthen the group's culture and sense of common purpose. The agency can also help by posting all relevant data sets in usable formats so that members of the network can use data visualization tools, such as Swivel or Many Eyes, to make sense of and comment on those data. The network can then do the heavy lifting of managing the process, collecting feedback, and evaluating submissions.

If an agency builds an open, transparent, meaningful framework, participants will come. Environmental activists, academics, corporate professionals, students, and environmental enthusiasts—more than just the usual corporate and interest group players—will have a way to contribute and get involved. Keep in mind that the EPA doesn't need a hundred thousand people to join a policy wiki committee on the issue of lead in the air. A few thousand participants, each working a few hours, helped the USPTO find crucial information it would otherwise not have had.

CIVIC JURIES

An even more ambitious approach to citizen consultation is represented by Danish consensus conferences, small-group citizen juries that convene to vet policymaking relating to complex scientific and technological issues.[4] Consensus conferences operate under the aegis of the Danish Board of Technology, an independent body that advises the Danish Parliament about science and technology issues like food safety and human health, information technology security, and free public transportation. Consensus conferences are used to analyze broad, complicated, and contentious social issues such as cloning and abortion. The method involves convening a focus group of about sixteen people from among interested members of the general public. Sometimes the group meets two days a week, for several weeks; at other times the meeting lasts for five days. The citizen group reads background information and attends presentations from a panel of professional experts. At the end of the meeting, the participants write position papers, which are published and distributed to Parliament.

The Danish juries meet face to face. But this method could easily be scaled up and adapted to enhance government accountability using the Internet. For example, instead of convening a jury to write position papers, the Department of Education could assign a citizen jury to oversee the work of appointed officials in its departments. (Even without the agency's consent or involvement it would be possible for a citizen jury to follow the work of a particular federal, state, or local official like fans track a movie star on a common blog.) Imagine designating separate juries to oversee the work of the assistant deputy secretary of the Office of Safe and Drug-Free Schools, the assistant secretary for Elementary and Secondary Education, and all other officials responsible for divisions within DOE. Each jury would serve online and for a limited term, to prevent members from becoming overburdened or entrenched. The policymaker overseen by the jury would be required (or might feel obliged in the case of the unofficial jury) to disclose and explain his official actions on a blog. Jurors, who might be paid, would log in regularly to read his reports, ask questions, request clarification, or challenge his actions. The official would be required to ask for the jury's recommendation before making any major decisions. He would not be required to follow its recommendation, but failure to do so would trigger a requirement for an official explanation. Both the recommendation and the official response would be a matter of public record.

Unlike federal advisory committees, which are handpicked by policymakers behind closed doors, civic juries could be convened through automated and transparent processes. Juries might be selected at random from a pool of volunteers. Civic jurors at the Department of Education could be drawn from a mix of volunteers, including some who work in education (teachers, administrators, food service workers, and so on) and others from outside the field who have an interest in education reform. Potential jurors would specify their profession and their interests in response to a web-based questionnaire. (In 2006–07 I prototyped and tested just such a system in a pilot project in Libya to solicit feedback on education policy from teachers, parents, and students.) As an alternative, members might be chosen at random from among the most active participants in a policy wiki community or from among those who participate in rulemaking activities.

This innovation is but one variation on the jury model that could enable ordinary people with or without special expertise to exert influence at the national level while informing policy and improving government practice. Such juries would resonate beyond the few dozen or few hundred people who serve. The mere existence of an avenue for engagement even by a small number of "us" creates an impetus for openness. Traditional opportunities for participation—like advisory committees, which are selected, not self-selected, and which take place face to face without any express accountability—do not foster civic engagement. By contrast, in the Mozilla model 10,000 users participated in making the web browser used by another 180 million. This engenders in the corporate culture—where there is no democratic obligation—the expectation that the expertise of people outside of the organization will be taken seriously. The participation of volunteers improves the company's product and increases the browser's appeal to its own community. People have a sense of ownership.

Beyond Notice and Comment

All three innovations—Peer-to-Patent, the policy wiki, and the civic jury—could be piloted today. While Peer-to-Patent continues at the USPTO, the EPA might try to involve an open network in drafting air quality evaluations, and the Department of Education could pilot the use of civic juries. Now more widespread experimentation with new techniques (and sharing of success and failures) is necessary. In particular because of the need to rationalize technology operations through centralization and enterprisewide management, it is that much more important to ensure that there are also outlets (programs and the personnel to champion them) for distributed innovation and experimentation across agencies and departments. New structures, like internal and external "labs" for testing social innovations, could also help to ensure that innovations in government are tried, tested, and disseminated. For example, the following innovations could all be implemented at low or no cost within the next year. Each one is paradigmatic of a different type of engagement that might be adapted in different contexts.

Crowdsourcing Communication: President's Question Time

Just as the British Parliament has the custom of a weekly "prime minister's question time," which gives members the opportunity to grill the PM on any and all matters of national policy, we can imagine a "question time" on the Internet at all levels of government. The president (or any government official) could establish a website on which people can pose questions, using a Digg-style recommender system to vet and prioritize the top questions. (The German chancellor already offers an online "direct to the chancellor" website, and there are independent versions of this idea, like Whitehouse2.org and askthespeaker.org). The public could "bubble up" the best ideas. The president could respond to the top three questions, as determined by the recommender system, during his weekly webcast and radio address or even during the State of the Union address. By letting public participation—not public opinion—drive the agenda for something as visible as the State of the Union, the president would send an important signal about openness and participation in government.

President Obama's cabinet appointees used this technique ("Open for Questions") during the transition period to solicit questions from the public. (Helping to design the participatory features of the transition website was one of my assignments in the Technology, Innovation, and Government Reform Working Group.) The new media team set up the website to enable people to prioritize questions about health care that Tom Daschle then answered in a recorded video. Subsequently, they asked questions about a range of policy topics, from foreign policy and the economy to science and technology. The incoming government also asked questions and solicited responses from the public, first to the question: How can government be a better supporter of the [social service] work that you're doing? Later, the transition instituted a Citizens Briefing Book to invite responses on a range of topics.

In the future, such conversational-style democracy could be improved through visual deliberation techniques that create community, rather than through questions and answers geared toward individuals. If participants could label their submissions, others can then easily sort, find, and respond to them. Visualizations and tree maps can be employed to reflect the process back to people. Beyond that, a corps of volunteer citizen moderators could help to sort and organize questions to make them optimally useful as input to decisionmaking, rather than just conversation by itself. Just as Peer-to-Patent makes public participation relevant to actual decisionmaking, by being tied in to actual White House practices, "question time" should spark meaningful engagement in a process that matters.

CHAMPIONING COLLABORATION: WHITEHOUSE.GOV

Overhauling the White House website (or any agency website) with an eye toward encouraging collaboration is a second possible low-cost, short-term innovation. Instead of simply showcasing trivia about the president and his family or soliciting suggested names for the president's dog, as Clinton did with Buddy in 1999 (and Bush did with the pardoned presidential turkey in 2007), the White House website should (also) be a forum for structured public participation and engagement in policymaking. People could be invited to submit questions for the president's question time via Whitehouse.gov. (By the time this is published, this may already be the case.)

In addition, the White House website can demonstrate models of collaboration both within government and outside of it. For example, the White House website could showcase examples—sorted, tagged, and organized—of civic engagement in local communities. Via a structured, web-based form, groups and individuals could be invited to submit stories about how they brought about change and engaged in good works— through Carrotmobbing, Obama Working, or other forms of activity. The focus of the website could change week by week. One week could feature stories from around the country about steps that people have taken to improve educational opportunities in their own communities; another could focus on examples of environmental reform. Even hard topics such as foreign policy could yield reports on efforts to create better understanding between peoples of different nationalities. Examples (in text, audio, and video) would be showcased on the website. This would help to encourage an ethic of participation and engagement and send a strong signal about a new kind of government.

COORDINATING COLLABORATION: BUILDING MINIMOVEMENTS

Government wields extraordinary convening power. The dot gov "brand" can be successfully leveraged to put people to work addressing national priorities. Whether on Whitehouse.gov or on a new website, the government could launch competitions for innovative, workable approaches that engage individuals and organizations with government to solve the most entrenched social problems. Such competitions would harness the public's energy, creativity, and goodwill and allow people and organizations to make a meaningful contribution to a large problem, while knowing that they are part of a broader movement.

The White House could sponsor such contests. In addition, every agency could experiment with publishing its detailed priorities in plain English (and Spanish, Russian, and other languages) and invite the public to devise creative and diverse solutions to the problems it has identified. A webmaster would set up a contest page. The theme of the contest, be it education or energy, might change each quarter. The president or his designate would convene a judging committee comprising cabinet and White House officials to select the winning solutions. The website would have a web-based form for members of the public to fill out to submit their proposals. The public would rate the submissions, and the top twenty-five ideas would then be forwarded to the judging committee. The president could announce the winner of that quarter's competition in his weekly radio address and instruct the relevant agency head to follow up and explore the proposal.

These competitions would be a way to bring crucial problems to the surface and elicit suggestions for solutions in a short, structured format. But this is also a way to help people find each other and create teams that can execute the proposal. Visualizations would reflect the work of the group back to itself and galvanize traction for each minimovement. Combined with software used by the website Pledgebank (If ten people do *x*, I'll do *y*), officials could help to generate extragovernment problem-solving activity. Following the competition, the winning idea would stay up on the site—or on a foundation website—and a conversation could ensue. The site could be a way to organize sign-ups and to allow foundations and businesses to adopt projects to fund. Groups in the private and nonprofit sectors have already experimented with such approaches. In 2008 American Express launched the Members Project to award $2.5 million to five projects that make a positive impact on the world as selected by its members. The Case Foundation also runs a lower-profile "crowd-sourced" philanthropy competition.

This could be a way to propose and organize a volunteer corps of technology professionals to aid in disaster relief by rebuilding computer networks and databases and restoring communications services in the event of a terrorist attack or natural disaster (Netroots advocate Andrew Rasiej worked on getting this idea into legislation). Similarly, this might be a way to get support for a volunteer science corps to conduct a baseline assessment of high school science labs, as science and technology specialist Tom Kalil has proposed. Using a series of guidelines developed by the National Science Teachers' Association and some well-produced instructional videos, volunteers would be able to conduct an assessment of the infrastructure, equipment, and safety of local school labs. Such a project might also seek to raise money from local businesses to improve the science facilities available to children.

Or to take one more example, if the EPA had posed the question about recycling mercury in lightbulbs (see chapter 1), the agency might have attracted proposals for remediation and induced companies to step up with solutions (or people to form a new company for this purpose). Similarly, if the EPA had articulated small business environmentalism as a priority, the Carrotmob idea—where consumers channeled their business to the San Francisco store most willing to invest in environmental retrofitting—might have emerged and been undertaken across the country. While many forms of civic engagement already occur outside government, agencies can use the web to set priorities, communicate challenges, learn from the public about problems that might demand agency attention, and give positive feedback for useful innovations (like the Carrotmob), which might then be copied and tried elsewhere. By using its bully pulpit to articulate an agenda, the agency focuses public attention and resources on important problems.

COLLABORATIVE BRAINSTORMING: THE POLICY JAM

The White House or agencies could also conduct online, structured brainstorming sessions with diverse experts to bring out ideas in connection with proposed presidential policy. While experimental in the political arena, such online brainstorming sessions have been practiced by IBM and UN World Habitat since 2001. The process could be an excellent way to run discussions about policy proposals to achieve energy independence or better schools or more transparent government. The White House could convene week-long, asynchronous brainstorming exercises on key policy questions, including ways to achieve more collaborative and participatory democracy.

In such brainstorming, people contribute and build on each other's ideas in a structured conversation under the guidance of moderators. Modeled on the IBM "jam," this method could be useful for eliciting new ideas and unintended consequences from proposed policies. For example, a collaborative government brainstorm might have five topics, one to talk about the future of transparency, another to discuss rulemaking, a third to focus on the role of advisory committees, a fourth to brainstorm ways to solicit expertise in new ways, and a fifth to discuss collaboration. The technology platform that IBM uses is a simple, modified wiki that requires no technical ability. Appropriate staff would develop the agenda for discussion and for outlining questions to address with the group. Experts could be both selected and self-selected to participate. The combination may help to ensure a diverse group (for example, a brainstorm about government innovation would include lawyers, consultants, technologists, political theorists, game designers, and experts in environmental and foreign policy, health care, and defense).

Because it is limited in duration, a jam helps to focus ideas toward generating practical proposals for implementation. It provides a forum to engage people with varying skills and expertise. And with an investment in creating good questions up front as well as enlisting good (volunteer) moderators, it can elicit ideas and solutions to complex problems in a group setting.

NETWORKED BRAIN TRUST

Senior political leadership could also create the impetus for universities to develop online systems for offering advice to the president, agency heads, and congressional staff. The major research universities, with the support of philanthropy, could build and operate an independent, open, online brain trust to augment the work of advisory committees. When the EPA needs data about air quality to write an air quality criteria document, it could turn to a network of environmental advisers, including experts on environmental science, climatology, geology, earth science, law, business, and communications from top universities. These experts would work in online groups, forcing both disagreements and consensus to the surface, and online, which would allow them to work with government without leaving their home institutions.

In parallel, the universities—at the administration's behest and encouragement—could convene a student version of the expert advisory network comprising undergraduates and graduate students from various disciplines. These students would act as a research corps, working in teams to answer questions and dig up information for political officials. By participating on the site, students could demonstrate mastery and expertise in a field, making themselves more attractive to employers while providing much needed research and assistance to underinformed government officials. Where the professorial experts are more inclined to opine, the student advisory network would be a place to solicit specific answers to concrete research questions demanding data and hard evidence.

MAKING PARTICIPATION MORE COLLABORATIVE: STRUCTURED NOTICE AND COMMENT

The president could also mandate, in connection with notice-and-comment rulemaking, that agencies articulate and seek answers to plain-English questions before drafting any final rule. Instead of issuing only a draft rule, agencies should be formulating and publishing interrogatories with the notice of proposed rulemaking as a matter of course.

This small innovation could lead to a sea change in consultative practice. It is then another small step from asking questions after the issuance of the notice to formulating them before the drafting process begins (with an advance notice of proposed rulemaking).

To begin with, agencies should start by asking questions. In current rulemaking practice, agencies rarely ask the public for more than an opinion on a pending regulation. (Some have made this a regular practice.) A draft regulation is posted wholesale with a request for comment. As a result, agencies sometimes receive hundreds of thousands of comments without any meaningful way to sort and read them. If, as in Peer-to-Patent, agencies established structures for outside engagement, asking specific, hard, focused questions, they would get useful answers. There is no reason such an innovation could not also apply to Congress, where there is no public consultation at all.

DECENTRALIZING PARTICIPATION

Moreover, when an agency publishes its list of consultative questions in connection with a notice of proposed rulemaking, it should solicit feedback through a broad range of channels, not only via its own website or regulations.gov. The agency's questions could be syndicated and pushed out to subscribing blogs and websites via a feed. Bloggers and interest groups that have an interest in air quality (Technorati, the blog search engine, pulls up eighty-six blogs dedicated to air quality and countless postings on the topic by general environmental weblogs) can then promote discussion and brainstorming on their own sites. Discussion could take place in the community, and feedback could subsequently be distilled and channeled back to the agency through comments to a notice of proposed rulemaking or participation in the new online consultation channels, which are eventually set up to take this feedback.

It would be a simple matter to create an EPA open-government button that people can place on their weblogs to advertise that they are citizen participants and subscribe to receive questions and host discussions on particular topics, such as air quality, from, say, the EPA.

ORGANIZING FOR INNOVATION

Innovation in government will happen, in part, because of forces naturally evolving in technology, culture, and society. The dispersion of social networking technologies creates greater familiarity with forming teams and groups.[5] The trend toward online distance work and collaboration across boundaries is making the necessary practices commonplace. These social and cultural shifts will inevitably spur innovations in outmoded practices of paper-based participation. Proliferating websites for civic participation from FixMyStreet to MyBikeLane (both designed as a way to submit complaints about potholes, traffic conditions, and malfunctioning red lights) may push on the door of government from the outside and help to acculturate both government professionals and citizens to a new level of engagement. The explosion of political participation rates in the presidential race of 2008, which accustomed people to an unprecedented level of participation in the electoral process, might in turn translate into a demand for more participation in governance.

The public may not continue to be satisfied with once-a-year voting and abstruse e-rulemaking when there can be engagement in online policy brainstorms, crowdsourcing of best practices suggestions, commenting on the blogs of government officials and on Whitehouse.gov, data visualization challenges, and more effective and modern federal advisory committees and peer review structures. Competition and demonstration from below (state and local) and from abroad might also be a factor in driving change. I have already recounted examples from Washington, D.C., Washington State, Alabama, Virginia, and other places where innovation is happening in the public sector of America's towns and cities.

In New Zealand, private citizens contributed to drafting the nation's new Policing Act, legislation that had not been revised since 1958, via a wiki.[6] The wiki received more than 25,000 visits over the course of 2007.

In Melbourne, Australia, the City Council ran a wiki-based collaborative project to create and then consult on Melbourne's ten-year plan.[7] The hope is that politically entrepreneurial projects (here and abroad) like Peer-to-Patent, which model the practices of collaborative governance, will show the way forward and enable others to undertake similar innovations.

But Peer-to-Patent had to be brokered from the outside. Without the law school to raise the money, convene supporters, and design the project, the USPTO by itself would not have undertaken Peer-to-Patent. The culture of expertise in government is too entrenched. Therefore if change is to come from within government, additional incentives are required that civil society cannot marshal alone. Just as having Vice President Gore as a champion led to more performance-based and efficient government in the early 1990s, vision and leadership—the bully pulpit—must be exercised if the political imperative of effective governance in the digital age is to come to pass. The United States seems to be on the right path. On his first day in office President Obama issued a memorandum to all federal executive heads on transparency and open government.

Most Western democracies have an electronic government chief or a chief information officer responsible for computerization in government. The British government has an Office of the e-Envoy, whose mandate is to "improve the delivery of public services and achieve long-term cost savings by joining up online government services around the needs of customers." The United Kingdom also has a CTO Council responsible for "flexible and cost-effective IT services across government that meet customer requirements." The Australians have an Information Management Office, which focuses on technical standards and tools. In the United States, where the Office of Management and Budget has incorporated an Office of E-Government, the e-government plan concentrates on procurement questions and on how to deliver services—such as paying taxes and parking tickets—to citizens more efficiently. The Clinger-Cohen Act of 1996 requires these government information technology operations to be run as efficiently and profitably as a business. Similarly, the Government Performance Results Act of 1993 requires agencies to write strategic plans that promote a new focus on "results, service quality, and customer satisfaction."

In contrast, the Swedes have adopted a less business-centric approach. The role of the Swedish minister for Democratic Issues and Public Administration is to address the quality of governance and opportunities for participation in Swedish government. In 2004 the minister promulgated a Plan for Public Administration in the Service of Democracy. That action plan includes such proposals as developing commissions of inquiry to "improve planning; to boost commissioners' knowledge; to improve the supply of skills; to consider effective follow-up," and experimenting with trial implementation of "citizen panels" that will "monitor quality in public administration" and conduct ongoing, empirical reporting and evaluation on the development of public administration. We can imagine that the U.S. chief technology officer might look more like the Swedish democracy minister than the e-envoy or the chief information officer, with the focus squarely on technological approaches to improving public administration and informing decisionmaking.

Before assuming office as president of the United States, Barack Obama announced that he would name the first chief technology officer of the federal government. With a chief information officer already in place in the Office of Management and Budget, the creation of this new position was intended to signal the importance of incorporating disruptive technologies not only in the thinking about policy but also in the practices of governance. The idea of this position is to have a counterpart to those who think about technology in terms of procurement or operations and, in addition, create responsibility for more open, participatory, and collaborative government. Whether they are CTOs or CIOs, it is vital to have leaders committed to fundamentally redesigning the workings of government and the relationship of government to the citizenry. While I talk about CTOs as a shorthand, it is key to have people by whatever title at the top, with the power of the president and the purse behind them, as well as leaders across the organization of government, who are primarily concerned with the processes and practices that produce more effective governance. Those on the inside of government need to collaborate with agency domain specialists as well as with those outside government, from not only industry, especially the technology sector, but also academia and the open-source and volunteer coding communities—to "embarrass the system" with good results.

Whatever the title (and whether in the United States or elsewhere), evangelists of persuasive personality and position—champions for a new collaboration agenda—are vital to driving change across the enormous and hidebound organizational structures of government. As Carmen Sirianni writes in *Civic Engagement and Collaborative Governance,*

[We must] transform the cultures of government institutions and non-profit contracting organizations in ways that can support citizen co-production, shared expertise, and other collaborative practices. No policy intended to encourage citizens to become engaged co-producers, or to persuade professionals to utilize their expertise to empower communities, can be expected to have substantial and sustained impact if the organization charged with implementing it [does] not re-orient some of [its] most fundamental organizational practices and mindsets.[8]

Be it a chief technology officer, a chief open-government officer, or Siriani's idea of a dedicated office of collaborative governance, there needs to be leadership to drive change from the top down as well as from the bottom up to "infect" the rest of the leadership. Because cabinet chiefs and agency heads must have substantive expertise in their "vertical" subject matter, it is helpful to also have a senior leader with "horizontal" expertise in the theory and practices of participation and collaboration who can focus on how to improve decisionmaking.

Over the long term, merely exhorting agency directors to incorporate more technology and conduct pilot programs is not enough. Personnel must be distributed throughout the organization who can seed innovations from the bottom up. Traditionally, agency heads are domain specialists and managers. Agency CIOs focus on infrastructure, while webmasters are divorced from the policymaking process. As a first priority, it is vital to ensure that there are technically knowledgeable personnel with a commitment to more open and collaborative government in jobs throughout the government. They must believe in the expertise and ability of the public. They must also be willing to say, "I don't know," and then turn to a network of collaborating experts for help.

To achieve success, the entire agenda of change cannot rest on one official, whether a CTO or a CIO. Collaborative governance depends upon having people throughout the agencies with the skills, ability, and willingness to innovate. Agency heads must be able to take risks and implement collaborative, web 2.0 strategies. If agencies are to establish "pilot programs to open up government decisionmaking and involve the public in the work of agencies not simply by soliciting opinions, but by tapping into the vast and distributed expertise of the American citizenry to help government make more informed decisions," as President Obama said on the campaign trail, they must also hire personnel with both technical and substantive know-how and a belief in open and collaborative government.[9]

There must also be senior leadership in a variety of positions, which are not thought of as particularly technological, who are committed to creating a more open government. For example, the Government Printing Office is a $1 billion-a-year service bureau in the executive branch that prints and publishes all the official journals of government, including the *Congressional Record,* the *Federal Register,* and the *Presidential Papers.* The director must be committed to publishing information in more usable, open, and visual formats if transparency is to be a meaningful goal. The National Archives and Records Administration, the keeper of the government's history, similarly must pursue a strategy of openness. The General Services Administration needs to update its web guidelines for agency webmasters to enable the use of innovative social media. The Office of Management and Budget needs to be committed to strategies, like viral competitions, that help to elicit innovative thinking across the institution.

THE NETWORKED CTO

There is no reason why the CTO or other government innovation leader must do all the work internally when he can rely on a network to extend his capacity. The Office of Chief Technology Officer should itself be a model for collaborative ways of working. Creating a network supported by a software platform to inform the CTO's work will be essential to identifying the best technology and practices to support innovation. The European Union has a new ePractice platform. This is a website where people with an interest in e-government, for example, can set up discussion groups to talk about projects relating to technology and government. ePractice is intended as a way for researchers to connect to one another across Europe. The site itself is quite clean, spare, and attractive and suggests one model for the CTO's advisory group.

The Internet Engineering Task Force—the large, open, international community concerned with the evolution of the architecture and the smooth operation of the Internet—offers the CTO as another possible model of collaboration. Since its inception in the late 1980s, the IETF has run itself openly and has invited participation on the basis of self-selection. As the organization grew in size and importance, it developed new practices for its own democratic self-governance. It has become part of the romantic lore of the cyber frontier that when the IETF plenary meets to approve a proposed resolution, the resolution is decided by having proponents and opponents hum and determining which hum is loudest! While the humming (which is a true story) is not the right model for making national policy, the idea of an open network of diverse, collaborating experts to generate good ideas is.

Above all, the CTO's office should not be a hierarchical and centralized government office. The idea is not to create another bureaucracy that will suffer from all the closed-door information deficits that already burden government agencies. Instead, the CTO could rely on a corps of expert, citizen volunteers—much like Peer-to-Patent's community of reformers—who would meet online to help plan his agenda, identify new technologies and best practices, design and develop pilot programs, and conduct evaluations. The involvement of such a community of reformers will help ensure that programs are honed to the needs of public participants as well as institutional players.

COLLABORATIVE GOVERNANCE LABS

The appropriate offices in government (which in the United States are presumably the CTO, the CIO, and the GSA) should set up, run, and fund innovative pilot projects (such as a policy wiki and a civic jury). Peer-to-Patent had to be created outside of government at great expense and with substantial difficulty. But if there were a government innovation lab, of the kind that every major high-technology company such as Google, IBM, and Microsoft has set up, then the next Peer-to-Patent idea or the consortium of university advisers or the civic jury initiative could be tried, tested, and deployed faster from within government with the assistance of outside advisers and technologists. I want to emphasize the importance of establishing such a project as a collaboration across government and with the public that can generate new ideas and channel many eyeballs toward the needs of the public sector.

The Office of the CTO could issue a request for assistance on a particular pilot project, and open-source programmers could be called upon to help. These challenges might come from agencies via the CTO or from the CTO himself. In much the same way as the Mozilla Foundation relies on its community of volunteers to develop the Firefox web browser (a complex set of tasks they accomplish on deadline and at a pace much faster than Microsoft develops its Internet Explorer browser), the CTO could turn to an outside network. In fact, a highly regarded organization like Mozilla or the World Wide Web Consortium, which sets technical standards relating to the web, could help to galvanize and organize the technical community to participate. The CTO's office itself would organize the process for distributed work on innovations. It would also address up front any legal impediments to establishing a volunteer technical corps that donates open-source software and services to the government as well as eliminating any design restrictions, such as the prohibition on the use of cookies, that could impair the use of social and visual technologies.

What technology entrepreneur, if asked, wouldn't want to lend her ability to help create effective web tools for the environmental protection agency? Or participate in a design process to advise on the development of such tools by the open-source community? What political scientist wouldn't love to have the chance not only to evaluate the impact of those tools but also to offer his opinion on how to make them better? What computer scientist wouldn't like the challenge of figuring out how to use rating and reputation systems to measure expertise in policymaking? What policymakers would not embrace the opportunity to sit down with technologists, lawyers, anthropologists, artists, economists, designers, and others to figure out how to do their job better? The best way to bring about collaboration is not top-down hierarchy and control but collaboration with a community committed to rough consensus and running code.

It is not necessary or desirable for the government to "own" or "build" all of its own technology. After all, the private sector and government collaborated on Peer-to-Patent successfully. The "lab" would usefully establish a process to connect a network of volunteer programmers to internal project management staff to address challenges issued by government officials. Countless technologists would be thrilled to participate in collaborative public sector innovation projects that benefited the government and the American people. Academics would line up to measure the social scientific impact of pilot programs. Because the resulting data would be open and available, there would be test beds other organizations could use for subsequent evaluation. Foundations or nongovernment organizations might step up to create and fund solutions as well.

Such a lab need not be physical. It could be a website for managing volunteers to test new methods and tools for citizen participation and government collaboration. Using volunteers could help to reduce the cost of innovation and experimentation. Having a place to play with new ideas—an experimental sandbox—before rolling out a new project on Whitehouse.gov or an agency website might make the Department of Health and Human Services more comfortable about doing a "world jam" with doctors. The Department of Housing and Urban Development would be able to run a contest for the best geolocational software applications using the agency's data feeds. The White House's new media team could fearlessly test out the use of genetic algorithm software to sort and winnow online comments rather than using the venerable White House website as a testing ground.

Such a network-based approach to managing the office would be taking to heart the values of collaboration, openness, decentralization, and innovation. There would be no need to implement all proposed innovations. The Threadless T-shirt company, for example, produces only half a dozen of the 800 design proposals customers submit each year via its website. The fact that the SourceForge repository for open-source software collaboration is teeming with languishing programming projects is not necessarily a bad thing. Rather, it may be a sign that people are choosing to work on the best ideas. Spurring this kind of engagement in the collaborative governance planning process would also lead to increased efforts by civic groups and those outside government to take action directly to develop solutions and attack problems in collaboration with government and driven by direction articulated by the CTO.

Projects should be evolutionary in nature and subject to iteration and improvement. By leveraging the expertise and assistance of the technology community to work, initially on a small number of pilot projects, it will become possible to prototype more rapidly. The CTO would develop the initial template and questions for soliciting the help of domain experts online to understand the problems faced by specific agencies. If the questions are asked with precision, those experts would share information about how decisionmaking works (and does not) in the EPA, in the Department of Transportation, and even in the White House. They would be able to critique current tools as well as citizen consultation practices.

If a project piloted in the lab were deemed successful, the CTO could work with the sponsoring agency to institutionalize such consultative practice; he would also assume responsibility for working with Congress to ensure adequate budgetary appropriations for the project going forward and with the president on drafting an appropriate executive order. The CTO would then be able to argue—based on practical, empirical, measurable success—for changes to the relevant substantive law or to the Administrative Procedure Act or Freedom of Information Act, as appropriate, and for agency appropriations to apply these new initiatives more widely. The CTO's office might also commission the development of tools for participation that can be reused across agencies. The CTO might also work with the National Science Foundation and outside philanthropies to support the development of government innovations and the related research to study their efficacy and improvement.

The Office of the CTO would curate the results of experiments taking place across all parts of government, evaluate and disseminate the results (in cooperation with the Government Accountability Office and the Office of Management and Budget), and coordinate this research with an open, public network of participating experts and enthusiasts. All research and data would be made openly and publicly available online in formats that are accessible, usable, and "mash-up-able" by the public. Academics and researchers would be invited to study and evaluate the progress of government programs. The CTO would publish the results. The Whitehouse.gov website might also publish highlights of the work and thereby draw attention to opportunities to participate and to the administration's more open, transparent, and trustworthy ways of working.

CHAPTER EIGHT

Lessons Learned

All mankind is divided into three classes: those that are immovable, those that are movable, and those that move.

—Benjamin Franklin

The financial crisis that began in 2008 highlighted the urgent need for effective strategies to address complex, unpredictable social problems. There is no better way to achieve effective governance of both public and private institutions today than through collaboration, not for its own sake, but to generate creative solutions to these kinds of challenges and to share the work of oversight and accountability.

Driven by competitive pressure, the private sector has recognized faster than government that success turns on mobilization of resources independent of traditional institutional boundaries. Jefferson's adage of two centuries ago captures this idea as applied to government: "I know of no safe depository of the ultimate power of the society but the people themselves." Effectively tapping that depository of expertise and action is the challenge and the opportunity of our era.

This urgent need to redesign the institutions of governance comes in parallel to a groundswell of interest in public engagement. The Obama-McCain presidential campaign demonstrated the willingness and ability of millions of Americans to work together to make a difference. Companies, universities, state and local governments, and civil society organizations are also ready to contribute. People are smart and willing to work together. Wikipedia is the constant reminder.

Yet there are too few outlets for participation in the shared work of managing society, participation in both traditional government practices and in innovative strategies that technology might enable to connect citizens and government to solve problems in new ways. Traditional agency public participation practices like peer review or federal advisory committees select participants by means of complex vetting processes. But only a handful can ever serve. The process of selecting participants creates an occasion for political litmus testing and manipulation. One-off comment processes are often unwieldy. Time consuming to run, they generally come too late in the decisionmaking process to offer much expertise and rarely bring in new voices from outside the Beltway.

The goal of Peer-to-Patent has been to devise a concrete strategy for marrying the techniques of web 2.0 to the practices of government decisionmaking in order to create more effective governance. The experience offers useful insights for how to design better practices to engage the public in government and how to create new collaborative opportunities within government and between government, the private sector, and individuals at scale. These "design lessons" are not technological per se. While technology is necessary to undertake collaboration efficiently, creating effective government institutions is not a job for webmasters. Rather, new governance structures and social practices are needed. Yet the good intention to want openness and engagement can often founder on the practical reality of knowing how to reengineer an institution and make collaboration manageable and useful.

The following ten lessons, first summarized and then discussed below, may help leaders in public and private organizations wishing to move toward more collaborative decisionmaking. These lessons apply both to information-gathering projects like Peer-to-Patent and to creating policy wikis, citizen juries, online brainstorming, and other innovations.

1. *Ask the right questions:* The more specific the question, the better targeted and more relevant the responses will be. Open-ended, "What do you think of *x*?" questions only lead to unmanageable and irrelevant feedback.

2. *Ask the right people:* Creating opportunities for self-selection allows expertise to find the problem. Self-selection can be combined with baseline participation requirements.

3. *Design the process for the desired end:* The choice of methodology and tools will depend on the results. But the process should be designed to achieve a goal. That goal should be communicated up front.

4. *Design for groups, not individuals:* "Chunk" the work into smaller problems, which can easily be distributed to members of a team. Working in groups makes it easier to participate in short bursts of time and is demonstrated to produce more effective results.

5. *Use the screen to show the group back to itself:* If people perceive themselves to be part of a minimovement, they will work more effectively together across a distance.

6. *Divide work into roles and tasks:* Collaboration requires parceling out assignments into smaller tasks. Visualizations can make it possible for people to perceive the available roles and choose their own. Wikipedia works because people know what to do.

7. *Harness the power of reputation:* Organizations are increasingly using bubbling-up techniques to solicit information in response to specific questions and allowing people to rate the submissions.

8. *Make policies, not websites:* Improved practices cannot be created through technology alone. Instead, look at the problem as a whole, focusing on how to redesign internal processes in response to opportunities for collaboration.

9. *Pilot new ideas:* Use pilot programs, competitions, and prizes to generate innovation.

10. *Focus on outcomes, not inputs:* Design practices to achieve performance goals and metrics. Measure success.

ASK THE RIGHT QUESTIONS

Many more people would get involved in government if they knew exactly what to do. Ze Frank, a technology humorist and political commentator, has demonstrated that, simply by asking, you can get people to do crazy, difficult things. In 2006 he challenged viewers of his daily web show to create an "earth sandwich" by putting pieces of bread on exactly opposite sides of the globe.[1] Two pieces of bread later—one in New Zealand and one in Spain—the sandwich was complete. Participation in unlikely quests is not limited to stunts. As an unknown teenager living in Finland, Linus Torvalds asked the distributed community of computer science professionals for help in adapting the Minux operating system teaching software to his home computer. The result was Linux and the worldwide open-source movement, which Torvalds continues to guide from Portland, Oregon.

The questions you ask shape the answers you receive. Just ask people to look at a patent and you will get what the Slashdot and Groklaw websites receive daily: thousands of undifferentiated comments on "Why I hate Microsoft" or "Why I hate the patent system." Such diatribes peter out after a day or so (if you're lucky). But ask a specific question and you'll get a specific answer. Ask people to submit prior art and specify that it must predate the invention. Ask people to cite the specific claims that are affected by the prior art. The more you ask for, the more people understand what is being asked of them and the more they get used to providing useful answers.

A critical part of knowing which questions to ask is to include the participating community in their selection. Peer-to-Patent, for example, invited the public to suggest patent applications that should be the subject of community attention. The Center for Patent Innovations that created Peer-to-Patent has extended this idea by launching a software platform to help any community, be it Linux software developers or those interested in breast cancer research, to identify patents that should be reexamined by the Patent Office. In a related move, the Department of State has launched the Diplopedia project to capture questions and answers about diplomacy that will help explain to the public what the agency does and how it functions.

Providing an online venue for articulating and answering questions has the added benefit of making problems visible in such a way that outside groups can also tackle them. For example, if the EPA set up an online system to solicit expertise in measuring air quality, other civic environmental groups could also tackle the problem. Again, the more specific the question, the better targeted and more relevant the responses will be. Tagging and labeling tools can then be introduced to make those submissions more searchable and useful. It is not necessary for the agency to control this dialogue. Instead, if the questions are clearly posed, others can assume the work. Consider the success of *Talking Points Memo,* an award-winning investigative journalism blog that brings together thousands of individuals to conduct distributed research.

Similar techniques can also be enlisted to ask people for their opinions, stories, anecdotes, and other nonexpert information. At Peer-to-Patent, we asked established communities, such as the Groklaw and Slashdot websites, to convene their own conversations about pending patent applications. We then asked them to forward the best of those conversations to us.

Ask the Right People

Another lesson of Peer-to-Patent is the importance of finding the right people to participate in answering questions and, as a corollary, the value of participant self-selection over traditional appointment and nomination methods. The Peer-to-Patent team did not—could not—identify all the world's experts on "thunking" (the subject matter of one of the applications). Only thunkers know who they are. Providing them with the opportunity to self-select was essential to boosting involvement.

Opening up an agency process to self-selection is not the same as traditional notice-and-comment rulemaking, which allows anyone to submit a comment to the agency. Notice-and-comment rulemaking attracts the usual Beltway lawyers, lobbyists, and interest groups, not outsiders. In contrast, Peer-to-Patent reaches the blogosphere—students and engineers, academics, and technologists—by promoting the opportunity to get involved via listservs and through channels that would reach non-patent professionals. Peer-to-Patent also weeds out potentially low-value participants by requiring contributors to respond to well-articulated questions through structured processes.

We could also imagine setting explicit standards for participation, whether on the basis of time commitment or qualifications. Diversity of skill or disposition may be taken into account when volunteers are sought. The success of Peer-to-Patent stems from a diverse community of reformers. Also, unlike in notice-and-comment rulemaking, participation in Peer-to-Patent demands joining an ongoing group whose members are responsive and responsible to one another. Peer-to-Patent also provides feedback to those groups in order to elicit the best submissions.

Self-selection also has the advantage of reducing the workload on officials of having to select, convene, and then maintain an expert group. Prestigious professionals may want care and feeding—attention paid to them as members of a standing committee. But an open network, whose members self-select to participate and from which volunteers can be chosen when needed, may decrease the workload on the agency. Although letting people self-select gives an agency less control over the consultative process, the agency can improve output from the volunteers by creating a sense of empowerment, freedom, and play. London School of Economics professor Claudio Ciborra writes in *Labyrinths of Information* about such self-organized practices:

> They tend to include an added element of ingenuity, experience, and skill belonging to the individual[s] and their community of practice rather than to the organizational systems. . . . Small forces, tiny interventions, and on-the-fly add-ons lead, when performed skillfully and with close attention to the local context, to momentous consequences, unrelated to the speed and scope of the initial intervention . . . on-the-fly appearance but deeply rooted in personal and collective skill and experience.

That said, new collaborative projects can usefully include both selected and self-selected expertise. If an agency has built up a network of experts who regularly advise it, the collaborative project might invite members of that network to self-select to participate in the new project. At the same time, the project might also reach out to bipartisan experts or those known to hold a view that would inform the discussion. This method also works with public consultation. The agency might solicit the input of a scientific advisory board of its choosing to discuss clean energy. That board, in turn, might hold an online brainstorming event with self-selected members of the public to elicit new ideas on the topic. By asking structured and specific questions, the board could generate information that the small group might not know. It might run a crowdsourcing exercise and ask the public to provide examples of best practices of pollution control or green cities. The board might ask members of particular science and environmental organizations to get involved.

Design the Process for the Desired End

Participation must not be undertaken for its own sake. As chapter 6 explains, the democratic mandate to engage in outreach under certain statutory conditions has led to anemic practices of participation, which are often of little relevance to decisionmakers and less value to the public. Instead, it is important to design the right process. This requires breaking down the desired end into discrete steps; understanding the problems at each stage from the perspective of different users or stakeholders; identifying the incentives for each group; and then pinpointing possible strategies, whether that strategy is a change of process, a legal amendment, or a special technology that might lead to the desired result. The pros and cons and the challenges of implementation for each approach should be identified.

This means that one-size-fits-all software solutions such as wikis or blogs do not substitute for rethinking underlying ways of working. For example, if participation in notice-and-comment rulemaking were designed such that the agency posed questions and then groups collaborated on responses to those questions, agencies might benefit from more useful expertise in connection with draft rules. The public's democratic right could be transformed into a more meaningful practice. Similarly, while the Freedom of Information Act affords the public a legal right to solicit information from an agency, if a mechanism (and a single website) were designed by which requests could be routed to the appropriate agency, the rationale for refusal uploaded, and the entire process rendered transparent and archived, the labyrinthine way FOIA requests now work could be transformed.

Designing for the desired end also means that groups need to understand clearly what is being asked of them. Being transparent about the purpose helps to ensure that people are not being asked to engage in make-work. One ubiquitous example drives the point home: We are familiar with having to type in the 6 or 7 captcha letters to identify ourselves as human before completing an e-commerce transaction. Internet users daily are forced enter 60 million captchas, amounting to 150,000 manpower hours each day. The Recaptcha project transforms this mindless typing exercise into a useful project by having people transcribe public domain books instead. Many of these classic books are now available as images and not text and cannot therefore be searched and used.

While we have no choice but to type in captcha or recaptcha when shopping, we do have a choice about participating in government processes. Hence when the U.K. prime minister's e-petitions website does not tell the public how their input will be used, it leads to thousands of duplicative and irrelevant proposals. The fact that petitions have no political weight at all is not articulated up front, resulting in criticism and dissatisfaction with the site. In Peer-to-Patent, we had to be open about the goals—goals that were different for patent examiners, patent practitioners, and public peer reviewers. There is no one right approach to asking and eliciting needed information. The choice of the methodology and tools will depend upon the desired results.

There is also no one right technology, though the technology does exist today and can, in many cases, be cheaply acquired to organize large-scale collaborative work. Certain kinds of questions require the use of networked computers to answer complex, data-intensive questions. The aggregation of information may be automated and the resulting intelligence both emergent and subject to interpretation by specialists. The SETI@Home project, for example, uses Internet-connected computers in the search for extraterrestrial intelligence (SETI). By linking computers together in a grid, SETI leverages the computing power of 3 million users to scan for sentient life. Another project, the Canadian Help Conquer Cancer initiative, connects the volunteered computer processing power of 330,000 computers. The resulting grid is the power equivalent of one of the fastest supercomputers, allowing the research team to analyze 86 million images and 9,400 unique proteins that could be linked to cancer.

These emergent solutions can be applied to human as well as machine intelligence—what I call a social grid rather than a computing grid—to arrive at predictive answers. Prediction markets (see chapter 6) demonstrate that groups can accurately and successfully make forecasts when large numbers of answers are aggregated, and information scientists are exploring the possibilities for harnessing such wisdom of the crowd to make prognostications about policy outcomes. However, these probabilistic mechanisms have limited applications. By itself, the wisdom of the crowd is actually quite dumb, pointing to a need to solicit expert intelligence, not simply an aggregation of votes or push-button opinions.

Peer-to-Patent is designed to solicit just such information, using wiki-style techniques for gathering information combined with Digg-style techniques for winnowing that information. Such a design is necessary to help the Patent Office identify a large number of discrete answers to a problem for which there is no one correct answer. Similarly, the NASA Clickworkers project, a citizen science project, used public volunteers with no prior scientific background to identify and classify the age of craters and land forms on Mars. On another front, the Central Intelligence Agency is exploring ways to set up a web-based system that will allow experts to identify and communicate potential security problems arising from environmental disasters like massive earthquakes and tsunamis.

DESIGN FOR GROUPS, NOT INDIVIDUALS

Working in groups rather than individually offers several important advantages both for the government agencies in need of usable information and solutions to problems and for those who participate in the process.

If Peer-to-Patent used the notice-and-comment approach, which directs individuals to submit information, instead of being designed for groups to work together, the process would have been difficult to manage and the resulting product less likely to be of help to the USPTO. But beyond mere utility, collaboration has the effect of mutual reinforcement and motivation. Enthusiasm for collective action is bolstered by the ability to be effective and powerful, and power is in turn created by a shared enthusiasm for working together. Whether examining a patent application, producing a community newsletter, or staging a revolution, people feel themselves to be part of something larger when they take part in a group-based, participatory process. Freud writes of the "oceanic feeling" of being enveloped by the group.[2]

The state of Virginia used a volunteer group to improve its physics curriculum statewide, since outdated physics textbooks were not scheduled for standards review until 2010 and lacked any content in emerging subjects such as modeling and simulation viewed as critical to Virginia's future technology economy. The Virginia Department of Education partnered with a nonprofit technology company to manage the process of creating the group (which included a peer review process). Around the core group of authors, the Virginia authority built a community of physics educators, who used and customized the materials. In 2009 the Department of Education published *Physics Flexbook,* an open-source collaborative high school textbook designed to supplement existing educational materials. From initial call for volunteers to finished product took six months and cost nothing.

Working in such groups makes it easier for individuals to participate in short bursts of time, without sacrificing other interests and commitments. Equally important, it creates many opportunities—like poking holes in dud patent applications—to make participation enjoyable and engaging. For the patent enthusiast and the person with knowledge to contribute, Peer-to-Patent is enjoyable because it has an impact. Who does not have fun answering a question to which she knows the answer?

Who does not enjoy demonstrating mastery and expertise? Who would not want public recognition as a prior artist? Many of the experiments with civic engagement emerging online seem to be fun and could be designed to be even more so. By adapting some of the techniques that draw players into collaborative games, such as World of Warcraft, these projects could do even more to sustain the enthusiasm that is at the heart of the most powerful online groups.

Use the Screen to Show the Group Back to Itself

As discussed in chapter 5 in detail, the importance of designing engagement practices to convey the sense of working together bears repeating as a key design lesson. People need to perceive themselves as part of a team, or minimovement, in order for them to work more effectively together across a distance. Of course, a minimum degree of openness and transparency is a baseline prerequisite. (Many government data, including patents, are stored as images rather than text, making that information difficult to use and not subject to search.) But making practices, people, and data intelligible in visual and graphic formats whenever possible gives the members of a collaborating group the nudge they need to organize across a distance.

In the past, the feeling of groupness depended on gathering many people together in a single place. Today, technology can take the place of physical proximity. The Sunlight Foundation, formed to uncover and document congressional abuses and errors, is one example of an organization that uses web-based interfaces effectively to run group collaborations. Its projects transform subjective, free-wheeling, dynamic amateurs into effective communities of congressional watchdogs. Wikipedia's clear outlines and rules lead to the planet's most comprehensive encyclopedia. "Mapping" techniques make it easier for members of a squad of volunteers who are working to inspect local school science labs or check broadband quality to sense themselves as part of a larger, national or regional movement and to know what work needs to be done.

Divide Work into Roles and Tasks

The two prescriptions for working in groups and using technology to show the group on the screen depend upon a third design requirement.

The work has to be parceled out into smaller tasks. Peer-to-Patent, like Wikipedia, works because there are smaller tasks that people can self-assign to do in a reasonable amount of time. The screen can make it possible for people to perceive the available roles and choose their own. But the process has to contemplate how the work will be "chunked."

Scratch, a wildly successful web-based software platform developed at the MIT Media Lab, provides a good analogy for thinking about how work can be broken down and structured. Scratch teaches kids to write software by giving them visual building blocks, each representing a basic function that can be "snapped" onto another block, like Lego pieces, to create an executable program that runs and performs a task, such as moving a cartoon character across the screen or making the character on the screen dance.

Similarly, the gathering and analysis of information upon which decisionmaking in government institutions depends can often be usefully parceled out into smaller parts. For example, Peer-to-Patent divides up the prior art submission process into discrete but interlocking functions that together yield information useful to the Patent Office. Users can assume the role of discussant, prior art uploader, annotator, or voter. The site's visual interface helps each participant assume a role, know what is expected of her, and contribute to the group work.

In a sense, parceling out assignments is no different from the way social movements have always operated. While some people write the handbills, others do the printing. Some drive people to the polls, while others make the coffee. The difference today is that the costs of coordinating distributed work have gone down. The visual nature of technology can make it possible for people to perceive the available roles and choose their own rather than having them assigned.

HARNESS THE POWER OF REPUTATION

Peer-to-Patent uses a rating system to encourage participants to vet each other's submissions and to take some of the burden of having to evaluate public submissions off the agency. Open, wiki-style, peer production enables many people to contribute information through the use of a common online environment, while the Digg-style ranking features help to limit the quantity and prioritize the quality of the public submissions.

Peer-to-Patent combines peer evaluation of content by means of an up-or-down vote with rating and reputation points for the participants themselves in the form of the prior artist award. Organizations are increasingly using such bubbling-up websites to solicit information in response to specific questions and allowing people to rate the submissions by means of starts, numbers, or thumbs up and down.

This style of crowdsourcing is a practical method to ask carefully circumscribed questions of a group. If drafted well, the request need not be to rate the best answers but simply, as in Peer-to-Patent, the most relevant ones. The crowdsourcing technique of posing a targeted question, allowing participants to submit answers, and then having them rate each other's response for relevance is in widespread use on political websites: Dell's Ideastorm, Netroots Nation's Ask the Speaker, Big Dialog's Ask the President Elect, White House 2, Google's Knol, and Ameritocracy. Such a technique could also, say, generate examples of successful open-government projects on a state and local level or identify the best green innovations.

Having users rate each other's information as a way to organize a large amount of input is only one way to use feedback to organize public participation practices. Peer-to-Patent also appoints prior artists on the basis of USPTO feedback. The rating and reputation of data and people can be combined to maximal effect.

Make Policies, Not Websites

Improved practices of engagement cannot be created through technology alone. A systems-based approach that looks at the problem as a whole, focusing on internal processes, helps to identify the opportunities for collaboration. Instead of focusing on the specific language of statutory patent reform in isolation, the New York Law School Peer-to-Patent team approached the patent application backlog as a larger problem of innovation in the system as a whole. We were able to zero in on practices of patent examination as a component that could improve institutional competence—a small change that might catalyze larger, systemic reform. Recall that in the CityScan project in Connecticut a community of teens and seniors used new tools to monitor the cleanup of rundown buildings. The project succeeded because the organizers of CityScan negotiated a strategy for working together with the government. They approached the project from back-end processes rather than looking only at the front-end use of tools.

Focusing on internal policies and practices shifts the attention from one-off instances of consultation to the creation of a culture and platform for ongoing, collaborative engagement. After all, Peer-to-Patent could have come up with a most beautiful website, but had the project not worked with agency officials to ensure that its technology responded to the needs of their workplace practices, the project could not have succeeded. In addition, we had to factor in the relevant patent law and policy to ensure that what we were proposing would either be legal or be able to find an appropriate work-around. Unlike a traditional technology design project for a corporate client, where a prototype is constructed in response to a request from the marketing department, Peer-to-Patent had to take into account the needs and incentives of agency officials, patent system stakeholders, and public volunteers.

Those wishing to create such participatory initiatives in the future must step back from participatory practices in isolation and, instead, map out how the agency gets expertise and where it falls short. The Office of Management and Budget sponsors the Expect More website to track the performance of government projects. It is not hard to imagine Participate More, a similar website that tracks the success of departmental efforts to engage expertise from "the edge." Only by understanding the complete picture of how the institution obtains expertise to make decisions can one then begin to construct the software platforms to fulfill the needs of collaborating groups.

PILOT NEW IDEAS

The newness of these technology-fueled approaches to governance requires an explicitly evolutionary approach. Peer-to-Patent was, after all, an experiment, which changed over time and will get better still. It is important to give personnel the incentives—budgetary and cultural—and the mechanisms for trying new ideas, failing, and trying again. Competitions that offer monetary rewards or reputational prizes offer an incentive to generate new ideas, whether from government officials within an agency or across departments or branches of government or from the public. Competitions could be open-ended invitations to brainstorm new ideas, though more structured requests for innovative ways to solve particular problems will lead to more concrete, better-defined answers. But encouraging participation and the generation of new ideas is far more important than ensuring precision in the ideas that are submitted. It is therefore important not to over-constrain the process.

In chapter 7 I talked about the idea of a government innovation lab as a potentially useful testing ground for new tools and processes. White house.gov and the home pages of agencies—which deliver authoritative information about law, policy, and vital citizen services—might not be the place to experiment with untested methodologies. But without experimentation there can be no innovation. Pilot programs that set clear expectations about their experimental nature are another way to try new approaches with a public audience. Peer-to-Patent makes it clear to users up front that the project is a trial based on a limited number of patent applications with inventor consent.

FOCUS ON OUTCOMES, NOT INPUTS

One of the central themes of this book is the importance of collaboration (as distinct from deliberation) as a form of participatory democracy. Typically, democratic theory focuses on the inputs to participation, namely the representative character of participants, the procedural rules by which they interact, and the fairness of access to the participatory process. By contrast, collaboration focuses on the outcomes of people's shared work. The assumption is that the ability to be powerful together benefits the individuals who get involved and, more important, leads to more effective outcomes. The results of collaborative projects should be measured for their success at achieving desired goals rather than on the basis of procedural criteria. In particular because collaboration—the processes and the tools to enable it—must first be designed and potentially redesigned, it is vital to assess what works and what does not.

Such a focus on outcomes therefore necessitates articulating the organization's core objective to be achieved, whether it is promoting a legislative agenda, achieving compliance with a new rule, ascertaining the best science to make a decision in the public interest, or encouraging creative solutions to a thorny problem. *Performance management* has become a popular public policy buzzword for the same concept. Performance management calls for rewarding workers on the basis of a program's outcomes rather than on the basis of credentials or inputs. It also implies generating more transparent data, which can be used to study the effectiveness of decisions and programs. But this is a new idea that ties together effective governance with citizen participation strategies.

THE BIGGER PICTURE: REDESIGNING GOVERNANCE

The Peer-to-Patent experience demonstrates the importance of thinking about how to *design* participation to address the institution's goals. Even the august National Academy of Sciences recognizes the value of designing the appropriate process to meet the challenge:

> Public participation should be fully incorporated into environmental assessment and decisionmaking processes, and it should be recognized by government agencies and other organizers of the processes as a requisite of effective action, not merely a formal procedural requirement. . . . Agencies undertaking a public participation process should, considering the purposes of the process, design it to address the challenges that arise from particular contexts. . . . There is no single best format or set of procedures for achieving good outcomes in all situations.[3]

If nothing else, Peer-to-Patent teaches us that design matters.[4] By design, I do not mean technology alone but also the combination of technology, law, and policy. In Peer-to-Patent, we approached the project as a design exercise. Our goal was not to build a website, a law, or a workplace practice but to create a collaboration system that would bridge the gap between the Patent Office and the scientific public. Thinking as designers freed us from thinking only as lawyers or technologists or patent specialists and pointed the way toward a new design science for government, that of designing digital institutions.

The aim of the team was to engage in what I term democratic software design (*democratic,* here understood with a small *d,* as a way of living and working). Democratic software design does not refer to the process of making the software but to the resulting civic, participatory, and collaborative uses. The task is particularly challenging because it is so new. Traditional software design focuses on ensuring that the screens through which people interact with the machine are familiar and easy to use. (There is a mantra in e-commerce that the shopping cart should be no more than one click away.) In contrast, democratic software design involves creating screens that guide people through novel and potentially complex practices that may be unknown to them, like public participation in a patent examination. It also requires situating designs in the social and legal context of hidebound institutions. Democratic software design cannot center on people's existing expectations but should push both institutional players and participating citizens to learn a new idiom of collaboration. Democratic design is reminiscent of what Buckminster Fuller calls "comprehensive, anticipatory design science."[5]

Using technology to drive law reform is explicitly evolutionary. We can iterate new versions of the social and institutional "operating system," but instead of Windows 1.0 and 2.0, we are striving to create better decisionmaking practices. The speed with which we can update software—as opposed to the long delays often involved in updating laws—allows us to respond efficiently to empirical data. Technologists believe in rough consensus, running code. Try something, see how it works, iterate, and try again.

EAST COAST CODE AND WEST COAST CODE

The idea of lawyers designing anything, let alone software, may be counterintuitive even to those who study cyberlaw. Typically, lawyers work through legal institutions—namely, Congress and the court system—to bring about reform. Lawyers generally do not regard technology design as within their purview. Lawyers write "East Coast" code: traditional legislation, regulation, and common law. They do not write "West Coast" code: software. Lawyers focus on technology policy, the law that controls access to and use of new technologies. For example, activists campaign for net neutrality provisions in telecommunications law to ensure that companies cannot discriminate among the websites, platforms, and tools traveling down their high-speed data pipes. Such "copy leftists" want to change the intellectual property laws to give a wider berth to fair use in the face of new tools for ripping, mixing, and burning. These statutes and doctrines that ensure open access to the conduits and content of communication help to ensure our individual rights and liberties in a new technological era.

There has been some recent attention paid to technology design by the courts. In April 2008 the Ninth Circuit Court of Appeals handed down a decision in *Fair Housing Council* v. *Roommate.com* that turned on the design, and not exclusively the content, of the website. The court determined that the site's mandatory drop-down menus, where users must specify answers to questions about sex, sexual orientation, and presence of children in the house, offend antidiscrimination laws. In other words, if questions had been presented on the screen as open ended, that is, "fill-in-the-blanks," the Roommate.com website might not have been liable. But because a customer could not use the service without use of the drop-down menus, the design created a discriminatory situation.

In another case, the liability of such peer-to-peer file-sharing services as Grokster for indirect copyright infringement hinged, in the court's analysis, in part upon design.[6] The organization of the website and the underlying communications protocols were deemed to have induced their users to infringe the copyrights of music publishers. The *Arriba Soft* case, also in the Ninth Circuit, turned on the question of whether, when a search engine makes a thumbnail-sized reproduction of an artist's work online, this constitutes fair use or if the technology aided and abetted infringement.[7]

In 2006 the Sixth Circuit Court of Appeals in *Stewart* v. *Blackwell* held that the use in certain Ohio districts of punch cards and other outdated voting technologies, which fail to provide notification and confirmation of a vote, lead to "statistically significant disparities between the levels of residual voting among African American and non–African American voters."[8] The court acknowledged that the choice of technology made the difference between the right to vote and disenfranchisement. The state later abandoned use of the machines.

Laws about access to polling places are essential, but voting machines that accurately count votes play as much, if not more, of a role in safeguarding our democracy. The design of the interfaces through which humans interact with technology, be it the computer, cell phone screen, or voting machine, can quite literally determine the scope of our rights to interact with government. Whereas intellectual property law prevents government from copyrighting public information, and transparency legislation mandates that government publish information online, software ensures that that information will be accessible. If data about healthcare or the environment are not in an open and user-friendly format, the design short-circuits opportunities for engagement. When an electronic rulemaking site says "click here to comment," it forecloses many opportunities for participation.

But as Peer-to-Patent teaches, lawyers and policymakers can also apply legal principles to the design of technological environments. When the country of Mongolia wanted to build out its telecommunications infrastructure, the responsible lawyers and policymakers reported that the greatest challenge the decisionmakers faced was not writing the legal rules on licenses but how to design the phone booth: the Mongolian government wanted to create a kiosk big enough for two Mongols in full sheepskin winter wear to stand in, but not big enough to use as a barn to corral their sheep. This vignette captures the notion that, instead of policy about technology, lawyers can create technology for policymaking and technology that helps to achieve the same goals as law.

Why should the White House website or the website for citizen participation in regulatory rulemaking (regulations.gov) be designed and built by engineers at Lockheed-Martin (as they are) instead of by the community of policymakers and experts inside and outside the agency who can identify values and goals, not just technological possibilities? If lawyers, policymakers, and government officials are indeed interested in the pursuit of social justice and the deepening of democracy, then it is incumbent upon these communities to care about technology and technological designs. Law and other professional schools ought to get into the business of "doing design" and equipping students with technological literacy as part of their training. At the very least, because technology is a means to communicate widely, it is a necessary means to achieving ends more effectively and efficiently.

By confining cyberlaw to litigation and legislation without including technology design, we limit the opportunity to experiment more rapidly and flexibly. Design science celebrates failing early and often until the right design is achieved. For lawyers, there is no success in failure. By not embracing the culture of design, however, we "domesticate" the field of cyberlaw unnecessarily. For example, high-profile and painfully slow litigation drives education reform, but well-designed student information systems that help educators manage student performance data—such as grade and attendance records, disciplinary and health information—may also promote educational equity. School officials could keep better track, for example, of those students in foster care who are shuttled from school to school and are therefore at risk of falling through the cracks. Designed wrong, this information—and the affected students—may get lost. Neither litigation nor legislation can overcome the problem. But computer scientists and engineers by themselves cannot build the legitimate, democratic institutions of the future. Knowing what technology makes possible does not imply an understanding of what the law allows. Changing the way that agencies work demands knowledge of how they organize information and communication.

Academics, for the most part, also have a poor track record at going beyond theory to practice. The demands of tenure and professional advancement emphasize publication over practicality, credit over collaboration, footnotes over feasibility, and social science over saving the world. Philanthropies, such as the Lance Armstrong Foundation, the Multiple Myeloma Foundation, and AOL founder Steve Case's foundation that studies brain cancer are all refusing to fund academic researchers unless they abandon the proprietary model, share data, and collaborate to produce cures. Left to their own devices, academics might also impose strictures to preserve replicable social science that may get in the way of trying replicable social practice. Just as medical cures need to work on people as well as mice, it is necessary to move from controlled, lab-based experiments about citizen participation to experiments situated in the real world: social science in situ.

By contrast, a law-plus-technology strategy such as Peer-to-Patent, which brings technologists together with lawyers, policymakers, educators, and other experts with complementary skills, made it possible to devise solutions that incorporated both kinds of code: code as law and code as software. Peer-to-Patent is, after all, a website. But it is also a process that depends upon a thorough understanding of the legal rules and policy context of the patent system. We needed to know how the screen should look but also how the examiner might do her job differently as a result of the technology. Politicians can post an e-mail address, but there must also be someone at the other end to read the mail and a process in place to make use of it. Even the most sophisticated web tools, blogs, wikis, and social networking sites designed for collaboration and engagement are ineffective without a willingness and ability to change the back-end processes of government.

The interdisciplinary approach of using technology together with law and policy is inherently hopeful and optimistic; it is not mired in political cynicism or compromise. Whereas Congress has not passed major patent reform legislation since 1952, the Peer-to-Patent pilot project went from

idea to prototype to software pilot in one year. To view reified legal institutions as the exclusive locus of law reform blinds us to the opportunities
that technology creates to be more inclusive of citizens participating in
government and solving problems outside of it.

POWER AND COLLABORATIVE DEMOCRACY

The potential for engaging people in government decisionmaking
through technology is about empowering individuals. Ordinary people
come together across distances to debate a proposal and also to decide
it. Communities bring collective wisdom to bear and also take action.

The political philosopher Hannah Arendt wrote: "Power corresponds
to the human ability not just to act but to act in concert. Power is never
the property of an individual; it belongs to a group and remains in existence only so long as the group keeps together."[9] When we set our minds
to something and work in concert to make it happen, we are powerful.
Put another way, together, we can accomplish what we cannot do alone.

Collaboration yields better information. We should want government
to make the best-informed decisions possible. But collaboration also
enables individuals to become more effective. As Kenneth Arrow, the
Nobel Prize–winning economist succinctly puts it, "Collective action is a
means of power, a means by which individuals can more fully realize
their individual values."[10] The more effective we become as individuals
by participating in communities of governance, the more powerful we
become as citizens participating in the life of our democracy.

We are drawn to the collaboration enabled by the Internet. We are
willing to engage in peer production. Even in the absence of hierarchical
firms or markets, we write for Wikipedia or contribute time to a MeetUp
or examine a patent application. It used to be that collective action
required geographical proximity: I had to be near you to join you. Technology revolutionizes our capacity for purposive collective action by geographically remote actors. Without physical presence or the need to man
the barricades, we discover what Howard Zinn calls "people power."[11]

Power is ultimately the defining concept of politics. It also has the
potential to be the defining political conception of the Internet. Power
can be understood as either relational or substantive. For those who
view power as relational, such as Hobbes, Michel Foucault, and Harold

Lasswell, it is defined as the ability to dominate other social groups. The organization and use of technology can be a means to the end of domination. Our view of bureaucracy as the sole source of legitimate decision-making authority emerges from this nasty, brutish, and short worldview of government. By contrast, collaborative democracy derives from a substantive view that focuses on the power, as Bertrand Russell describes, to "produce intended effects" or what Edmund Burke calls the "liberty, when men act in bodies."[12] We can conceive of "power over" as "power to" and produce the operational mechanisms for collective action.

The traditional link between the public and policymaking has been the voting booth. But that once-a-year process is severely anemic; it deprives government of all that citizens have to offer and strips citizenship of the robust opportunities for greater participation and engagement. While we have ballot measures and referenda, these direct democratic measures allow for only a thumbs-up or thumbs-down vote. And deliberation limits involvement to only talk. Ordinary citizens have more to offer than voting or talking. They can contribute their expertise and, in so doing, realize the opportunity now to be powerful. The official no longer needs to be the sole decisionmaker. Instead, new technology can help bridge the chasm between public participation and public policy in issues ranging from climate change to patents. Collaborative governance is an idea whose time has come.

NOTES

CHAPTER ONE

1. One study found that the signaling value of patents accounted for increased investment in the semiconductor industry. If a start-up doubles the number of its patent applications, it is likely to see a 24 percent rise in early-stage valuation. David Hsu and Rosemary Ziedonis, "Patents as Quality Signals for Entrepreneurial Ventures," *Academy of Management Best Paper Proceedings* (2008), p. 2.

2. Sealed crustless sandwich, U.S. Patent 6004596 (filed December 8, 1977; rejected in reexamination December 16, 2003).

3. U.S. Constitution, Article I, sec. 8, cl. 8.

4. U.S. Patent and Trademark Office, "Performance and Accountability Report Fiscal Year 2007" (www.uspto.gov/web/offices/com/annual/2007/2007 annualreport.pdf [July 2008]), p. 13.

5. See for example Bioinformatic transaction scheme, U.S. Patent 20080208916 (filed May 1, 2008); Basic poetry generation, U.S. Patent 7,184,949 (filed May 10, 2002).

6. USPTO, Patent Examiner Qualifications (www.uspto.gov/go/ac/ahrpa/ohr/jobs/qualifications.htm [July 2008]).

7. Under *Code of Federal Regulations* 37, sec. 1.56 (known as Rule 56), the applicant has a duty to use candor and good faith with the Patent Office in the examination process. This means that he must disclose any present and conscious awareness of material information, but it does not create an affirmative duty to search.

8. Patent Act, 37 U.S.C., sec. 102 (2000) (novelty as a requirement of patentability).

9. See letter from Thomas Jefferson to James Hutchinson, March 12, 1791, in *The Papers of Thomas Jefferson,* vol. 19, edited by Julian P. Boyd (Princeton University Press, 1974), p. 614. ("Congress having referred to me a petition from a person of the name of Isaacs, setting forth that he has discovered an easy method of rendering sea-water potable, I have had a cask of sea-water procured, & the petitioners have created a small apparatus in my office, in order to exhibit his process. Monday morning 10 o'clock is fixed on as the time for doing it. It would give me great satisfaction to be assisted on the occasion by your chemical knowledge, & the object of the letter I have taken the liberty of writing is to ask whether it would be convenient for you to be present at the time & place before mentioned, which, besides contributing to a public good, will much oblige, Sir, Your most obedient & most humble servant, Th. Jefferson.")

10. USPTO website (www.uspto.gov/go/cio/oitp/ [September 29, 2008]).

11. USPTO, "Patent Public Advisory Committee Meeting: Public Session, Feb. 9, 2007" (www.uspto.gov/web/offices/com/advisory/acrobat/ppac_transcript_020907.pdf [August 2008]), pp. 13–15. See also U.S. Government Accountability Office, "Intellectual Property: USPTO Has Made Progress in Hiring Examiners, but Challenges to Retention Remain," GAO-05-720 (2005), p. 28 ("Depending on the type of patent and the skill level of the examiner, each examiner is expected to process an average of 87 applications per year at a rate of 19 hours per application"); Kevin Maney, "Patent Applications So Abundant That Examiners Can't Catch Up," *USA Today,* September 21, 2005, p. B3.

12. This number is projected to reach 1.4 million in 2012. See USPTO, "Strategic Report 2007–12" (www.uspto.gov/web/offices/com/strat2007/stratplan20072007-2012.pdf [August 2008]), p. 11.

13. Federal News Radio, interview with John Doll, June 15, 2007 (www.federalnewsradio.com).

14. World Intellectual Property Organization, *The World Patent Report: A Statistical Review* (Brussels: United Nations, 2008), p. 23.

15. Solar Navigator.net, "IMDB: The Internet Movie Data Base" (www.solarnavigator.net/films_movies_actors/imdb_internet_movie_data_base.htm [September 2008]).

16. Oh My News International (english.ohmynews.com/index.asp [September 2008]).

17. Moon Ihlwan, "In Korea, NHN Makes Google a Midget," *Business Week Online,* September 9, 2008 (www.businessweek.com/globalbiz/content/sep2008/gb2008095_505433.htm [September 2008]).

18. Asa Dotzler, "180 Million Firefox Users: Great Birthday Present," June 5, 2008 (weblogs.mozillazine.org/asa/archives/2008/06/180million_fir.html [October 15, 2008]).

19. Beth S. Noveck, "Peer-to-Patent: A Modest Proposal," July 14, 2005 (cairns.typepad.com/blog/2005/07/index.html [July 2005]).

20. Daniel Terdiman, "Web Could Unclog Patent Backlog," July 14, 2005 (www.wired.com/science/discoveries/news/2005/07/68186 [October 2008]).

21. *2007 IBM Annual Report* (www.ibm.com/annualreport/2007 [March 2008]).

22. James Bessen and Michael J. Meurer, *Patent Failure* (Princeton University Press, 2008), p. 22.

23. Linda S. Sanford, *Let Go to Grow* (New York: Prentice-Hall Professional Technical Reference, 2006), p. 4. Sanford calculates that 16 percent of 1,008 large companies survived during the thirty-year period 1962–98.

24. USPTO Official Gazette Notice, "Pilot Concerning Public Submission of Peer Reviewed Prior Art," June 26, 2007 (www.uspto.gov/web/offices/pac/dapp/opla/preognotice/peerreviewpilot.pdf [October 2008]).

25. Nicholas Varchaver, "Patent Review Goes Wiki," *Fortune,* August 16, 2006, p. 18; Alan Sipress, "Open Call from the Patent Office," *Washington Post,* March 5, 2007, p. A1.

26. Peer-to-Patent website (www.peertopatent.org).

27. "Peer-to-Patent First Anniversary Report" (June 2008) (dotank.nyls.edu/communitypatent/P2Panniversaryreport.pdf [September 2008]), p. 6.

28. Carl J. Schramm and Robert E. Litan, "The Growth Solution," *American* (July/August 2008): 3.

29. Jonathan Schwartz, "ZFS Puts Net App Viability at Risk?" October 24, 2007 (blogs.sun.com/jonathan/entry/harvesting_from_a_troll [October 2008]).

30. Barack Obama, "Science, Technology, and Innovation for a New Generation," November 14, 2007 (www.brackobama.com/pdf/issues/technology/fact_sheet_innovation_and_technology.pdf [October 2008]).

31. U.S. Chamber of Commerce, "Recommendations for Consideration by the Incoming Administration" (Washington: 2008), p. 7.

32. Jay Rosen, "The Future of Professionally Created Content," Legal Futures Conference, Stanford University, March 8, 2008.

33. "Evolution of Security" (www.tsa.gov/blog [September 2008]).

34. Eric Schmidt, "Technology, Economic Growth, and Open Government," New America Foundation, November 18, 2008 (www.newamerica.net/events/2008/eric_schmidt).

35. Thomas A. Kalil, "Leveraging Cyberspace," *IEEE Communications Magazine,* July 1996, pp. 82–86.

36. Don Tapscott and Anthony Williams, *Wikinomics: How Mass Collaboration Changes Everything* (New York: Portfolio, 2006).

37. IBM, "Majority of Global CEOs Plan Fundamental Change and Expect New Forms of Innovation to Drive Growth, According to IBM Study," news release, March 1, 2006 (www-03.ibm.com/press/us/en/pressrelease/19289.wss [October 2008]).

38. IBM Social Computing, "World Jam" (www.research.ibm.com/Social-Computing/WorldJam.htm [September 2008]); IBM, "IBM Invests $100 Million in Collaborative Innovation Ideas," news release, November 14, 2006 (www.03.ibm.com/press/us/en/pressrelease/20605.wss [October 2008]).

39. Karim R. Lakhani and Jill A. Panetta, "The Principles of Distributed Innovation," *Innovations* 2 (2007): 97–112.

40. Jeff Howe, "The Rise of Crowdsourcing," *Wired* 14.06, June 2006 (www.wired.com/wired/archive/14.06/crowds.html [December 2008]), pp. 1–4; Jeff Howe, *Crowdsourcing: Why the Power of the Crowd Is Driving the Future of Business* (New York: Crown Business, 2008), pp. 63–70.

41. Tapscott and Williams, *Wikinomics: How Mass Collaboration Changes Everything*.

Chapter Two

1. Max Weber, *Essays in Sociology,* edited by H. H. Gerth and C. Wright Mills (Oxford: Routledge, 1991), p. 216.

2. J. B. Ruhl and James Salzman, "In Defense of Regulatory Peer Review," *Washington University Law Review* 84 (2006): 1–61.

3. Philip E. Tetlock, *Expert Political Judgment: How Good Is It? How Can We Know?* (Princeton University Press, 2005), p. 20.

4. Ibid., p. 15.

5. Scott E. Page, *The Difference: How the Power of Diversity Creates Better Groups, Firms, Schools, and Societies* (Princeton University Press, 2007).

6. Joaquin Sapien, "Industry-Packed Federal Advisory Board Told DOE to Double U.S. Coal Consumption," May 19, 2008 (www.propublica.org/article [October 2008]).

7. Sonya Lunder and Jane Houlihan, "EPA Axes Panel Chair at Request of Chemical Industry Lobbyists," March 2008 (www.ewg.org/reports/decaconflict [October 2008]).

8. Union of Concerned Scientists, "Restoring Scientific Integrity in Policymaking: Scientists Sign-On Statement" (www.ucsusa.org/scientific_integrity/abuses_of_science.html [October 2008]).

9. Union of Concerned Scientists, "Interference at EPA: Science and Politics at the U.S. Environmental Protection Agency," April 23, 2008 (www.ucsusa.org/EPAscience [October 2008]).

10. Chris Mooney, *The Republican War on Science* (New York: Basic Books, 2005).

11. Government in the Sunshine Act, P.L. 409, 94th Cong. (September 13, 1976).

12. John Ashcroft, Memorandum for All Heads of Departments and Agencies, "The Freedom of Information Act," October 12, 2001.

13. Sunshine Week, "More People See Federal Government as Secretive; Nearly All Want to Know Where Candidates Stand on Transparency," March 15, 2008 (www.sunshineweek.org/sunshineweek/secrecypoll08 [October 2008]); Gup, *Nation of Secrets: The Threat to Democracy and the American Way of Life* (New York: Doubleday, 2007).

14. Amanda Terkel, "Bush Administration Hides More Data, Shuts Down Website Tracking U.S. Economic Indicators," February 13, 2008 (www.think progress.org/2008/02/13/economic-indicators [October 2008]).

15. Paul Kiel, "Bush Admin: What You Don't Know Can't Hurt Us, 2007 Version" November 23, 2007 (www.tpmmuckraker.talkingpointsmemo.com/ archives/004766.php [October 2008]).

16. Ibid.

17. American Inventors Protection Act, P.L. 113, 106th Cong. (November 29, 1999).

18. U.S. Patent and Trademark Office, *Manual of Patent Examining Procedures,* sec. 904.02(c) (8th ed., 2001) ("This policy also applies to use of the Internet as a communications medium for connecting to commercial database providers"); U.S. Patent and Trademark Office, "Patent Internet Usage Policy," 64 *Federal Register* (June 21, 1999) ("If security and confidentiality cannot be attained for a specific use, transaction, or activity, then that specific use, transaction, or activity shall NOT be undertaken/conducted"), p. 33060.

19. Carrotmob (www.carrotmob.org [October 2008]).

20. Obama Works (www.whyobamaworks.org [October 2008]).

21. Tech for Obama (www.techforobama.com [October 2008]).

22. Silicon Valley for Obama (www.sv4obama.com [October 2008]).

23. WashingtonWatch (www.washingtonwatch.com [October 2008]).

24. OpenSecrets (www.opensecrets.org [September 2008]); Fundrace (http:// fundrace.huffingtonpost.com [October 2008]).

25. PublicMarkup (www.publicmarkup.org [October 2008]); see also Ellen Miller, "You Can Markup the Bills on the Mortgage Industry Bail Out," September 22, 2008 (blog.sunlightfoundation.com/2008/09/22 [October 2008]).

26. MapLight (www.maplight.org [October 2008]).

27. Connecticut Policy and Economic Council (www.city-scan.org [October 2008]).

28. Frank Richard Cowell, *The Athenaeum: Club and Social Life in London, 1824–1974* (London: Heinemann, 1975).

29. Stephen M. Kosslyn, "On the Evolution of Human Motivation: The Role of Social Prosthetic Systems," in *Evolutionary Cognitive Neuroscience,* edited by S. M. Platek, T. K. Shackelford, and J. P. Keenan (MIT Press, 2006); A. W. Wooley and others, "Using Brain-Based Measures to Compose Teams: How Individual Capabilities and Team Collaboration Strategies Jointly Shape Performance," *Social Neuroscience* 2 (2007): 96–105.

30. Edward Day Collins, "Committees of Correspondence of the American Revolution," *Annual Report of the American Historical Association* (1901): 245–71.

31. Harvey Anderson, "Intellectual Property and Free Expression," lecture, Stanford University, May 27, 2008 (notes on file with author).

32. Mitchell Baker, Mozilla Foundation chairman of the board, "Summer 2008 Goals," May 14, 2008 (blog.lizardwrangler.com/2008/05/14 [October 2008]).

33. "Energy Bill Bans Incandescent Lightbulbs." For more on mercury in lightbulbs, see the EPA website (www.epa.gov/epawaste/hazard/wastetypes/universal/lamps/index.htm [October 2008]). For more on the congressional mandate, see Matthew Wald, "A U.S. Alliance to Update the Lightbulb," *New York Times,* March 14, 2007, p. C3.

34. Henry Fountain, "A Cloth to Cut the Mercury Risk from Lightbulbs," *New York Times,* July 8, 2008, p. F3.

35. Frank Newport, "Bush's 69% Job Disapproval Rating Highest in Gallup History," April 22, 2008 (www.gallup.com/poll/106741 [October 2008]); "Congressional Approval Falls to Single Digits for First Time Ever," July 8, 2008 (www.rasmussenreports.com/public_content/politics/mood_of_america/congressional_performance [October 2008]).

36. "Series of Tubes" (en.wikipedia.org/wiki [October 2008]). Also see the Series of Tubes weblog (www.seriesoftubes.net [October 2008]). The remark also spawned a graphic, "The Series of Tubes Subway Map" (www.boingboing.net/2007/07/20 [October 2008]).

37. See, for example, Andrew Chadwick, *Internet Politics: States, Citizens, and New Communications Technologies* (Oxford University Press, 2006).

38. Beth Simone Noveck, "A Democracy of Groups," *First Monday* (December 2005) (www.firstmonday.org/issues/issues10_11/noveck/).

39. Thomas E. Cronin, *Direct Democracy: The Politics of Initiative, Referendum, and Recall* (Harvard University Press, 2006).

40. Charles Krauthammer, "Ross Perot and the Call In Presidency," *Time,* July 13, 1992, p. 84.

41. Center for Tele-Democracy (fp.auburn.edu/tann [October 2008]). See also Direct Democracy League (www.ddleague-usa.net [October 2008]).

42. Eugene Volokh, "How Might Cyberspace Change American Politics," *Loyola Los Angeles Law Review* 34 (2001): 1213–20.

43. The company was Vivarto Inc., founded by Mikael Nordfors. Its website is still online (www.vivarto.com [October 2008]).

44. "The U.S. Congress Votes Database" (projects.washingtonpost.com/congress/rss [October 2008]); Darlene Meskell, "New Opportunities for Involving Citizens in the Democratic Process," *USA Services Inter-Governmental Newsletter* 20 (Fall 2007): 1–3 (www.usaservices.gov/events_news/documents/USA ServicesNewsletterFall-07.pdf [December 2008]).

45. Bruce A. Ackerman and James Fishkin, *Deliberation Day* (Yale University Press, 2004); James S. Fishkin, *Debating Democracy and Deliberation: New*

Directions for Democratic Reform (Yale University Press, 1991); James Bohman, *Public Deliberation: Pluralism, Complexity, and Democracy* (MIT Press, 1996).

46. Diana C. Mutz, *Hearing the Other Side: Deliberative versus Participatory Democracy* (Cambridge University Press, 2006).

47. Cass Sunstein, *Why Societies Need Dissent* (Harvard University Press, 2003), p. 118.

48. Ann Macintosh and Stephen Coleman, "Promise and Problems of E-Democracy: Challenges of Online Citizen Engagement" (Paris: OECD, 2003).

49. Peter M. Shane, ed., *Democracy Online: The Prospects for Political Renewal through the Internet* (New York: Routledge, 2004).

50. Karen Czapanskiy and Rashida Manjoo, "The Right of Public Participation in the Law-Making Process and the Role of the Legislature in the Promotion of This Right," *University of Maryland School of Law Legal Studies* 42 (2008): 31.

51. Alexander Meiklejohn, *Political Freedom: The Constitutional Powers of the People* (New York: Harper, 1960).

52. Edward Wyatt with Charles V. Bagli, "Visions of Ground Zero: The Public; Officials Rethink Building Proposal for Ground Zero," *New York Times,* July 21, 2002, p. A1.

53. See for example Howard Zinn, *A Power Governments Cannot Suppress* (San Francisco: City Lights, 2007).

54. Michael Sorkin, *Starting from Zero: Reconstructing Downtown New York* (New York: Routledge, 2003), pp. 57–61.

55. Michael Schudson, *The Good Citizen: A History of American Civil Life* (New York: Free Press, 1998).

56. There are numerous proponents of this "strong" theory of civic engagement: Benjamin R. Barber, *Strong Democracy* (Princeton University Press, 1984); Richard E. Sclove, *Democracy and Technology* (New York: Guilford, 1996); Theda Skocpol and Morris P. Fiorina, eds., *Civic Engagement in American Democracy* (Brookings, 1999).

57. Jack M. Balkin, "Digital Speech and Democratic Culture: A Theory of Freedom of Expression for the Information Society," *New York University Law Review* 79 (2004): 1–58.

58. The ideal type of citizens' group is one that is "composed of representatives of all strata of its community; it would be unbiased, courteous, well-organized, adequately financed, articulate." Donald Guimary, *Citizens Groups and Broadcasting* (New York: Praeger, 1975), p. 148.

59. Andy Oram, "In Search of Microelites: How to Get User-Generated Content," November 14, 2007 (radar.oreilly.com/2007/11/in-search-of-microelites-how-t.html [October 2008]).

60. Joseph Nye, "Picking a President," *Democracy Journal* (Fall 2008): 19–28.

61. *Sony Corp. of America v. Universal City Studios,* 464 U.S. 417 (1984).

62. Prioritizing Resources and Organization for Intellectual Property Act of 2008 (ProIP Act) S. 3325. Nate Anderson, "Big Content Gloats as Bush Signs Pro-IP Act," *ArsTechnica,* October 14, 2008 (http://arstechnica.com/news.ars/post/20081014-bush-signs-pro-ip-act-big-content-gloats.html [December 2008]); John Borland, "RIAA Settles with 12-Year-Old Girl," September 9, 2003 (http://news.cnet.com/2100-1027-5073717.html [October 2008]); Eric Bangeman, "RIAA versus Grandma, Part II: The Showdown That Wasn't," December 16, 2007 (arstechnica.com/news.ars/post/20071216.html [October 2008]). See also *MGM Studios Inc.* v. *Grokster, Ltd.,* 545 U.S. 913 (2005) (peer-to-peer file-sharing case) (arstechnica.com/news.ars/post/20081014.html [October 2008]).

Chapter Three

1. U.S. Patent and Trademark Office, "Patent Organization" (www.uspto.gov/web/offices/pac/index.html [October 2008]).

2. TC 2100 has 87,301 applications awaiting first action by an examiner and 151,698 total applications pending. In 2008, TC 2100 was combined with another art unit and renamed TC 2400. Jack Harvey continues to direct.

3. Patent Act of 1952, as amended. 35 U.S.C. 101 et seq.

4. "Confidential status of applications; publication of patent applications," 35 U.S.C. 122 (November 29, 2000).

5. "Infringement of patent," 35 U.S.C. 271 (December 8, 2003); "Damages," 35 U.S.C. 284 (November 29, 2000); "Injunctions," 35 U.S.C. 283 (July 19, 1952), "Attorney fees," 35 U.S.C. 285 (July 19, 1952); "Contents and term of patent; provisional rights," 35 U.S.C. 154 (November 2, 2002); *eBay Inc* v. *MercExchange, L.L.C.,* 547 U.S. 388 (2006) (discussing injunction limitations and requirements in patent cases).

6. For another study of the heuristics of documents like patent applications or, in this case, IMF country reports, see Richard Harper, *Inside the IMF: An Ethnography of Documents, Technology, and Organizational Action* (Academic Press, 2007); Geoffrey Bowker and Susan Leigh Star, *Sorting Things Out: Classification and Its Consequences* (MIT Press, 2008); Annelise Riles, ed., *Documents: Artifacts of Modern Knowledge* (University of Michigan Press, 2006).

7. Abraham Lincoln, "Lecture on Discoveries and Inventions (Feb. 11, 1859)," in *Abraham Lincoln: Speeches and Writings, 1859–1865,* edited by Don E. Fehrenbacher (New York: Library of America, 1989), p. 11.

8. See Saul Lach and Mark Schankerman, "Incentives and Invention in Universities," *RAND Journal of Economics* 39 (June 22, 2008): 403–33; Association of University Technology Managers, "Emory Is Top-Ranked University in Latest Survey of Commercialized Research," February 26, 2007 (www.highbeam.com); "Bayh-Dole University and Small Business Patent Procedures Act," P.L. 96-517, sec. 6(a) (December 12, 1980).

9. Eben Moglen, "The Global Software Industry in Transformation," annual lecture, Scottish Society for Computers and Law, Edinburgh, June 26, 2007 (www.archive.org/details/EbenMoglenLectureEdinburghJune2007DVD [December 2008]).

10. Joseph Stigliz, "Give Prizes Not Patents," *New Scientist,* September 16, 2006, p. 21.

11. Malcolm Gladwell, "In the Air," *New Yorker,* May 12, 2008.

12. Frank Lewis Dyer and Thomas Commerford Martin, *Edison: His Life and Inventions* (New York: Harper and Brothers, 1910); see also The Incandescent Lamp Patent, Supreme Court of the United States, 159 U.S. 465 (1895).

13. Roger Bilstein, *Flight in America: From the Wrights to the Astronauts* (Johns Hopkins University Press, 2001), p. 28; Robert P. Merges and Richard R. Nelson, "On the Complex Economics of Patent Scope," *Columbia Law Review* 839 (1990): 16–17 ("More importantly for our purposes, the validation of Edison's broad patent slowed the pace of improvements considerably").

14. James Bessen and Michael J. Meurer, *Patent Failure* (Princeton University Press, 2008).

15. James Bessen and Michael J. Meurer, "Do Patents Stimulate R&D Investment and Promote Growth?" (www.patentlyo.com/patent/2008/03/do-patents-stim.html [October 2008]).

16. Mark Lemley and Bhaven Sampat, "Is the Patent Office a Rubber Stamp," Working Paper 999098, Second Annual Conference on Empirical Legal Studies, Stanford (papers.ssrn.com/sol3/papers.cfm?abstract_id=999098 [October 2008]).

17. See Cecil D. Quillen Jr. and Ogden H. Webster, "Continuing Patent Applications and Performance of the U.S. Patent and Trademark Office," *Federal Circuit Bar Journal* 11 (2001): 13; Cecil D. Quillen Jr., Ogden H. Webster, and Richard Eichmann, "Continuing Patent Applications and Performance of the U.S. Patent and Trademark Office: Extended," *Federal Circuit Bar Journal* 12 (2002): 38 (lowering figures by 12 percent from earlier calculations).

18. This chapter owes a debt to anthropologists of policymaking, such as Don Brenneis, who study the intersection between information, expertise, and communicative practice in law and policy.

19. *Autogiro Co. of America* v. *United States,* 384 F.2d 391 (1967); see also Diogenes Laertius, "Myson," in *The Lives and Opinions of Eminent Philosophers,* translated by Charles Duke Yonge (H. G. Bohn, 1853) ("Men ought not to seek things for words, but for words in things; for that things are not made on account of words, but that words are put together for the sake of things").

20. Edward C. Walterscheid, *The Nature of the Intellectual Property Clause: A Study in Historical Perspective* (Buffalo: William S. Hein, 2002).

21. David G. Post, *In Search of Jefferson's Moose: Notes on the State of Cyberspace* (Oxford University Press, forthcoming).

22. U.S. Patent 6805351, issued October 19, 2004.

23. Allan S. Lichtman and Rosemary R. Lichtman, "Professional malpractice board game apparatus," U.S. Patent 4068848, issued January 17, 1978. To add to the pressure, examiners are given a financial incentive (in the form of productivity bonuses) to grant patents quickly. See Gajan Retnasaba, "Why It Is Easier to Get a Patent in September," May 23, 2008 (ssrn.com/bstrct=1121132 [October 2008]) (USPTO incentive scheme rewards examiners who allow patents).

24. John Buell, "Weed-cutting golf club," U.S. Patent Application 10/965431 (filed October 14, 2004).

25. *Topliff* v. *Topliff*, 145 U.S. 156 (1892).

26. *Senmed Inc.* v. *Richard-Allan Medical Industries*, 888 F.2d 815 (Fed. Cir. 1989).

27. Tom Krazit and Anne Broache, "BlackBerry Saved," March 3, 2006 (news.cnet.com/BlackBerry-saved/2100-1047_3-6045880.html?tag=mncol;txt [October 2008]).

28. Darko Kirovski, "Off-line economies for digital media," U.S. Patent Application 11/296194, published June 14, 2007; see also "Off-line economies for digital media" (peertopatent.org/patent/20070136608/activity [October 2008]).

29. James Toupin, "Navigating Recent Cases," March 17, 2008 (www.ipo.org/AM/PrinterTemplate.cfm?Section=IPO_Daily_News_&template=/CM/ContentDisplay.cfm&ContentID=17638 [October 2008]).

30. See Lee Petherbridge, "Positive Examination," *IDEA* 46 (2006): 182–83. Also see *Code of Federal Regulations* 37, sec. 1.63(b)(3) (2006) ("An applicant is required to disclose any information that is material to the prosecution of the patent"); *CHISUM* 6, sec. 19.03(2)(b)(i) ("An applicant and his or her patent attorney [traditionally] were under no duty to conduct a search of the prior art"). Sometimes applicants file no prior art at all; see for example *Patent Chronicles,* March 23, 2005 (www.patentchronicles.com [October 2008]). The USPTO has proposed a rule change to "encourage patent applicants to provide the USPTO the most relevant information related to their inventions in the early stages of the review process."

31. "Citation of prior art," 35 U.S.C. 301 (November 29, 1999).

32. *Code of Federal Regulations* 37, sec. 1.99 (November 29, 2000) ("Third-party submission in published application").

33. 35 U.S.C. 284 (July 19, 1952) ("Damages"). *Chaparral Industries, Inc.* v. *Boman Industries, Inc.,* 697 F.Supp 1113, 1124 (1988); *Vulcan Eng'g Co.* v. *FATA Aluminum, Inc.,* 278 F.3d 1366, 1378 (2002) (setting forth the standard for willfulness).

34. Jack Harvey, e-mail to author, April 1, 2008.

35. See USPTO, *Manual of Patent Examining Procedure,* sec. 1134.01 (8th ed., 2001); *Code of Federal Regulations* 37, sec. 1.99 (2006). The patent examiner may not respond to the third party except to process the fee. Robert Clarke, deputy director, Office of Patent Legal Administration, presentation at meeting

of the USPTO, February 16, 2006 (cairns.typepad.com/peertopatent/files/community_patent_and_pto213v2.ppt [October 2008]).

36. 35 U.S.C. 122(c) (July 19, 1952) ("The Director shall establish appropriate procedures to ensure that no protest or other form of pre-issuance opposition to the grant of a patent on an application may be initiated after publication of the application without the express written consent of the applicant").

37. Matthew Kim, senior patent examiner, e-mail to author, June 19, 2008.

38. "File Integrity," *Patent Office Professional Association Newsletter* 85 (November 1985): 3 (complaints about one million missing or misfiled documents); "File Integrity Is an Automation Problem Too," *Patent Office Professional Association Newsletter* 98 (March 1998): 3 (concern that automation will only exacerbate the problem and make it less transparent).

39. Eliot Weinberger, "Notes on Susan," *New York Review of Books,* August 16, 2007.

40. John Doll, phone interview by author, October 10, 2007.

41. "Improving the Patent Process," John Doll, interview by Federal News Radio, June 15, 2007 (www.federalnewsradio.com/?sid=1168400&nid=250 [October 2008]).

42. Bhaven N. Sampat, "Determinants of Patent Quality: An Empirical Analysis," September 2005 (siepr.stanford.edu/programs/SST_Seminars/patentquality_new.pdf_1.pdf [October 2008]).

43. "Need a Journal?" *Patent Office Professional Association Newsletter* 89 (April 1989): 4.

44. "POPA and PTO Reach Reorganization Agreement," *Patent Office Professional Association Newsletter* 97 (July 1997): 7.

45. Excerpts from USPTO, *Human Capital Survey Employee Responses* 7 (July 2007).

46. "Automation," *Patent Office Professional Association Newsletter* 85 (July 1985): 3–4.

47. Arxiv (www.arxiv.org [October 2008]).

48. See for example Osapa (www.linuxfoundation.org/en/Osapa [October 2008]) (The goal is to reduce the number of poor-quality patents issued by increasing accessibility to open-source software code and documentation that can be used as prior art during the patent examination process).

49. Christopher Wong, "Community Service: Adapting Peer Review to the Patenting Process," *I/S: A Journal of Law and Policy for the Information Society* 4 (2008): 45.

50. USPTO, *Manual of Patent Examining Procedure,* sec. 904.02(c) (8th ed., 2001).

51. Brewster Kahle, interview by author, August 22, 2007.

52. USPTO, *The 21st Century Strategic Plan,* 2003 (www.uspto.gov/web/offices/com /strat21/stratplan_03feb2003.pdf [October 2008]) (proposing that

the USPTO investigate market-driven initiatives to "achieve greater examiner productivity by reducing their prior art search responsibilities").

53. USPTO, *U.S. Patent Activity, Calendar Years 1790 to the Present* (www.uspto.gov/web/offices/ac/ido/oeip/taf/h_counts.htm) (295,926 patent applications in 1997 compared to 456,154 patent applications in 2007).

54. World Intellectual Property Organization, *WIPO Patent Report: Statistics on Worldwide Patent Activity*, 2007 (www.wipo.int/ipstats/en/statistics/patents/patent_report_2007.html#P173_14118).

55. USPTO, *U.S. Patent Activity, Calendar Years 1790 to the Present* (www.uspto.gov/web/offices/ac/ido/oeip/taf/h_counts.html [December 2008]).

56. European Patent Office, *Patents around the World* (www.epo.org/focus/patent-system.html).

57. USPTO, *U.S. Patent Classification System* (www.uspto.gov/go/classification/selectnumwithtitle.htm [October 2008]).

58. In 2007 the USPTO issued 347 design patents for the shape of golf clubs and only 29 for baseballs.

59. Plant Patent Act, 35 U.S.C. 161–64; Plant Variety Protection Act of 1970, 7 U.S.C. 2321–582; Act of February 4, 1887, ch. 105, 24 Stat. 387.

60. The U.S. Supreme Court opened the floodgates of patent activity with its 1980 ruling in *Diamond* v. *Chakrabarty*, 447 U.S. 303 (1980). In deciding that a bacterium capable of breaking down crude oil, and thus useful in the cleanup of oil spills, was patentable, the High Court declared the scope of patentable subject matter to include living organisms. In his conclusion, Chief Justice Warren E. Burger wrote that Congress had intended patentable subject matter to "include anything under the sun that is made by man."

61. In re Alappat, 33 F.3d 1526, at 1544 ("a useful, concrete and tangible result"); *Diamond* v. *Diehr*, 450 U.S.C. 175 (1981) at 187 ("Our earlier opinions lend support to our present conclusion that a claim drawn to subject matter otherwise statutory does not become non-statutory simply because it uses a mathematical formula, computer program, or digital computer"); *State Street Bank & Trust Company* v. *Signature Financial Group, Inc.*, 149 F.3d 1368 (Fed. Cir. 1998); in re Fisher, 421 F.3d 1365 (Fed. Cir. 2005).

62. Rochelle Cooper Dreyfuss, "The Federal Circuit: A Case Study in Specialized Courts," *New York University Law Review* 64 (1989): 26–30.

63. Fred Warshofsky, *The Patent Wars: The Battle to Own the World's Technology* (New York: Wiley, 1994), p. 65.

64. In a comparison of appeals cases from 1953 to 1978 and from 1982 to 1990, the share of District Court decisions finding validity and infringement that were upheld increased from 62 percent to 90 percent. Decisions of invalidity and no infringement were reversed 12 percent of the time before the Federal Circuit's creation and 18 percent afterward. Moreover, the rate of preliminary injunctions increased dramatically. See John R. Allison and Mark A. Lemley, "How Federal Circuit Judges Vote in Patent Validity Cases," *Florida State University Law*

Review 27 (2000): 745–54 ("Judges appointed after 1982 voted to hold a patent valid 164 times out of 298, or 55.0% of the time"); see also Dreyfuss, "The Federal Circuit." As Dan L. Burk and Mark Lemley remark, "The Federal Circuit has bent over backwards to find biotechnological inventions nonobvious, even if the prior art demonstrates a clear plan for producing the invention." Dan L. Burk and Mark A. Lemley, "Is Patent Law Technology-Specific?" *Berkeley Technology Law Journal* 17 (2002): 1155–56. But compare Donald R. Dunner, "The United States Court of Appeals for the Federal Circuit: Its First Three Years," *American Intellectual Property Law Journal* 13 (1985): 185–86 ("What [the results] show is anything but a bias in favor of patents—either from a validity or an infringement standpoint").

65. In re Alappat 33 F.3d 1526 (1994).

66. Drug Price Competition and Patent Restoration Act of 1984, P.L. 98-417, 98 Stat. 1585 (1984) (codified as amended 21 U.S.C. 355 (1994). Extension of patent term, 35 U.S.C. 156.

67. 35 U.S.C. 154; TRIPS Article 33.

68. John F. Duffy, "A Minimum Optimal Patent Term," Berkeley Center for Law and Technology, January 6, 2005 (repositories.cdlib.org/bclt/lts/4 [October 2008]).

69. "USPTO Should Reassess How Examiner Goals, Performance Appraisal Plans, and the Award System Stimulate and Reward Examiner Production Final Inspection Report," IPE-15722, September 2004, p. 11, n. 12. (From 1999 to 2003 the complexity factor increased 4.25 percent. From 1990 through 2003 the complexity factor increased 11 percent, or an average of 0.85 a year based in part on some new technologies.)

70. John Doll, interview by author, October 10, 2007.

71. Dennis Crouch, "Does Size Matter? Counting Words in Patent Specifications," December 20, 2007 (www.patentlyo.com/patent/2007/12/does-size-matte.html [October 2008]); Dennis Crouch, "Rising Claim Counts," December 23, 2007 (www.patentlyo.com/patent/2007/12/rising-claim-co.html [October 2008]) ("Of the sample measured, the average total claims in 1975 was 10.6 while in 2001 it had jumped to 18.9").

72. The shortest claim in history is only one word, claiming "Element-95" in U.S. patent 3156523 (www.questel.orbit.com/Piug/piugl2006/0733.html [October 2008]).

73. U.S. patent application 20030196788 ("Producing hydrocarbons and non-hydrocarbon containing materials when treating a hydrocarbon containing formation," first inventor Harold J. Vinegar [Shell Oil] has 8,958 claims) (ipbiz.blogspot.com/2004/11/us-patent-applications-with-thousands.html [October 2008]).

74. "Ronald A. Katz" (en.wikipedia.org/wiki/ronald_a._katz [October 2008]).

75. Department of Commerce, Patent and Trademark Office, Changes to Practice for Continued Examination Filings, Patent Applications Containing

Patentably Indistinct Claims, and Examination of Claims in Patent Applications; Final Rule, 72 *Federal Register* 46716 (August 21, 2007) (www.uspto.gov/web/offices/com/sol/notices/72fr46716.pdf [October 2008]) ("require[s] an applicant who presents more than five independent claims or more than twenty-five total claims in an application to help focus examination by providing additional information to the Office in an examination support document").

76. *Tafas v. Dudas,* 07–cv-0846 (E.D.Va 2007).

77. USPTO, *Human Capital Survey Employee Responses.*

78. See U.S. Government Accountability Office, "Intellectual Property: USPTO Has Made Progress in Hiring Examiners, but Challenges to Retention Remain," GAO-05-720 (2005) ("Depending on the type of patent and the skill level of the examiner, each examiner is expected to process an average of 87 applications per year at a rate of 19 hours per application"); Kevin Maney, "Patent Applications So Abundant That Examiners Can't Catch Up," *USA Today,* September 21, 2005, p. 3B.

79. Alan P. Douglas, "Column of the President," *Patent Office Professional Association Newsletter* 81 (June-July 1981).

80. U.S. Department of Commerce, Office of Inspector General, "Patent and Trademark Office: Board of Appeals and Interferences: High Inventory and Inadequate Monitoring Threaten Effectiveness of Appeal Process," Audit Report BTD-10628-8-0001, September 1998, p. 11.

81. National Research Council, *A Patent System for the 21st Century,* edited by Stephen A. Merrill, Richard C. Levin, and Mark B. Myers (Washington: National Academy of Sciences, 2004), p. 104.

82. John A. Squires, "Mr. Director (Please) Tear Down This Wall," AIPLA spring meeting, May 14, 2008 (www.aipla.org/Content/ContentGroups/Speaker_Papers/Spring_Meeting/200812/Squires)

83. John Love, deputy commissioner for patent examination policy, U.S. Patent and Trademark Office, "Patent Relations with the PTO," AIPLA spring meeting, May 10, 2007 (www.aipla.org/Content/Microsites139 [October 2008]).

84. Joseph Rolla, "Presentation to the Boston Patent Law Association" (www.uspto.gov/web/offices/pac/dapp/opla/presentation/bostonplaslidestext.html [October 2008]).

85. See Edward C. Walterscheid, *The Nature of the Intellectual Property Clause: A Study in Historical Perspective* (Buffalo: William S. Hein, 2002), pp. 107–10.

86. Mark Twain, *A Connecticut Yankee in King Arthur's Court* (New York: Signet Classics, 2004 [1889]), p. 58.

87. Venetian Statute on Industrial Brevets (1474); An Act for the Encouragement of Learning, by Vesting the Copies of Printed Books in the Authors or Purchasers of Such Copies, During the Times Therein Mentioned (Statute of Anne), 8 Anne c.19 (1709).

88. *Philips v. AWH Corp.,* 376 F.3d 1382 (Fed. Cir. 2004).

NOTES TO PAGES 64–68 **205**

89. Carlos Gutierrez, letter to Patrick Leahy, April 3, 2008 (www.ogc.doc. gov/ogc/legreg/letters/110/S1145Apr0308.pdf [October 2008]).

90. Method of swinging on a swing, U.S. Patent 6368227 (April 9, 2002); reexamination, C.N. 90006289, Cl. 472/118 (May 21, 2002).

91. Adam Jaffe and Josh Lerner, *Innovation and Its Discontents: How Our Broken Patent System Is Endangering Innovation and Progress, and What to Do about It* (Princeton University Press, 2004), p. 22.

92. Dan Cooperman, "The Patent System and the Future of Innovation," speech, Legal Futures Conference, Stanford Law School, March 8, 2008 (www. law.stanford.edu/display/images/dynamic/events_media/20080308_CIS_Legal-Futures_190-3.qtl [December 2008]).

93. Brad Smith, "Microsoft Calls for Reforms to the U.S. Patent System," March 10, 2005 (www.microsoft.com/presspass/features/2005/mar05/03-10 patentreform.mspx).

94. Theodore Eisenberg and Margo Schlanger, "The Reliability of the Administrative Office of the U.S. Courts Database: An Initial Empirical Analysis," *Notre Dame Law Review* 78 (October 2003) (papers.ssrn.com/sol3/papers. cfm?abstract_id=413181 [October 2008]).

95. PricewaterhouseCoopers, "2008 Patent Litigation Study: Damages, Awards, Success Rates, and Time to Trial" (www.pwc.com/extweb/pwc publications.nsf [October 2008]).

96. Jason Schlosser, "Judge Slashes $307 Million Patent Verdict for Rambus," August 14, 2006 (news.lp.findlaw.com/andrerws/bt [October 2008]).

97. *TiVO Inc.* v. *EchoStar,* 516 F.3d 1290 (Fed. Cir. 2008).

98. Julie Creswell, "So Small a Town, So Many Patent Suits," *New York Times,* September 24, 2006, p. 2 (citing *LegalMetric,* "National Litigation Report").

99. AIPLA, "Report of the Economic Survey, 2007" (www.aipla.org/Content/ NavigationMenu/Professional_Development/Law_Practice.htm [October 2008]).

100. Ibid.

101. George S. Ford, Thomas M. Koutsky, and Lawrence J. Spiwak, "Quantifying the Cost of Substandard Patents: Some Preliminary Evidence," Policy Paper 30 (Washington: Phoenix Center).

102. Manny W. Schecter, "Prior Art: Open Collaboration Is Medicine for Our Ailing Patent System," *BNA, Patent, Trademark, and Copyright Journal* 72 (October 20, 2006): 682–85; quotation, 684.

103. Bessen and Meurer, *Patent Failure,* p. 8.

104. U.S. Patent 6058417 (information presentation and management in an online trading environment), filed October 23, 1998; granted May 2, 2000.

105. Professional Inventors Alliance, "Save the Patent," April 7, 2008 (www. docs.piausa.org/PIAUSA/08-04-07-PIAUSA-NYT [October 2008]).

106. Ryan Thomas Grace, "Method and instrument for proposing marriage to an individual," U.S. Patent Application 10/378423 (filed March 3, 2003).

107. Bessen and Meurer, *Patent Failure,* p. 8.

Chapter Four

1. Martha Lagace, "John Seely Brown Piece—Screen Language: The New Currency for Learning," Harvard Business School, *Working Knowledge: A First Look at Faculty Research,* May 13, 2002 (hbswk.hbs.edu/archive/2930.html [October 2008]).

2. For an extended discussion of physics and culture, see Beth Simone Noveck, "A Democracy of Groups," *First Monday* 10 (December 2005) (www.firstmonday.org/issues/issues10_11/noveck/ [December 2008]).

3. I like the metaphor so much I named my web log the Cairns blog and posted an extended explanation of the metaphor here (cairns.typepad.com/about.html [October 2008]). See also "The Deliberative Interface," July 3, 2005 (http://cairns.typepad.com/blog/2005/07/the_deliberativ.html [October 2008]).

4. Steven R. Pearson and others, "Method for providing recovery from a failure in a system utilizing distributed audit," U.S. Patent 5832203, November 3, 1998.

5. U.S. Patent and Trademark Office, "Applicant's Consent to Third-Party Comments in Published Applications and Consent to Pilot Participation" (www.uspto.gov/web/patents/peerpriorartpilot [October 2008]). Pursuant to the USPTO rules for Peer-to-Patent, applications are posted for four months from the publication date. Since an applicant must consent within thirty days of publication, however, the ultimate window might be three months instead of four.

6. "Peer-to-Patent First Anniversary Report" (early data about the project); "The Peer to Patent Project: Community Patent Review" (further information and updates) (http://dotank.nyls.edu/communitypatent [October 2008]).

7. Paul Broyles and Patrick Gibbons, "User-selectable, management-alert format," U.S. Patent 20070118658, May 24, 2007.

8. At the end of the pilot's first year, the National Science Foundation awarded the Peer-to-Patent team a research grant to study the effect of tagging on citizen participation.

9. Tree mapping was developed by the Human-Computer Interaction Lab at the University of Maryland (www.cs.umd.edu/hcil/treemap [October 2008]). See also Ben Shneiderman, "Treemaps for Space-Constrained Visualization of Hierarchies" (www.cs.umd.edu/hcil/treemap-history/index.shtml [October 2008]).

10. See http://peertopatent.org/patent/20070118658/discussion (October 2008).

11. "Third-Party Submission in Published Application," 37 *Code of Federal Regulations* 1.99 (September 20, 2000).

12. "Image file wrapper," U.S. Patent 20070118658 (http://portal.uspto.gov/external/portal/pair [October 2008]).

13. Eric S. Raymond, *The Cathedral and the Bazaar* (Cambridge, Mass.: O'Reilly, 2001), p. 30.

14. Bailenson is the founder of the Virtual Human Interaction Lab (http://vhil.stanford.edu [October 2008]). His publications can be found on the same website (http://vhil.stanford.edu/pubs/ [October 2008]).

15. Aaron Britt, "On Language: Avatar," *New York Times,* August 10, 2008, p. MM12.

16. Jeremy N. Bailenson and others, "Facial Similarity between Voters and Candidates Causes Social Influence," *Public Opinion Quarterly* (2008) (http://vhil.stanford.edu/pubs/2008/bailenson-facial-similarity.pdf [October 2008]).

17. Joan Morris DiMicco, "Changing Small Group Interaction through Visual Reflections of Social Behavior," Ph.D. dissertation, MIT, 2005; Joan DiMicco and Walter Bender, "Group Reactions to Visual Feedback Tools," paper prepared for the Second International Conference on Persuasive Technology, April 26–27, 2007, Stanford. Her papers are available at www.joandimicco.com (October 2008).

18. DiMicco, "Changing Small Group Interaction," p. 15.

19. WNYC, *Brian Lehrer Show,* "30 Issues in 30 Days" (www.wnyc.org/30issues [October 2008]). Using wiki tools, participants nominated topics, suggested content, provided research, and voted on results for discussion on air. The project ran through October 2008.

20. Noveck, "A Democracy of Groups."

21. Steven Weber, *The Success of Open Source* (Harvard University Press, 2004).

22. Noah D. Zatz, "Sidewalks in Cyberspace: Making Space for Public Forums in the Electronic Environment," *Harvard Journal of Law and Technology* 12 (1998): 149.

23. Joi Ito, "Leadership in World of Warcraft," March 13, 2006 (joi.ito.com/weblog/2006/03/13/leadership-in-w.html [October 2008]).

24. Conference, Convergence of the Real and Virtual, May 9–11, 2008 (mysite.verizon.net/wsbainbridge/convergence.htm [October 2008]).

25. John Seely Brown and Josh Thomas, "The Gamer Disposition," *Harvard Business Review Online,* February 14, 2008 (conversationstarter.hbsp.com/2008/02/the_gamer_disposition.html [October 2008]).

26. "The Group Brain Project" (http://groupbrain.wjh.harvard.edu/ [October 2008]).

27. Noveck, "A Democracy of Groups."

28. Scott E. Page, *The Difference: How the Power of Diversity Creates Better Groups, Firms, Schools, and Societies* (Princeton University Press, 2007). See also Ray Reagans and Ezra Zuckerman, "Networks, Diversity, and Productivity: The Social Capital of Corporate R&D Teams," *Organization Science* 12 (2001): 502; Jose Ramasco, "Social Inertia and Diversity in Collaboration Networks," *European Physical Journal: Special Topics* 143 (2007): 47–50.

29. Northwestern Law School, "Northwestern Law Announces Accelerated JD, Other Proposals," news release, June 20, 2008 (www.law.northwestern.edu/news/newsdisplay.cfm?ID=191 [October 2008]).

30. Stephen M. Kosslyn, "On the Evolution of Human Motivation: The Role of Social Prosthetic Systems," in *Evolutionary Cognitive Neuroscience,* edited by S. M. Platek, T. K. Shackleford, and J. P. Keenan (MIT Press, 2006), p. 546.

31. Cass Sunstein and Richard Thaler, *Nudge* (Yale University Press, 2008). This important study in behavioral economics illustrates the idea of choice architectures (the attributes that influence our propensity to make certain choices). See also Amos Tversky and Daniel Kahneman, "The Framing of Decisions and the Psychology of Choice," *Science* 211 (1981): 453–58.

32. "Godwin's Law" (http://en.wikipedia.org/wiki/Godwins_law [October 2008]).

33. Don Tapscott and Anthony D. Williams, *Wikinomics: How Mass Collaboration Changes Everything* (New York: Portfolio, 2006), p. 144; "Slashdot FAQ: Comments and Moderation" (http://slashdot.org/faq/com-mod.shtml [October 2008]).

34. Clay Shirky, *Here Comes Everybody* (New York: Penguin, 2008), p. 291.

35. Nancy Scola, "Public Submitted Thousands of Debate Questions Online, Not Millions (Updated)," October 8, 2008 (www.techpresident.com/blog/entry/31240 [October 2008]).

36. Netroots Nation, "Questions for Nancy Pelosi" (www.askthespeaker.org [October 2008]).

37. Ed O'Keefe, "Obama Asks Dean to Drop Restrictions on Debates" (voices.washingtonpost.com/channel-08/2007/05/obama_asks_dean_to_waive_copyri.html [October 2008]). See also Lawrence Lessig, "Free Debates: Round Two" (www.lessig.org/blog/2008/09/free_debates_round_two.html).

38. "E-Petitions" (petitions.number10.gov.uk/ [October 2008]).

39. Neil Franklin, e-petitions project manager, interview by author, September 12, 2008.

40. "Feedback scores, stars, and your reputation" (pages.ebay.com/help/feedback/scores-reputation.html [October 2008]) (description of ratings system). See also "What Is Feedback and How Does It Affect My Reputation?" (pages.ebay.com/help/feedback/questions/feedback.html [October 2008]).

41. Peter Kollock, "The Production of Trust in Online Markets," in *Advances in Group Processes,* vol. 16, edited by E. J. Lawler and others (Greenwich, Conn.: Elsevier, 1999). Separating the two sides of the transaction by time or space (such as purchasing something by mail or on credit) introduces greater risks: the party who moves second must be considered trustworthy or have some other form of guarantee. The formal infrastructure that exists to manage these risks is vast and includes such elements as credit card companies, credit rating services, public accounting firms, and—if the exchange goes bad—collection agencies and the court system.

42. International Business Machines, "IBM Sets Record for Most U.S. Patents Earned in One Year, Announces the 'Inventors Forum' to Collaborate with Small

and Mid-Size Enterprises," news release, January 11, 2007 (www-03.ibm.com/press/us/en/pressrelease/20868.wss [October 2008]).

43. President's Commission on the Patent System, "To Promote the Progress of Science and Useful Arts" (1966), p. 73.

44. Michael Liedtke, "Microsoft Backs Novell's Linux Platform" (www.usa today.com/tech/news/2006-11-02-windows-linux_x.htm?POE=TECISVA [October 2008]).

45. "Patent Litigation Run Amok," December 21, 2007. This anonymously posted blog was taken down once the identity of its author (Patent Troll-Tracker) was revealed. A copy is on file with author.

46. "Todd Dickinson to Take AILPA Helm," August 15, 2008 (www.patent lyo.com/patent/2008/08/todd-dickinson.html [October 2008]).

47. David Clark, "A Cloudy Crystal Ball: Visions of the Future," July 16, 1992 (xys.ccert.edu.cn/reference/future_ietf_92.pdf [October 2008]). The full quote is, "We reject kings, presidents, and voting. We believe in rough consensus and running code."

48. Biotechnology Industry Organization, "BIO Expresses Concerns Regarding New Patent Reform Legislation," news release, June 19, 2007 (www.bio.org/ip/domestic/20070719.asp [October 2008]).

49. Peter K. Yu, "The International Enclosure Movement," *Indiana Law Journal* 82 (2007): 859.

50. Richard Stallman, "Prior Art Won't Solve the Software Patent Problem," September 15, 2006 (www.linux.com/articles/57167 [October 2008]).

51. Peer-to-Patent, "Workshops and Events" (dotank.nyls.edu/community patent/workshopsandevents_locations.html [October 2008]).

52. ABA Committee on the Status and Future of Federal e-Rulemaking, "Achieving the Potential: The Future of Federal e-Rulemaking: A Report to Congress and the President," 2008 (ceri.law.cornell.edu/documents/final-report-pr-2.pdf [December 2008]); Penn Program on Regulation, "Task Force to Federal Regulators: Open Your Doors to the Public and Let in More Sunshine: Transparency and Public Participation in the Rulemaking Process," 2008.

53. Project on Law and Democratic Development, "International Working Group on Online Consultation and Public Policy Making" (www.reconnecting democracy.org [October 2008]).

54. Juerg Haefliger, William F. Bruckert, and James S. Klecka, "Tuning core voltage of processors," U.S. Patent 20070174746, July 26, 2007; also see peer-topatent.org/patent/20070174746/activity (October 2008).

55. Broyles and Gibbons, "User-selectable, management-alert format."

56. Jack Harvey, "Results of Pilot: U.S. Patent and Trademark Office Perspective," paper prepared for AIPLA spring meeting, May 14, 2008 (www.aipla.org/Content/ContentGroups/Speaker_Papers/Spring_Meeting/200812/Harvey-jack-slides.pdf [October 2008]).

57. Jack Harvey, "Pilot Concerning Public Submission of Peer Reviewed Prior Art," paper prepared for AIPLA spring meeting, May 14, 2008 (www.uspto.gov/web/patents/peerpriorartpilot/peer051408aipla.pdf [October 2008]).

58. "Method for configuring a wind farm network" (peertopatent.org/patent/20070255832/activity [October 2008]); "Recommending contacts in a social network" (peertopatent.org/patent/20080059576/activity [October 2008]).

59. Her Majesty's Treasury, "Recommendation 23," *Gowers Review of Intellectual Property* (November 2006): 85.

60. "Japan Patent Office Launches Community Patent Review," July 28, 2008 (cairns.typepad.com/peertopatent/2008/07/japan-patent-of.html [October 2008]).

61. See Erica Naone, "Moving Freely between Virtual Worlds: Players Hope to Connect Their Separate Domains to Form a 3-D Internet," *MIT Technology Review,* October 29, 2007, p. 2.

CHAPTER FIVE

1. See Brian Robinson, "Group Advocates Data-Driven Policymaking," *Federal Computer Weekly,* April 23, 2007 (www.fcw.com/online/news/102541-1.html [October 2008]). See also Daniel Esty and Reece Rushing, "Governing by the Numbers: The Promise of Data-Driven Policymaking in the Information Age," April 2007 (www.americanprogress.org/issues/2007/04/pdf/data_driven_policy_report.pdf [October 2008]).

2. Billy Beane, Newt Gingrich, and John Kerry, "How to Take American Health Care from Worst to First," *New York Times,* October 24, 2008, p. A27.

3. For the D.C. data feeds and Apps for Democracy, see data.octo.dc.gov (December 2008).

4. The example of dangerous toys and the Consumer Product Safety Commission owes a debt to the 2008 Stanford seminar Networked Governance. Tasked with designing ways of producing more effective citizen participation in government, one team of students hit upon this idea. The presentation of their idea is on YouTube (www.youtube.com/watch?v=RpCN_-rnFo [December 2008]).

5. Nate Ritter, "How Geeks Can Help in Disasters," October 25, 2007 (blog.perfectspace.com/2007/10/25/how-geeks-can-help-in-disasters-san-diego-fire-2007 [October 2008]).

6. Steve Lohr, "Google and IBM Join in Cloud Computing Research," *New York Times,* October 8, 2007, p. 8.

7. Will Dick, "Virtual Alabama: Seeing the Sense in Sharing," working paper, nGenera Insight (September 2008) (www.ngenera.com/convs/show/9421-measuring-government-2-0 [October 2008]).

8. Federal Financial Institutions Examination Council (www.ffiec.gov/ [October 2008]).

9. Tyson Evans, "Charles Blow, NYT Visual Journalist," April 1, 2008 (update.snd.org/news/entry/charles-blow-nyt-visual-columnist [October 2008]).

10. Edward Tufte, *Envisioning Information* (Cheshire, Conn.: Graphics Press, 1990), p. 12.

11. Steve Lohr, "Digital Tools Help Users Save Energy, Study Finds," *New York Times,* January 10, 2008, p. C1.

12. Debate Hub (debatehub.c-span.org [October 2008]).

13. J. C. R. Licklider and Robert W. Taylor, "The Computer as Communication Device," *Science and Technology* 76 (1968): 22.

14. Cass Sunstein, "The Daily Me," in *Republic.Com* (Princeton University Press, 2001).

15. Arnold Pacey, *Meaning in Technology* (MIT Press, 1999), pp. 39–57 (discussing Alfred Crosby's description of the "shift to the visual" in history).

16. The classic text is Tufte, *Envisioning Information.* See also Stuart Card, Jock MacKinlay, and Ben Shneiderman, eds., *Readings in Information Visualization* (Academic Press, 1990).

17. See www.many-eyes.com (October 2008).

18. "Swivel: Where Curious People Explore Data" (www.swivel.com [October 2008]).

19. Tufte, *Envisioning Information,* p. 50.

20. See www.airnow.gov (October 2008).

21. See www.kitab.nl/tunisianprisonersmap (October 2008).

22. See www.freebase.com (October 2008).

23. See www.ashoka.org/changemakers (October 2008).

24. See www.delver.com (October 2008).

25. See www.naver.com (October 2008).

26. Erica Naone, "Mapping Professional Networks: IBM's Atlas Tool Aims to Help Businesses Visualize Connections between Colleagues," December 28, 2007 (www.technologyreview.com/Infotech/19985/?nlid=777&a=f [October 2008]).

27. J. M. DiMicco and N. Yankelovich, "Constellation: Using Visualization to Find the Path to Experts," poster presentation, ACM conference, Organizational Computing and Groupware Technologies (Group 2007), November 2007 (www.joandimicco.com/pubs/dimicco-yankelovich-group07-poster-constellation.pdf).

28. Dawn Nunziato, "The Death of the Public Forum in Cyberspace," *Berkeley Technology Law Journal* 20 (2005), p. 7.

29. David R. Johnson, "How Online Games May Change the Law and Legally Significant Institutions," *New York Law School Law Review* 49 (2004): 51.

30. Micah L. Sifry, "Obama across America: Seeing the Big Picture" (www.techpresident.com/blog/entry/31556 [October 2008]).

31. See youtube.com/videoyourvote (October 2008). The project is a partnership with the ACLU's Voting Rights Project, BlackBoxVoting.org, Center for American Politics and Citizenship, Center for Governmental Studies, Center for

the Study of the American Electorate, Citizen Media Law Project, Common Cause, Flip Video Spotlight, electionline.org, Howcast.com, Lawyers' Committee for Civil Rights under Law, Overseas Vote Foundation, People for the American Way, Pew Center for the States, Rock the Vote, Video the Vote, Voto Latino, Why Tuesday? and Election Protection.

32. Congress passed the Government in the Sunshine Act in 1994, requiring that meetings of those federal agencies headed by "collegial bodies" be open to the public. Affecting fifty agencies, including most of the major independent regulatory commissions, the Sunshine Act also provides the legislative framework to ensure openness. But the requirement to meet in the open has led staffers who are not bound by these rules to meet behind closed doors. Government in the Sunshine Act, P. L. 94-409, 90 Stat. 1241 (1976), codified at 5 U.S.C. 552(b).

33. OMB Watch, "21st Century Right to Know" (www.ombwatch.org/article/archive/551 [November 2008]).

34. Freedom of Information Act, P. L. 89-487, 80 Stat. 250 (1966), current version at 5 U.S.C. 552 (1996).

35. Paperwork Reduction Act, P. L. 104-13, 109 Stat. 163 (1995), codified at 44 U.S.C. 3501-20.

36. Darrell M. West, "Global Perspectives on E-Government," in *Governance and Information Technology: From Electronic Government to Information Government,* edited by Viktor Mayer-Schönberger and David Lazer (MIT Press, 2007), p. 19.

37. The Consumer Product Safety Improvement Act of 2008 (P. L. 110314) provides for the creation of a public database.

38. Jerry Brito, "Hack, Mash, Peer: Crowdsourcing Government Transparency," *Columbia Science and Technology Law Review* 9 (2008): 119–22.

39. A report from the University of Michigan states that the next presidential administration should make a renewed commitment to expanding the availability of government information and services online. See National Quality Research Center, American Customer Satisfaction Index (ACSI). The center's E-Gov Satisfaction Index of October 28, 2008, indicates that citizen satisfaction with e-gov is near an all-time high.

40. See www.public.resource.org/index.html (October 2008).

41. Carl Malamud, "The Importance of Being Edgar" (mundi.net/cartography/EDGAR/index.html [December 2008]).

42. James Grimmelmann, "Copyright, Technology, and Access to the Law: An Opinionated Primer," June 17, 2008 (james.grimmelmann.net/essays/CopyrightTechnologyAccess [December 2008]).

43. Data must be complete, primary, timely, accessible, machine-processable, nondiscriminatory, nonproprietary, and license-free. See "Got Data?" (wiki.opengovdata.org/index.php/OpenDataPrinciples [October 2008]).

44. David Robinson and others, "Government Data and the Invisible Hand," *Yale Journal of Law and Technology* 11 (Fall 2008) (papers.ssrn.com/sol3/papers.cfm?abstract_id=1138083[October 2008]).

45. Web Content Managers Advisory Council, "Requirements Checklist for Government Web Managers" (www.usa.gov/webcontent/reqs_bestpractices/reqs_checklist.shtml [October 2008]).

46. See W. David Stephenson, "Automated Data Feeds Make Smart Regulation Possible Now" (www.huffingtonpost.com/w-david-stephenson/automated-data-feeds-make_b_128208.html [October 2008]).

47. Curtis W. Copeland, "Electronic Rulemaking in the Federal Government," Congressional Research Service Report RL3421018, October 16, 2007 (www.opencrs.com/document/RL34210 [October 2008]).

48. See Darlene Meskell, "New Opportunities for Involving Citizens in the Democratic Process," *GSA* no. 20 (Fall 2007): 2–4. See also Stephen Frantzich and John Sullivan, *The C-Span Revolution* (University of Oklahoma Press, 1996).

49. EPA Geospatial Data Access Project (www.epa.gov/enviro/geo_data.html [October 2008]).

50. National Neighborhood Indicators Partnership (www2.urban.org/nnip [October 2008]).

51. Cindy Skrzycki, "1,700 Pages of Rules, Fewer Dead Trees," *Washington Post,* December 18, 2007, p. D3.

52. OMB Watch, "21st Century Right to Know," p. 10.

53. See www.pugetsound.epageo.org/ (October 2008).

CHAPTER SIX

1. See Sam Peltzman, *Political Participation and Government Regulation* (University of Chicago Press, 1998); H. Margaret Conway, *Political Participation in the United States* (Washington: CQ Press, 2000).

2. James O. Freedman, "Crisis and Legitimacy in the Administrative Process," *Stanford Law Review* 27 (April 1975): 1056.

3. Gerald Frug, "The Ideology of Bureaucracy in American Law," *Harvard Law Review* 97 (April 1984): 1333.

4. Administrative Procedure Act, ch. 324, 60 Stat. 237 (1946) (codified as amended in scattered sections of 5 U.S.C.).

5. Beth Simone Noveck, "The Electronic Revolution in Rulemaking," *Emory Law Journal* 53 (2004): 455, n. 98.

6. Cornelius M. Kerwin, *Rulemaking: How Government Agencies Write Law and Make Policy* (Washington: CQ Press, 1994), p. 116.

7. Administrative Procedure Act, 5 U.S.C. sec. 553(c).

8. Thomas Jefferson, letter to Samuel Kercheval, July 12, 1816, in *Classics of American Political and Constitutional Thought,* edited by Scott J. Hammond, Kevin R. Hardwick, and Howard L. Lubert (Indianapolis: Hackett , 2007), p. 745.

9. Cary Coglianese, "The Internet and Citizen Participation in Rulemaking," Working Paper RWP 04-044 (Harvard University, Kennedy School of Government, 2004), p. 7.

10. Marissa Martino Golden, "Interest Groups in the Rule-Making Process: Who Participates? Whose Voices Get Heard?" *Journal of Public Administration Research and Theory* 8 (1998): 250-64.

11. Peter L. Strauss, "ABA Ad Law Section's E-Rulemaking Survey," *Administrative and Regulatory Law News* 29, no. 3 (Spring 2004): 8.

12. Environmental Protection Agency, "Controlling Power Plant Emissions: Public Comments" (www.epa.gov/mercury/control_emissions/comment.htm [October 2008]).

13. Cameron Scott, "9 Seconds," *SFGate.com,* October 23, 2008 (www.sfgate.com/cgi-bin/blogs/sfgate/detail?blogid=49&entry_id=31846).

14. Federal Advisory Committee Act, P. L. 92-463, 86 Stat. 770 (1972) (codified at 5 U.S.C. App. 2).

15. Negotiated Rulemaking Act, P. L. 101-648, 104 Stat. 4976 (1990) (codified at 5 U.S.C. secs. 561–70); see also Phillip J. Harter, "Assessing the Assessors: The Actual Performance of Negotiated Rulemaking," *New York University Environmental Law Journal* 9 (2000): 32–56.

16. "[Once] an agency decides to establish a negotiated rulemaking committee, the agency shall publish in the *Federal Register* and, as appropriate, in trade or other specialized publications, a notice which shall include . . . a list of the persons proposed to represent such interests and the person or persons proposed to represent the agency." 5 U.S.C. sec. 564(a)(4) (1990).

17. National Research Council, "Public Participation in Environmental Assessment and Decision Making" (Washington: 2008), pp. 3–9.

18. Cary Coglianese, "Assessing the Advocacy of Negotiated Rulemaking: A Response to Philip Harter," *New York University Environmental Law Journal* 9 (2001): 386–447.

19. Christopher Mooney, *The Republican War on Science* (New York: Basic Books, 2006).

20. Thomas McGarity and Wendy Wagner, *Bending Science: How Special Interests Corrupt Public Health Research* (Harvard University Press, 2008).

21. J. B. Ruhl and James Salzman, "In Defense of Regulatory Peer Review," *Washington University Law Review* 84 (2006): 1–61.

22. Ibid., p. 25.

23. Presidential Commission on the Space Shuttle *Challenger* Accident (Rogers Commission), *Report of the Presidential Commission on the Space Shuttle* Challenger *Accident* (Washington: GPO, 1986), appendix F.

24. Sheila Jasanoff, *The Fifth Branch: Science Advisors as Policy Makers* (Harvard University Press, 1990), p. 61; see also Joshua B. Bolten, "Issuance of OMB's 'Final Information Quality Bulletin for Peer Review,'" Memorandum M-05-03, Office of Management and Budget, December 16, 2004.

25. Government Accountability Office, "Federal Research: Peer Review Practices at Service Agencies Vary," GAO/RCED-99-99 (1999).

26. See for example the following publications by the Government Accountability Office: "Peer Review: EPA Needs Implementation Procedures and Additional Controls," GAO/IRCED-94-98 (1994); "Peer Review: Reforms Needed to Ensure Fairness in Federal Agency Grant Selection," GAO/PEMD-94-1 (1994); "Peer Review: Compliance with the Privacy Act and Federal Advisory Committee Act," GAO/GGD-94-48 (1991); "Federal Advisory Committees: GSA's Management Oversight and GAO Comments on Proposed Legislative Amendments," GAO/T-GGD-89-1 (1998); "Federal Advisory Committee Act: General Services Administration's Management of Advisory Committee Activities," GAO/GGD 89-10 (1988); "University Funding: Information on the Role of Peer Review at NSF and NIH," GAO/WED-87-87FS (1987). See also Lars Noah, "Scientific 'Republicanism': Expert Peer Review and the Quest for Regulatory Deliberation," *Emory Law Journal* 49 (2000): 1034–83 (various ways peer review is used in government).

27. Mohammed Kashef, "Scientific Peer Review in the Public Sector," 2005 (dotank.nyls.edu/communitypatent/peerreview_dec05.pdf [October 2008]) ("[Peer review] is an integral practice to the development of quality research in the private and public sectors in industry and in education, because the process of peer review allows even a large group of scientists, regardless of geographic proximity, to collaborate on the evaluation of innovation").

28. Bolten, "Issuance of OMB's 'Final Information Quality Bulletin for Peer Review.'"

29. American Association for the Advancement of Science, "Another Decline for EPA R&D in 2009: AAAS R&D Funding Update on R&D in the FY 2009 EPA Budget" (www.aaas.org/spp/rd/epa09p.pdf [October 2008]).

30. Information Quality Act, P. L. 106-555 app. C, 114 Stat. 2763A-154 (2000); "Guidelines for Ensuring and Maximizing the Quality, Objectivity, Utility, and Integrity of Information Disseminated by Federal Agencies," republication, 67 *Federal Register* 8452 (February 22, 2002).

31. Ibid.

32. Stephen M. Johnson, "Junking the 'Junk Science' Law: Reforming the Information Quality Act," *Administrative Law Review* 58 (2006): 37–80.

33. Mooney, *The Republican War on Science,* p. 103.

34. Jasanoff, *The Fifth Branch,* pp. 69–76; Wendy E. Wagner, "The 'Bad Science' Fiction: Reclaiming the Debate over the Role of Science in Public Health and Environmental Regulation," *Law and Contemporary Problems* 66 (2003): 67–71;

Sidney A. Shapiro, "Politicizing Peer Review: The Legal Perspective," in *Rescuing Science from Politics: Regulation and the Distortion of Scientific Research*, edited by Wendy Wagner and Rena Steinzor (Cambridge University Press, 2006).

35. Bolten, "Issuance of OMB's 'Final Information Quality Bulletin for Peer Review,'" p. 6.

36. Alan Charles Raul and Julie Zampa Dwyer, "'Regulatory *Daubert*': A Proposal to Enhance Judicial Review of Agency Science by Incorporating *Daubert* Principles into Administrative Law," *Law and Contemporary Problems* 66 (2003): 7 (arguing that the principles of *Daubert* should be applied to administrative agencies "to encourage reviewing judges to be less deferential, and thus more probing, of agency science"); see also *Daubert* v. *Merrell Dow Pharm., Inc.*, 509 U.S. 579 (1993).

37. E-Government Act of 2002, H.R. 2458/S. 803, section 206.

38. Beth S. Noveck, "The Electronic Revolution in Rulemaking," *Emory Law Journal* 53 (2004): 433.

39. Daniel C. Esty, "Environmental Protection in the Information Age," *New York University Law Review* 79 (2004): 172.

40. See Stuart W. Shulman and others, "Electronic Rulemaking: A Public Participation Research Agenda for the Social Sciences," *Social Science Computer Review* 21 (2003): 163–64; *Code of Federal Regulations* 36, sec. 219.9.

41. Government Accountability Office, "Electronic Rulemaking: Efforts to Facilitate Public Participation Can Be Improved," GA-03-901 (2003).

42. Cary Coglianese, "Citizen Participation in Rulemaking: Past, Present, and Future," *Duke Law Journal* 55 (2006): 954.

43. Orly Lobel, "The Renew Deal," *Minnesota Law Review* 89 (2004): 342; for a citation, see Paul S. Berman, "Global Legal Pluralism," *Southern California Law Review* 80 (2007): 1155.

44. See for example David Schoenbrod, *Saving Our Environment from Washington: How Congress Grabs Power, Shirks Responsibility, and Shortchanges the People* (Yale University Press, 2006).

45. Breaking the Logjam (www1.law.nyu.edu/conferences/btl/index.html [October 2008]).

46. Angus Macbeth and Gary Marchant, "Improving the Government's Environmental Science," *New York University Environmental Law Journal* (forthcoming) (available at www1.law.nyu.edu/conferences/btl/index.html).

47. Cass R. Sunstein, *Infotopia: How Many Minds Produce Knowledge* (Oxford University Press, 2006).

48. See Kenneth J. Arrow and others, "Statement on Prediction Markets," AEI-Brookings Joint Center for Regulatory Studies, May 2007 (http://ssrn.com/abstract=984584 [October 2008]); these authors define prediction markets as "markets for contracts that yield payments based on the outcome of an uncertain future event, such as a presidential election"; see also James Surowiecki, *The Wisdom of Crowds* (New York: Anchor Books, 2005); Sunstein, *Infotopia*.

49. Steve Lohr, "Betting to Improve the Odds: Companies Use Prediction Markets to Funnel Ideas from the Work Force," *New York Times,* April 9, 2008, p. H1.

50. Iowa Electronic Markets (www.biz.uiowa.edu/iem/ [October 2008]); Hollywood Stock Exchange (www.hsx.com [October 2008]).

51. Media Predict (www.mediapredict.com [October 2008]).

52. Kluster (www.kluster.com [October 2008]).

53. Philip Tetlock, *Expert Political Judgment: How Good Is It? How Can We Know?* (Princeton University Press, 2005).

54. Roberto Unger, *What Should Legal Analysis Become?* (London: Verso, 1999), p. 39.

55. Gary E. Marchant and Andrew Askland, "GM Foods: Potential Public Consultation and Participation Mechanisms," *Jurimetrics* 44 (2003), p. 101.

56. Ibid.

57. See Beth S. Noveck and David R. Johnson, "Breaking the Logjam: An Environmental Law for the 21st Century," *New York University Environmental Law Journal,* 17 (2009).

58. Danah Boyd, "Can Social Network Sites Enable Political Action?" in *Rebooting America,* edited by Allison Fine and others (New York: Personal Democracy Press, 2008).

59. Bureau of Labor Statistics, news release, "Number of Jobs Held, Labor Market Activity, and Earnings Growth among the Youngest Baby Boomers: Results from a Longitudinal Survey," June 28, 2008.

60. Irving Wladawsky-Berger, "Social Networks and Organizational Governance," October 15, 2007 (blog.irvingwb.com/blog/2007/10/social-networks.html [October 2008]).

61. Irving Wladawsky-Berger, "Participatory Governance," October 11, 2008, (blog.irvingwb.com/blog/2008/10/participatory-governance.html [October 2008]).

CHAPTER SEVEN

1. Scott Page, *The Difference: How the Power of Diversity Creates Better Groups, Firms, Schools, and Societies* (Princeton University Press, 2007), p. xvii.

2. Clean Air Act, 42 U.S.C. 7401 (2006).

3. Clean Air Act, 42 U.S.C. 7408(2) (2006).

4. Danish Board of Technology, "Consensus Conference" (www.tekno.dk/subpage.php3?article=468&toppic=kategori12&language=uk [October 2008]).

5. David Chartier, "Social Networks Exploding: May Appear in Government," *ArsTechnica,* October 26, 2008 (arstechnica.com/news.ars/post/2008 1026-studies-social-networks-exploding-could-outmode-government.html [October 2008]).

6. For the guide to citizen participation in the Wiki Policing Act of 2008, see www.e.govt.nz/policy/participation/guide-to-online-participation.

7. For the Melbourne Ten-Year Plan Wiki, see www.futuremelbourne.com.au.

8. Carmen Siriani, *Investing in Democracy: Civic Engagement and Collaborative Governance* (Brookings, 2009), p. 77.

9. Barack Obama, "Science, Technology, and Innovation for a New Generation," November 14, 2007 (www.barackobama.com/pdf/issues/technology/Fact_Sheet_Innovation_and_Technology.pdf [October 2008]).

CHAPTER EIGHT

1. "If the Earth Were a Sandwich" (www.zefrank.com/sandwich/ [October 2008]).

2. Sigmund Freud, *Civilization and Its Discontents* (New York: W. W. Norton, 2005), pp. 36, 41, 46–47.

3. Thomas Dietz and Paul C. Stern, eds., *Public Participation in Environmental Assessment and Decision Making* (Washington: National Research Council, 2008), pp. 9-3, 9-7.

4. See Richard Farson, *The Power of Design* (Norcross, Ga.: Greenway Communications, 2006).

5. R. Buckminster Fuller, *Your Private Sky* (Frankfurt: Springer Verlag, 2001), p. 256.

6. *MGM Studios, Inc.* v. *Grokster,* 545 U.S.913 (2005).

7. *Kelly* v. *Arriba Soft Corporation,* 336 F.3d 811 (9th Cir. 2003).

8. *Stewart* v. *Blackwell,* 444 F.3d 843 (2006).

9. Hannah Arendt, *Crisis of the Republic* (New York: Harcourt, Brace, Jovanovich, 1972), p. 143.

10. Kenneth Arrow, *Social Choice and Individual Values* (Yale University Press, 1951).

11. Howard Zinn, *A People's History of the United States, 1492–Present* (New York: HarperCollins, 2003), p. 251.

12. Bertrand Russell, *Power: A New Social Analysis* (London: Allen and Unwin, 1938); Edmund Burke, *Reflections on the Revolution in France* (London: Dodsley, 1791), p. 9.

INDEX